T0330197

Single Parents and Child Support Systems

NEW HORIZONS IN SOCIAL POLICY

Series Editors: Patricia Kennett and Misa Izuhara, *University of Bristol, UK*

The New Horizons in Social Policy series captures contemporary issues and debates in social policy and encourages critical, innovative and thought-provoking approaches to understanding and explaining current trends and developments in the field. With its emphasis on original contributions from established and emerging researchers on a diverse range of topics, books in the series are essential reading for keeping up to date with the latest research and developments in the area.

For a full list of Edward Elgar published titles, including the titles in this series, visit our website at www.e-elgar.com.

Single Parents and Child Support Systems

An International Comparison

Edited by

Kay Cook

Professor of Sociology, Department of Humanities and Social Sciences, Swinburne University of Technology, Australia

Thomas Meysen

Managing Director, SOCLES International Centre for Socio-Legal Studies, Germany

Adrienne Byrt

Postdoctoral Research Fellow, Centre for Transformative Media Technologies, Swinburne University of Technology, Australia

NEW HORIZONS IN SOCIAL POLICY

Cheltenham, UK • Northampton, MA, USA

Published by
Edward Elgar Publishing Limited
The Lypiatts
15 Lansdown Road
Cheltenham
Glos GL50 2JA
UK

Edward Elgar Publishing, Inc.
William Pratt House
9 Dewey Court
Northampton
Massachusetts 01060
USA

A catalogue record for this book
is available from the British Library

Library of Congress Control Number: 2023951219

This book is available electronically in the **Elgar**online
Sociology, Social Policy and Education subject collection
http://dx.doi.org/10.4337/9781800882409

ISBN 978 1 80088 239 3 (cased)
ISBN 978 1 80088 240 9 (eBook)
Printed and bound by CPI Group (UK) Ltd, Croydon, CR0 4YY

Contents

Contributors

Adedayo Adelakun has been called to the Nigerian Bar as a Barrister and Solicitor of the Supreme Court of Nigeria. He holds a master's degree in Peace and Conflict studies from the National Open University of Nigeria. He is currently studying towards a master's degree in law at Lead City University, Nigeria.

Olanike S. Adelakun is an expert in the broad field of international family law with specific interest in women's rights, child protection and assisted reproductive technologies. She is a lecturer at the school of law of the American University of Nigeria and currently a visiting researcher at New York University School of Law. She has published widely in her field of engagement.

Marisa Lo Bartolo completed her Bachelor of Arts, Gender Studies Major, at the University of Melbourne in 2016. Later in 2021, she completed a Graduate Certificate in Domestic and Family Violence at RMIT University. She is currently working at Good Shepherd Australia New Zealand as a Policy and Advocacy Advisor, focusing on policy and advocacy relating to family violence. She has a strong interest in primary prevention of family violence, the recovery process after family violence, and keeping an intersectional lens at the centre of all work.

Christina Boll is Head of the department for Families and Family Policies at the German Youth Institute (DJI) and a Guest Professor of Economics at the University of Applied Labour Studies (HdBA). Her research interests lie at the intersection of family and labour economics, with a particular interest in life course analysis, intra-couple labour division, human capital and earnings.

Rhonda Breitkreuz is Professor and Chair in the Department of Human Ecology at the University of Alberta. Breitkreuz researches the ways in which social policies impact wellbeing, gender equality, and access to resources for individuals and families in both Canada and internationally. She is the founder and director of the Global Research Network on the Economic Empowerment of Women. This network is comprised of an interdisciplinary group of international scholars that aims to enhance women's economic and social wellbeing in six global regions.

Adrienne Byrt is a Postdoctoral Research Fellow and design sociologist at Swinburne University of Technology, where she researches family and gender-based violence prevention and intervention. Her research spans the sociology of families, design methods, and feminist theory, with a view to enact social justice and transformative policy and service delivery.

Yiyoon Chung is a Professor of Public Administration at Konkuk University in Seoul, Korea. She completed her Ph.D. in Social Welfare at the University of Wisconsin–Madison in the United States. Her research interests focus on empirical analysis of social policies and their effects on the welfare of disadvantaged children and families. Her articles have been published in peer-reviewed journals including Demography, Journal of Policy Analysis and Management, and Social Service Review.

Kay Cook is a Professor and the Associate Dean of Research in the School of Social Sciences, Media, Film and Education at Swinburne University of Technology. Her research explores how new and developing social policies such as welfare-to-work, child support and child care policies, transform relationships between individuals, families and the state. Her work seeks to make the personal impact of these policies explicit in order to provide tangible evidence to policy makers to affect more humanistic reform.

Laura Cuesta is an Assistant Professor in the School of Social Work at Rutgers, the State University of New Jersey. Dr. Cuesta's research focuses on understanding how countries approach social problems emerging from dramatic changes in family structure. Dr. Cuesta takes a comparative perspective to understand social problems and public policy responses to mitigate their negative consequences, particularly poverty and income inequality.

Alisha Griffin currently directs her own independent consulting firm, AGWks LLC. She served the State of New Jersey in the child protective/welfare service arena and New Jersey and California as the Director of Child Support. Ms Griffin has been Director of the National Family Preservation Network, the National Child Support Enforcement Association, and the National Council of Child Support Directors. She also served as a member of the US delegation to the Special International Convention held to improve cooperation among States for the international recovery of child support and other forms of family maintenance.

Angela Guarin is an Assistant Professor in the School of Government at the Universidad de los Andes in Bogota, Colombia. Dr. Guarin's research broadly examines how poverty, inequality, and social policies impact the lives of vulnerable children and families. Her work is empirical and focuses on both domestic and international comparative research. Dr. Guarin's research aims to inform evidence-based policymaking in order to improve social policies' capacity to assist families with children.

Mari Haapanen Mari Haapanen is a doctoral student at Invest doctoral program, Department of Social Research, University of Turku. Her research focuses on the economic well-being of shared care families and child support policies.

Mia Hakovirta is a Professor of social work at the University of Turku, Finland. She conducts cross-national research on family and child support policy with a focus on separated families and their economic well-being. Her work has been published in leading academic journals on social policies and family change.

Yoonkyung Kim is a Researcher in the Korean Institute for Healthy Family and a visiting professor in Sookmyung Women's University. She worked as a director of Child Support Counseling Headquarters (2015–2018), Child Support Enforcement Headquarters (2019), and Family Counseling Headquarters (2020–2021) in the Korean Child Support Agency. Her recent research interests focus on supervised visitation, and she also works as a consultant for supervised visitation in Family Centers.

Eric Lee is Head Attorney for Los Angeles County Child Support Services Department. He received his J.D. from Southwestern University School of Law and his B.A. from the University of California, San Diego. He has worked in child support for more than 20 years where he has led his department's Intergovernmental Relations division for the past 7 years.

Thomas Meysen is managing director at SOCLES International Centre for Socio-Legal Studies. He has published widely across child and youth welfare, violence against women, family law, and child protection. Thomas Meysen leads interdisciplinary research teams to reform social policy and family law.

Zarina Md Nor received her PhD from Royal Melbourne Institute of Technology (RMIT) University, Melbourne, Australia. Her expertise is in Economics and Finance, and she is currently teaching these subjects to her students at Universiti Sains Malaysia. Her research interest is in Family Economics and Family Finance, focusing on low-income single mothers and child support issues in Malaysia. She is a member of the International Network of Child Support Scholars (INCSS) and NCSEA International Subcommittee.

Hannah Roots BA, LLB, MBA, is a lawyer and internationally recognized expert in the field of international child support. She works on projects in Canada, the United States, and in Europe to help governments implement the 2007 Hague Convention on Child Support and other Forms of Family

Maintenance, and to enhance their child support programs to better serve international families.

Sarah Sinclair is an applied economist and senior lecturer at RMIT University Melbourne. Recognised for her influential work in child support policy, Dr. Sinclair has contributed significantly to the field through her publications and community engagement. Her research findings shed light on the complex dynamics of child support and explore ways to improve policies and systems that directly impact the well-being of children and their families. Through her research, she seeks to shape and improve the landscape of child support, ensuring the fair and equitable distribution of resources to those who need it most.

Christine Skinner is Emeritus Professor at the Department of Social Policy and Social Work in the University of York. She is an expert in child support policy with over 20 years' experience researching the lives of separated families. Christine's' research has impacted on UK policy developments, and she has acted as specialist policy adviser to the House of Commons Select Committee, the National Audit Office and the Ministerial 'Expert Steering Group on Relationship Support Services'. She has advised policy making bodies on child support in Korea, France, and Australia and she has conducted comparative analysis of child support schemes across many countries.

Introduction to *Single Parents and Child Support Systems*

Kay Cook, Thomas Meysen, and Adrienne Byrt

This book takes a novel approach to child support policy analysis by locating the transfer of payments between separated parents within a wider social policy ecosystem. While work has begun to compare child support systems across countries, such studies have focused primarily on technical legal, administrative, and policy settings. In contrast, this book examines how child support policies align conceptually with other social policies. When child support is embedded within a broader suite of policy settings, its potential contribution to improving children's wellbeing can be understood. As such, the aim of the collection is to advance the conceptualisation of comparative post-separation family policy research while allowing best-practice principles of child support program implementation to be identified across contexts.

Child support is money paid by a non-resident parent to a resident parent for the purpose of supporting children following parental relationship breakdown (OECD, 2011). In the overwhelming majority of cases worldwide, payments are made by a non-resident father to a resident mother, reflecting the deeply gendered distribution of work and care that is almost universal. In doing so, child support recognises and compensates mothers for the opportunity costs incurred as a result of being a child's primary carer. As a result, child support does not exist in a policy vacuum, but exists in reference to other policies that shape the opportunity costs of motherhood, and post-separation motherhood, such as parental leave, childcare, welfare, and employment policies (Hakovirta, Cook and Sinclair, 2020).

Children's right to parental child support payments, and the state's role in facilitating and enforcing these, is set out in the United Nations Convention on the Rights of the Child (1990) which 196 states have ratified. Of the ten countries included in this collection, all bu the U.S. are parties to the Charter. Across the countries included here, there is significant variation in how child support sits within government institutions and systems. At one end of the spectrum, Nordic and Northern European countries provide guaranteed payments when non-resident parents do not transfer child support to the resident parent. At the other end of the spectrum, African, Southern Asian and South

American countries have weaker institutions to facilitate the assessment and transfer of payments. In between, liberal welfare regimes often use child support payments to reduce welfare benefit outlays.

However, while comparative research in the field of post-separation policy analysis is burgeoning, current research is either limited to very specific studies of policy or legal mechanisms across countries (see for example recent examples published by Beaumont et al., 2014; Claessens and Mortelmans, 2022; Chung and Kim, 2019; Cuesta, Hakovirta and Jokela, 2018; Hakovirta et al., 2019; 2020; Skinner et al., 2017a; 2017b; Walker, 2015), or generic accounts of policy types, such as 'fatherhood' or 'child' policies that do not take into consideration how these policies work or are experienced on the ground (see for example Rush, 2015).

To provide a way for comparative policy, legal and family researchers to locate individual child support systems within wider socio-political contexts and allow comparisons across systems, the book starts by setting out how children's and resident, often single, parents' economic welfare can be conceived across countries with respect to the responsibilities of the state, the market and the family. Following a comparative analysis of the features and functions of child support programs across countries, ten country-specific chapters map how post-separation child support policy reinforces or breaks from the gender and family logics that underpin each country's suite of relevant welfare and family policies. The countries included span Nordic, Liberal, Conservative/ Corporatist welfare regimes, and emerging social policy comparators from Africa, South America and Asia, including one Sharia law regime.

The book concludes with a review of the resourcing of children's care across the ten case study countries, as distributed between the state, the market and separated families. By positioning child support as a means of operational-ising the opportunity costs of children's care, the collection examines how child support policies reference, reinforce or contradict the gendered logics of pre-separation and other family policies that exist within wider regimes of welfare and family policy in each national context.

ADVANCING COMPARATIVE CHILD SUPPORT POLICY

At present, comparative child support policy work is legal in nature, such as work on the development and implementation of the Hague Convention on the International Recovery of Child Support and Other Forms of Family Maintenance (Beaumont et al., 2014; Walker, 2015) or focused on the techni-cal details of child support policy across countries (see for example: Hakovirta et al., 2020; Skinner et al., 2017b; Skinner, Bradshaw and Davidson, 2007). These works provide important insight into what child support policy does, but they do not situate child support within the context of other social policies that deeply influence how child support policy is structured. Examples of implicated policies include welfare benefits, childcare and maternal employment policies that shape the distribution of work and care pre-separation and thus also post-separation.

The journal article by Hakovirta, Cook and Sinclair (2020) lays the groundwork for the proposed book, as it compared post-separation child support policy with the logics inherent in pre-separation family policies existing in Australia and Finland, albeit with a narrower focus on how gender equality was enacted. The study found that each country's child support program flipped the gendered logic of the wider welfare system when moving from pre- to post-separation policy contexts. For example, in Finland, pre-separation family policies foregrounded gender equality in the form of equal access to parental leave and generous childcare provisions to enable maternal employment. Australian pre-separation policies, by contrast, favoured a gendered division of labour, with mothers being discursively positioned as the major parental leave recipients and high childcare costs preventing mothers' return to employment. However, post-separation, Finnish child support policy was deeply gendered, with fathers having to provide payments to mothers even when they shared care of children equally. In Australia, child support policy was completely de-gendered, taking into account each parent's income and care of children on an equal basis. The paper concluded that gender-equal treatment post-separation (as in Australia) could not provide gender-equal outcomes post-separation, as gender-unequal outcomes were instead entrenched by the unequal opportunities that existed pre-separation.

In this collection, the ideas raised by Hakovirta, Cook and Sinclair (2020) are taken further, looking across a diverse range of countries to examine how pre- and post-separation policies, and varying configurations of state, market and family sources of income, shape single mothers' and their children's well-being. The collection examines the logics evident within and across countries, illustrating where policies or social norms work at cross purposes, or where assumptions about child support program rules and implementation belie the reality of women's income, work and care.

THEORETICAL FRAMING

In the book, responsibilities for children's economic welfare following the separation of their parents will be analysed with respect to the institutional spheres of the family, the state, and the market. Social policies, legal settings and cultural norms shape the configuration of support available to carers in countries, both in the form of income available to carers as well as the resources provided to carers to support their caring activity. In making resources available to and prescribing legal or policy requirements for separated parents, countries position how the market, the family and the state should be configured to provide the most 'suitable' sources of support. As Edwards and Magarey (1995, p. 8) noted several decades ago:

> for feminists, thinking in terms of the triad of the state-market-family is essential if academic analysis and policy-making are to take account of the gendered nature of the relationship between these institutional spheres.

Following the lead of these pioneering gender policy researchers, in this text, we move beyond an examination of child support in isolation to locate it within a system of support available to children in separated families. While child support is specifically designed to provide direct financial resources to children, this familial form of support sits alongside state income support. As previous research has shown (Fletcher, 2022; Skinner et al., 2012), in some countries, familial support – in the form of child support – is recouped by the state when beneficiaries are income support recipients, negating familial support in place of state-provided assistance. At the same time, states can compel separated parents to seek both familial and market support. For example, in some countries, seeking child support is mandatory for benefit recipients, predominantly single mothers, who must also engage in welfare-to-work programs (De Gendre et al., 2021; Kiely and Butterworth, 2014). Such programs seek to reconfigure the balance of the state, the market and the family as the most appropriate sources of support for single parents and the children in their care.

Within each of the institutions of the family, the state and the market, the state plays a significant role in shaping the policy and legal context that dictates the nature and conditions of each. For example, within the institution of the family, if families live apart, family law assigns responsibilities to parents for their underage children. Looking through the lens of the economic situation of the child, the traditional gender distinction was to appoint the care to the mother and the financial support to the father. However, family forms and the gender roles of parents therein have become more diverse. How states respond to increasing diversity and complexity – and how the institution of the family is resourced or governed by the state is a site of analysis. The book provides an overview of the demographics context of single parent families, on social welfare, and on the legal situation in the particular countries, with a priority on child support. Responsibilities of the state, or the lack of such, shape family life of post-separation families. Limited access to social security, or welfare-to-work requirements, can compel single parents to work, which brings the existence, availability and subsidy of childcare facilities into focus. To contextualise child support within the intersection of state, market and family policies, the book will examine the responsibilities for child support, day-care, and social benefits and how law and policy reflect their interdependence. Finally, the book will examine whether support provided by the state empowers single parents and strengthens their agency, or instead leads to the responsibilisation of single parents without supporting their capacity to combine work and care. The latter refers to the process by which neoliberal economic policies displace responsibility for welfare and safety from the state onto communities and individuals (Goddard, 2012). The market comes into play as the means through which individuals should secure these. The book will reflect on how law and policy count on self-regulating market mechanisms, including the labour administration and the market in a set of coordinated responsibility, and ensure that a safety net is built.

OVERVIEW OF THE COLLECTION

This collection lays the groundwork for a knowledge base to enable international comparison in relation to the legal-institutional structures and socio-cultural backgrounds and enhance understanding of the interplay between society/families, law/state/policy, and the economy. It also broadens the developing worldwide, interdisciplinary network of researchers in the field of child support and builds a forum for expert debates in international publications, research, and other forms of exchange. The structure of the collection is as follows.

Chapter 1 presents an overview of how child support systems are technically managed in Australia, Canada, Columbia, Finland, Germany, Malaysia, Nigeria, South Korea, the United Kingdom, and the United States of America. To lay the groundwork for each country's discussion of the role of child support in relation to a wider array of work and family policies, this chapter sets out the alignments and divergences in child support's organisation and management across countries.

In Chapter 2, a conceptual framework that identifies the broader societal tensions across countries in presented. Child support policy and law have evolved across countries in recent decades, with the introduction of more technical measures of the costs of children, taking into consideration both parents' income and the sharing of care across households. At the same time, while some highly technical, advanced child support systems have seen a proliferation in tools to manage the complexity of child support payments, other countries are only beginning to take steps to embed child support into their suite of measures to financially support children post-separation. In advanced systems with highly technical calculations of children's entitlements, increasing family complexity as separated parents re-partner, add new children, and re-separate complicates lone parents' need for child support income and paying parents' capacity to pay. At the same time, increasing income uncertainty and precarity places increasing pressure on welfare states, child support formulas, and parent needs. As such, Chapter 2 sets out a framework for understanding child support within this rapidly evolving social context, including the pressure points faced by families in both countries with advanced welfare states and those where resident parents are instead directed to the family and the market to secure the financial resources required for children's upkeep. Thus, this chapter explores the ways in which gender differences persevere yet are negated in the context of child support provision post-separation. This conceptual framework outlines the broad socio-cultural tensions across all countries and explicates the gendered lens through which the child support systems presented in this collection can be understood.

At the core of the book, Chapters 3 through to 12 present reports on the national child support systems in different countries. These will mark out the wide variety of systems operating worldwide and enable critiques and contrasts between them (to be done in the conclusion, Chapter 13) with respect to the relative emphasis and contribution of the family, state and market in supporting single parent families, and as reflected in child support policy. The countries included provide an overview of the key child support policy regimes as well as those systems existing in divergent and emerging cases. This diversity will enable the boundaries and assumptions of liberal, conservative and Nordic regimes to be identified and critiqued.

The countries covered not only reflect the classic three-fold classification by Esping-Andersen (1990), differentiating between 'liberal' welfare states (Anglo-American), conservative and 'corporatist' welfare states (continental Europe), and social democratic welfare states (Nordic countries), but also the collection adds to the differentiation by including a state from Eastern Europe and reflects the continental European differences between countries from Middle and Southern Europe. Also, Asian countries, including an Islamic country, an African and a Latin American country are represented.

The collection concludes with a brief discussion on the importance of viewing child support policy through the lens of the gendered triple bind to extend the interrogation of incomplete or inadequate systems across countries.

REFERENCES

Beaumont, P., Hess, B., Walker, L. and Spancken, S. (2014). *The recovery of mainte-nance in the EU and worldwide.* Oxford: Hart Publishing.
Chung, Y. and Kim, Y. (2019). How cultural and policy contexts interact with child support policy: A case study of child support receipt in Korea and the United States. *Children and Youth Services Review, 96*, pp. 237–249.
Claessens, E. and Mortelmans, D. (2022). Honesty is the best approach. The importance of fairness perceptions in child maintenance agreements. *Relaties en Nieuwe Gezinnen, 12*(1).

Cuesta, L., Hakovirta, M. and Jokela, M. (2018). The antipoverty effectiveness of child support: Empirical evidence for Latin American countries. *Social Policy Administration, 52*(6), pp. 1–19.

de Gendre, A., Schurer, S. and Zhang, A. (2021). *Two decades of welfare reforms in Australia: How did they affect single mothers and their children?* (No. 14752). Institute of Labor Economics (IZA).

Edwards, A. and Magarey, S. (1995). *Women in a restructuring Australia: work and welfare.* Allen & Unwin.

Esping-Andersen, G. (1990). *The three worlds of welfare capitalism.* Princeton University Press.

Goddard, S. (2012). Cosmopolitan Power in International Relations: A Synthesis of Realism, Neoliberalism, and Constructivism. *Political Science Quarterly, 127*(2), 316–318.

Hakovirta, M., Cook, K. and Sinclair, S. (2020). Gender equality prior to and following separation: Nordic and liberal policy inconsistencies. *Social Politics.* https://doi.org/10.1093/sp/jxaa010

Hakovirta, M., Skinner, C., Hiilamo, H. and Jokela, M. (2019). Child poverty, child maintenance and interactions with social assistance benefits among lone parent families. *Journal of Social Policy*, pp. 1–21.

International Network of Child Support Scholars (2019). Glossary: INCSS. Available at: www.incss.org/glossary

Kiely, K. M. and Butterworth, P. (2014). How has Welfare to Work reform affected the mental health of single parents in Australia? *Australian and New Zealand Journal of Public Health, 38*(6), 594–595. http://doi.org/10.1111/1753–6405.1230

OECD (2011). Doing Better for Families. Paris.

Rush, M. (2015). *Between two worlds of father politics.* Manchester, England: Manchester University Press.

Skinner, C., Bradshaw, J. and Davidson, J. (2007). Child support policy: An international perspective. Corporate Document Services Leeds.

Skinner, C., Cook, K. and Sinclair, S. (2017a). The potential of child support to reduce lone mother poverty: Comparing population survey data in Australia and the UK. *Journal of Poverty and Social Justice, 25*(1), pp. 79–94.

Skinner, C., Hakovirta, M. and Davidson, J. (2012). A comparative analysis of child maintenance schemes in five countries. *European Journal of Social Security, 14*(4), pp. 330–347.

Skinner, C., Meyer, D. R., Cook, K. and Fletcher, M. (2017b). Child maintenance and social security interactions: The poverty reduction effects in model lone parent families across four countries. *Journal of Social Policy, 46*(3), pp. 495–516.

Walker, L. (2015). *Maintenance and child support in private international law.* Bloomsbury Publishing.

1. Poverty, gender and child support systems in comparative perspective

Adedayo Adelakun, Olanike S. Adelakun, Marisa Lo Bartolo, Christina Boll, Rhonda Breitkreuz, Adrienne Byrt, Yiyoon Chung, Kay Cook, Laura Cuesta, Alisha Griffin, Angela Guarin, Mari Haapanen, Mia Hakovirta, Yoonkyung Kim, Eric Lee, Thomas Meysen, Zarina Md Nor, Hannah Roots, Sarah Sinclair, and Christine Skinner

INTRODUCTION

The payment of child support has a significant influence on the financial situation of separated parents and their children. While the technical management of payment calculations and transfers often comes to dominate the discourse about child support policy, and even acts as a proxy for the nature of child support, the way in which systems are structured and operated provide important insights into national child support logics and values. To delve into these issues and examine alignments and divergences in child support organisation and management across countries, this chapter provides an overview of how child support systems are technically managed in ten countries, worldwide.

The following description of the various child support regimes is divided into four sections, following the chronology of access to the child support system, to the calculation of payment amounts, through to the collection of payments, and finally, their enforcement. The material presented here is designed to support each of the subsequent country-specific chapters and place the discussion of each national system's particular technical characteristics within an international, comparative perspective. As such, this chapter does not critique each system; rather, it offers a way of understanding their distinctiveness, shared purposes, and technical procedures. It describes how the features of national child support systems differ or are constant across countries, and how they underpin each country's current struggles with how to resource children living apart from one parent.

Across the countries included in this collection, child support is organised either through an administrative agency, through the courts, or through a combination of these two systems, known as a 'hybrid' approach (Table 1.1). In Australia and the UK, the child support systems are managed through administrative services. Countries such as Canada and South Korea (Korea, hereafter), are characterised as judicial, whereby private agreements are only enforceable if filed with a court and in which only enforcement is administratively supported. The child support systems in Colombia, Finland, Germany, and Nigeria are organised through hybrid means, where in cases in which authentic instruments are agreed upon and filed at a child support agency, the resulting agreement can be enforceable. In the US, all forms can be found in the different states.

Table 1.1   Child support system organisation

	Administrative	Judicial	Hybrid
Australia	X		
Canada		X	
Colombia			X
Finland			X
Germany			X
Korea		X	
Malaysia			X
Nigeria			X
United Kingdom	X		
United States			X

With respect to the purpose of the child support system, there is considerable variability across countries, as well as variation in the explicitness of the purpose of the child support system. For example, Colombia and Malaysia explicitly state the focus of their child support systems in their legal frameworks, while others document it in policy statements. In several countries, the policy goals are focussed on enhancing the child's (financial) well-being (Colombia, Korea, Nigeria). The recovery of child support, as stated in art. 27(4) of the UN Convention on the Rights of the Child (1989), is ultimately privatised by framing it as a parental responsibility which may be increased (Canada, Colombia, Malaysia, Nigeria, the UK, the US) or shared (Finland). However, while parental responsibility is foregrounded, children's right to receive support, and the state's role in ensuring parents provide such support, are less explicit. Although poverty reduction has emerged as a focus of the system in Canada, Colombia, the UK, and the US, it is not necessarily supported by state responsibility. For example, in the UK and the US, reduction of welfare expenditure is explicitly stated in official policy documents. In some countries, child support policy originally aimed to achieve poverty reduction (Australia) or provide support for 'fallen' and later 'unmarried' mothers (Germany). However, the responsibility of the state to ensure single parent family financial welfare was ultimately relegated as discussions about technical solutions to calculate a just amount of child support were foregrounded (Cook, 2021; Garfinkel et al., 1998; Gorlick and Brethour, 1998; Lens, 2002; Seccombe, James and Walters, 1998; Skinner, Bradshaw and Davidson, 2007). As Cook (2021) explained, while the broader aim of child support appears to centre on providing children with resources from both parents, poverty is rarely alleviated through child support payments, particularly when welfare benefits are also taken into account (Hakovirta, 2011; Skinner et al., 2017; OECD, 2011).

ACCESSING CHILD SUPPORT SYSTEMS

Following on from the various purposes of child support outlined in the literature (Cook, 2021; Hakovirta, 2011; Skinner, Bradshaw and Davidson, 2007), the first major division between national child support systems is whether it is mandatory to seek child support or not (Table 1.2). No country mandates that child support is sought for all children of separated parents. Just over half of the countries included here (Finland, Malaysia, Nigeria, and the UK) have no mandated requirements, while the others make child support mandatory in a limited number of circumstances. Typically, these circumstances include the establishment of child support during divorce proceedings (Colombia, Germany, and Korea), or child support is required for welfare recipients (Australia, some Canadian provinces [Employment Support and Income Assistance Regulations 2019], Germany). In some countries, such as Finland, while payments are completely voluntary, parents can only be provided with guaranteed child support if agreements are registered. In Australia, establishing a child support order is only required if the parent with care is in receipt of Family Tax Benefits. However, due to the generous means-testing of this cash payment, approximately 85 per cent of single parents are affected by this measure.

Almost all countries included here regard child support as an optional process that parents can either agree on between themselves, or which resident parents (overwhelmingly mothers) can choose to pursue. Where agreements are voluntary, the state can still become involved, either in the process of

Table 1.2   *Is seeking child support mandatory?*

	Yes	No	In some cases
Australia			X
Canada			X
Colombia			X
Finland		X	
Germany			X
Korea		X	
Malaysia		X	
Nigeria		X	
United Kingdom		X	
United States			X

determining payment amounts, or lodging private agreements for the purpose of their later enforcement. Germany provides an expansive, voluntary administrative support system. If single parents receive welfare benefits of any kind they are required to seek support either through legal or administrative channels. When administrative services are engaged, the most likely outcome is a notarised enforceable private agreement (authentic instrument). If no appropriate agreement can be reached between parents, or payments are not made voluntarily, the services can move to represent the child at the family courts to establish an order and/or enforce child support.

With respect to making agreements, the UK is one of the only jurisdictions where a voluntary service can be provided by the state. There is no requirement for separated families to have a child support arrangement. However, if parents want to establish an order, and cannot agree on terms, they must first seek support from the Child Maintenance Option service before accessing the Child Maintenance Service (CMS). In the UK, there are two main types of child maintenance: statutory and non-statutory arrangements. Statutory child maintenance arrangements are those which have been arranged with the CMS or its predecessor, the Child Support Agency (CSA). Non-statutory arrangements in the UK include all other arrangements, such as voluntary financial or non-financial arrangements, shared care arrangements, or court orders requiring parents to make financial payments.

In other jurisdictions, agreements made between parents, or by the courts, may then be lodged or ratified for oversight and enforcement purposes. For example, in Canada, parents may make a private agreement, but to be enforceable, it must be filed with a court ('Family Law Act', SBC 2011;

'Family Maintenance Enforcement Act', RSBC 1996). In Malaysia, there are two separate legal systems through which child support can be claimed: the family court for non-Muslims, and the sharia court for Muslims. Malaysian parents can obtain child support through court orders or voluntary agreement, where court orders formalise child support claims that can then be enforced. However, when both parents have reached mutual understanding, an out of court child support settlement can be used instead. In Nigeria, there is a choice for the applicant seeking child support to apply to the customary court, magistrate court, high court (in the case of a pending divorce) or the social welfare department of the Ministry of Women Affairs. Some choose to apply to NGOs or to go public on community-based radio programs. In Finland, parents agree on child support arrangements which are then ratified by the Municipal Social Welfare Board (SWB) or the court to determine if the agreement is in the best interests of the child. The court will process the dispute in cases where parents disagree. For parents who are dissatisfied with the ratified agreement, a 'fairer' agreement in court can be pursued (Hakovirta and Hiilamo, 2012).

In contrast to the voluntary systems just described, where the onus for initiating and pursuing the process ultimately rests with the resident parent, in some countries, parents are compelled to seek child support by the state. There are two state processes through which child support was found to be made compulsory, either through divorce proceedings or as a condition of benefit eligibility, reflecting familial and liberal welfare state traditions, respectively. In Colombia and Korea, married parents who are getting a divorce must make an agreement in order to finalise divorce proceedings. Divorce proceedings in Germany must include a child support agreement or order. In Colombia, unmarried couples who have a registered cohabitation must make an agreement in order to finalise the union dissolution, but unmarried parents may decide against making a child support arrangement. By contrast, in Australia, seeking child support is compulsory for the 85 per cent of single parents who receive Family Tax Benefit cash payments (Department of Human Services, 2019). The same requirement applies to Germany. What these voluntary and compulsory systems reveal is the primacy of parental 'choice' when it comes to ensuring their children's right to receiving support from both parents (United Nations, 1989). In almost all cases, mothers are responsible for initiating the process and either seeking payments privately from their ex-partners or taking legal action against them. At the same time, mothers typically face costs as they pursue their children's right to support (Table 1.3).

Table 1.3   Costs to seek child support

	Yes	No	Depends
Australia		X	
Canada	X (in most cases)		
Colombia	X		
Finland		X	
Germany	X (judicial system)	X (admin services)	
Korea		X	
Malaysia	X		
Nigeria			X
United Kingdom	X		
United States	X	X (state policies)	

Costs of Seeking Support

In most of the countries included in this collection, there are direct costs that applicants (mainly mothers) must pay to enter the court system (Canada, Colombia, Finland, Germany, Korea, Malaysia, Nigeria, the UK, the US). In most instances, these are the costs associated with legal representation. For example, in Canada and Germany, a lawyer is required to obtain a court order as in Canada Legal Aid is not available to establish a child support order. Similarly, in Colombia, married parents must pay divorce proceedings fees and legal representation costs if not pursuing free services provided by the child support system. If parents cannot afford a lawyer, they must represent themselves or, in countries where parents enter the judicial system to resolve child support disputes, then legal fees are payable. However, parents still can make use of the cost-free representation by the administrative support services (Germany, Korea, Malaysia, Nigeria, the UK, the US). In some courts, governments provide limited assistance for self-represented litigants or mediation services (Canada).

Access to administrative support is free for parents in Australia, Finland, and Germany. In Korea, free access to the system was available to all single parents for the first six years after the service first began in 2015. Since 2021, however, the revised administrative rules dictate the service preference to low-income single parents. Actual user distribution is yet unknown. In other countries included in this collection, access to administrative services requires a fee. US federal law sets an application fee of $35 USD and an additional fee of $25 USD if more than $500 USD have been collected for non-public assistance cases. However, policies are not uniform across states in the US, where some charge fees while others waive fees. The UK imposes fees on both parents to encourage them to make agreements privately, and to recoup some of the costs of operating the system. Parents pay a one-off fee of £20 to register on the child support system. In addition, a 'pay and collect' function charges for this service, whereby the non-resident parent must pay 20 per cent extra on top of their calculated payment amount and the resident parent with care receives 4 per cent less than the calculated amount when using collect and pay. In 2019–2020, £41.54 million was collected in fees (of which £6.77m was from receiving parents) (House of Commons, 2023).

Besides the direct costs to parents to access administrative services, parents can face indirect costs associated with sourcing, copying and providing the extensive amount of documentation required to calculate child support orders. In all countries where parents must attend court or administrative hearings in person, parents must also cover transportation to and from appointments and hearings. Indirect costs also include forgone earnings due to the time invested in pursuing a child support arrangement. Finally, child support can impose emotional and psychological costs on applicants whether parents engage with child support through the courts, an administrative system or privately between themselves. These non-financial costs can be exacerbated or eased by the type of system and the process through which payments are calculated and pursued.

CALCULATING PAYMENT AMOUNTS

How child support payments are calculated entails symbolic as well as technical dimensions. Symbolically, how children share in their parents' income post-separation can be determined based on a number of principles, including the financial needs of children, the capacity of parents to pay, or seeking to continue to pre-separation proportion of income provided to children. When families separate, the costs of living separately increase, while parents' earning capacity can be reduced by their need to care for children. As such, the principles used to calculate payments can cause financial hardship for paying parents and can equally leave caring parents with a shortfall of funds (Hakovirta, 2011; Skinner et al., 2017). It is the balance that countries strike between children's needs, parents' capacity to pay, and the equitable sharing of income with children that serves as a flashpoint for ongoing tensions in national child support policymaking, particularly when these payment calculations are prescribed in administrative formulae (Natalier, 2018; Skinner et al., 2017).

In all of the countries included, non-resident parents' capacity to pay is either the sole, or a primary consideration in calculating payment amounts (Table 1.4). Either the income of the payer (Germany, Malaysia/Nigeria: Muslim population, the UK, 6 States in the US) or of both parents is taken into account (Australia, Colombia, Finland, Korea, Malaysia/Nigeria: Non-Muslim

population, 43 States in the US). In circumstances where a child has extraor-
dinary needs (Canada), the main carer earns a particularly high income
(Germany), or when parents share care (Canada, Germany), exceptions are
made. In Malaysia and Nigeria, which operate separate systems for Muslims
and non-Muslims in each country, non-Muslims have both parents' incomes
included, while the sharia courts in the respective countries only take the
father's income into consideration. Four countries treat both parents' incomes
equally in the calculation of child support orders (Australia, Colombia,
Finland, Korea). These countries consider both parents' incomes, either in the
judicial determination of payments, or when applying a child support formula.
While not explicitly gendered, as is the case in sharia law, the exclusion of
the resident parent's income shifts the focus exclusively on the non-resident
parent's capacity to pay.

The child's needs are additionally taken into account in half of the countries presented here (Australia, Colombia, Finland, Germany, Malaysia, and
Korea). In the US, 6 states calculate based on a percentage of the payer's
income. The remaining 43 states, the District of Columbia, Virgin Islands and
Guam calculate based on an income shares model, or Melson model, linked to
the child's needs. Continuity of the child's living standard (before separation)
is explicitly (Germany, Korea) or implicitly (Australia, Colombia, Finland,
Malaysia) included in the concept of calculations when linking the child's
needs and payer's capacity.

Table 1.4   Principles underpinning payment calculations

	Needs based	Capacity to pay	Continuity of expenditure
Australia	X	X	
Canada		X	
Colombia	X	X	
Finland	X	X	
Germany	X	X	X
Korea		X	X
Malaysia	X	X	
Nigeria		X	
United Kingdom		X	
United States	X	X	

Operationalising parents' capacity to pay is achieved by scaling orders based
on payer's income and setting caps on maximum payments. As mentioned,
some countries balance payer's capacity to pay with child's needs, which in

some of the countries leads to private negotiations or discretionary, judicial decision-making (Colombia, Finland, Malaysia). Such decision-making may include an assessment of the needs of resident children, the incomes of each parent, and non-resident parents' responsibilities to other children, both resident and non-resident. In some cases, however, balancing children's needs with payer's capacity is pre-determined and calculated through judicially determined mechanisms such as a child support formula (Germany), or costs of children tables (Australia; DHS, 2019). The guidelines published by the Korean family court for the range of child support amounts are not legally binding. As such, it remains unclear whether the enactment of this principle is routine or to what extent judicial discretion is used.

Table 1.5   The upper and lower limits of child support calculations

	Minimum liabilities	Maximum liabilities	Notional income imputed for assessments
Australia	Yes	Yes	Yes
Canada	No	No	Yes
Colombia	Yes	No	Yes
Finland	No	No	No
Germany	Yes	Yes	Yes
Korea	Yes	Yes	Yes
Malaysia	No	No	No
Nigeria	No	No	Depends
United Kingdom	Yes	Yes	No
United States	No	No	Yes

When determining payments, five of the ten included countries set minimum payment amounts (Table 1.5), with only four of the same countries having maximum payment calculations. The other countries had no limits on the amount of child support that could be set. In most countries, when payers do not participate in child support assessment processes, through such measures as not lodging tax returns, withholding income data, or being deliberately unemployed or underemployed, states can impute income for the purposes of determining child support assessments (Australia, Canada, Colombia, Germany, Korea, the US). In Nigeria, while the law requires that the parent's notional income be considered with respect to 'earning capacity', in practice this is not considered.

As the proceeding discussion has identified, decisions that states make about how to calculate child support has significant implications for addressing the needs of children, and the extent to which they share in both parents' resources. There are myriad ways to calculate the financial resources available to be shared with children, particularly in relation to the extent caring responsibilities are shared. When care is shared between parents, the costs of children are also more or less shared accordingly. However, not all countries assess the extent to which children are sharing in their parents' resources through co-residence, either outlined in the guidelines (US) or calculated via overnights with the payer (Australia, Finland, the UK). The remaining countries do not provide for legal provisions or guidelines to calculate shared caring responsibilities since such family constellations are still rare (Colombia, Korea, Malaysia, Nigeria), or due to reforms lacking behind societal developments which leads to exceptions only when care times are (almost) equally shared (Canada, Germany).

While there is limited recognition of the de-gendering of earnings across countries, on care time, far fewer countries assess both parents' contribution to the care of children in the calculation of child support obligations. Only Australia and most states in the US explicitly include the proportion of care provided by each parent in their calculation of child support orders. Where care is shared in the UK and Finland, deductions to the amount of child support to be paid are provided to paying parents. At the other extreme, in Nigeria and Malaysia, it is expected that children will reside with mothers and continue to be paid for by fathers following parental separation. The country-specific chapters provide detail of the prevalence of shared care, and the way that their systems work with respect to wider gender-equality issues.

Over time, parents may seek modification of their child support orders or enforceable authentic instruments due to changing parental or child circumstances. All countries had provisions for parents to renew orders or agreements should the needs of the child or the circumstances of the parent change. The same applies to legal changes. However, modifications might not be taken up due to the costs involved. In several countries, parents' circumstances must have changed significantly for child support orders to be modified or agreements to be renegotiated (Australia, Finland, Germany, Korea). In Germany, orders or authentic instruments can be stipulated dynamically so that changes in formulae are taken into account automatically. The UK has a threshold whereby an employed payer's income had to change by a minimum of 25 per cent before a reassessment could be sought. Most states in the US set the threshold at 20 per cent. At the other extreme, the Australian formula has ten reasons, including changes to income, care-time, children's needs including school fees and healthcare costs, and asset changes applicable to either parent, for which reassessments could be sought.

Table 1.6   *Methods of child support payment collection*

	Agency	Court	Private
Australia	X		X
Canada	X		X
Colombia			X
Finland	X		X
Germany	X		X
Korea			X
Malaysia			X
Nigeria		X	X
United Kingdom	X		X
United States	X		X

COLLECTION OF PAYMENTS

Once child support orders or authentic instruments are determined, the next process through which payments pass is that of child support collection. Here, some countries enlist administrative agencies to collect and transfer payments (Australia, Canada, Finland, Germany, the UK, the US). All countries allow – or some encourage – parents to transfer payments privately (Table 1.6). Only Nigeria involve the courts in collecting payments. Here, where the court perceives that the non-resident parent may not obey the order of the court to pay the resident parent directly, the court may make an order for them to pay to the court instead. However, in most cases, the non-resident parent may also agree to pay directly to the resident parent based on a private arrangement.

When making payments, lump sum payments are legally possible in most jurisdictions. They are typically rare (Finland, Korea, the US) and/or at the discretion of the court (Canada, Colombia, Nigeria). In other countries lump sum payments are not allowed (Germany, Malaysia, the UK).

Payment Receipt for Social Assistance Recipients

While child support is designed to ensure the fulfilment of the right of the child-to-child support payments from the parents, when a child's resident parent is in receipt of social assistance, some states intercept payments to reduce welfare expenditures (Table 1.7).

In some Canadian provinces/territories, any payments received while a parent is on social assistance are retained by the government, while in a few

*Table 1.7   Who receives payments when resident parents are social
                  assistance recipients?*

	State	Parent	Other
Australia	X	X	
Canada			Varies by province/ territory
Colombia		X	
Finland		X	
Germany	X		
Korea		X	
Malaysia			No social assistance
Nigeria			No social assistance
United Kingdom		X	

provinces/territories, all payments are passed through to the resident parent without any deduction from future social assistance payments. In Australia, while all child support paid to social assistance recipients is passed on to parents, this money is counted as income for the purpose of benefit payment calculations. As a result, child support recipients receive less state support as a result of child support payments – which is in effect an implicit claw-back mechanism (Skinner et al., 2017). Finland also provides the full value of payments to resident parents, but there is no 'disregard' of this income when calculating parents' state benefit entitlements (Hakovirta et al., 2020). Likewise, in Korea, a dollar transferred as child support will reduce a dollar from welfare support and possibly negate welfare eligibility for parents within the National Basic Living Security System that guarantees a minimum income. In Germany, the child support claim changes over to the state authority that has paid social benefits. In the US, only payments exceeding the amount of social benefits is paid to the child.

Other countries reviewed here do not tie child support payments to social assistance benefits. Either this is because payments are made privately and the state is not in a position to interfere and calculate benefit implications (Colombia, Korea), because states have chosen to pass on the full value of payments to resident parents (UK), or because social security payments are not widely available (Malaysia, Nigeria). In Korea, only advance payments with limited scope and accessibility are designed to be collected from the non-resident parent by the state.

Guaranteed Payments

In order to ensure a stable and predictable income for resident parents, some countries provide advanced, or guaranteed payments. However, state payment of private payer obligations is internationally unusual (Skinner et al., 2007; Hakovirta and Hiilamo, 2012), as more typically, as the countries reviewed here demonstrate, states are unwilling to intervene to advance residents their expected child support income (Table 1.8).

Table 1.8   *The availability of advanced/guaranteed payments*

	Yes	No
Australia		X
Canada	X (Quebec)	X (All other provinces/territories)
Colombia		X
Finland	X	
Germany	X	
Korea	X	
Malaysia		X
Nigeria		X
United Kingdom		X
United States		X

For those jurisdictions that do provide advanced payments (Quebec, Germany, Finland, Korea), parents must first experience a default on their expected child support, which then must be registered with the state who will subsequently provide a compensatory benefit payment. In Finland, the social insurance institution (Kela) pays guaranteed child support in case of default of child support payments, while a child support debt accumulates for the liable parent. Kela then collects the debt from the liable parent to recoup the advanced payments made (Kela, 2022). In Germany, guaranteed payments are provided if child support is not (fully) paid. After policy reform in 2017, most conditions have been dropped, especially the limited period for advance payments and the age limit. However, the recipient parent must not have (re)married. After the age of 12, guaranteed payments are only made if no social assistance is paid for the child(ren).

Korea is one of the most recent countries to introduce legislation to guarantee payments for parents with a child support order. Here, there is a small and very selective advance payment program, called 'short-term emergency financial assistance' administered by the Korean Child Support Agency.

These payments are provided only to low-income resident parents who do not receive a support payment where there are additional risks to children, such as a child's serious illness or the risk of utility disconnection due to non-payment. This program, like Finland, assumes subsequent cost recovery from the non-resident parent. But, due to the nature of the program (small, very selective, and implemented as an agency program rather than a national policy), most experts and single parents in Korea assume that the nation has no advance payments system. The existence of this belief is evidenced by the fact that bills proposing advanced child support payments are repeatedly recommended to the National Assembly.

In stark contrast to Korea, Malaysia has moved in the opposite direction with respect to advanced child support payments. Previously, for Muslim families, advanced payments were able to be ordered by the Family Unit of the Shariah Court. However, as in other countries, unpaid child support was regarded as a debt to the state, the recouping of which would compensate the state for its advanced payment outlays. The Malaysian program only lasted for a short time, as it was found to be financially unsustainable given that absent fathers did not contribute.

In all other countries, except for the Canadian province of Quebec, unpaid child support is a debt borne entirely by resident parents. Given the disproportionate levels of financial hardship experienced by sole mothers, internationally, the unpredictability and unreliability of child support income is of significant concern. The final section of this chapter turns to examine how countries enforce child support obligations.

ENFORCEMENT OF PAYMENTS

While most countries allow, and at times encourage, parents to make agreements about child support payments privately, in most instances, these agreements are enforceable. Typically, this involves filing a privately made agreement with a court (Canada, Nigeria, Korea, the UK) or administrative agency (Australia, Germany). In Colombia, private agreements are enforceable if they meet three conditions: 1) it is stated (i.e., all elements of the child support obligation are written: amount, mode, frequency, and method of payment), 2) it is clear (i.e., there is no uncertainty regarding any elements of the child support obligation), and 3) it is enforceable (i.e., the requisites to pursue it have been met; for instance, paternity has been established or can be presumed).

Despite the option to have private agreements and authentic instruments enforced, this was not regarded as common across countries, as the financial and logistical barriers were often too great. Rather, the enforcement of private agreements was left to individuals, reflecting states' preference for voluntary payments as opposed to enforcement options (Table 1.9).

Table 1.9   Prioritisation of voluntary or enforced payments

	Voluntary	Enforced
Australia	X (majority)	X (minority)
Canada	X	
Colombia	X	
Finland	X	
Germany	X	
Korea	X	
Malaysia	X	
Nigeria	X	
United Kingdom	X	
United States		X

In almost all countries, with the exception of the United States where wage with-holding is the preferred collection source and Australia in some circumstances, voluntary payments are prioritised. In Australia, more than half of the child support caseload (and an estimated 15 per cent of all separated parents who do not receive any government payments) transfer payments privately. As such, it is in a minority of cases that enforcement tools such as wage-withholding are employed. For all other countries included here, voluntary payments are the default. In some instances, (Canada, Colombia, Germany, Korea, Nigeria, the UK) enforcement tools such as wage-withholding can be enacted if a payee parent seeks administrative or judicial intervention after debts have accrued. In Malaysia, parents can voluntarily opt for wage-withholding when establishing their orders, but voluntary commitment to such tools is prioritised.

One of the major problems with enforcing child support is the fact that most payments are made privately. Exceptions to this are the administrative child support systems in Finland, Germany, and the US in which payments are usually made through the administrations and thereby monitored. Beyond returning to the state to seek advanced or guaranteed payments – in a limited number of countries and in a limited range of circumstances – there are few tools available to recipient parents to ensure that their children receive payments. At the same time, however, most of the countries reviewed here had incentives or sanctions that could be applied to encourage or enforce payments. With respect to Australia and the US, Oldham and Smyth (2018) discussed the pendulum of soft to hard enforcement options – seeking to

Single parents and child support systems

Table 1.10   *What enforcement measures apply?*

AUS	• Wage garnishment
	• Interception of tax returns
	• International travel departure prohibition orders
CAN	• Wage attachment
	• Attachment of tax refunds and government benefits (other than welfare)
	• Attachment of pensions
	• Attachment of lottery winnings
	• Attachment of estate pay-outs or other types of non-income payments
	• Seizure of personal property (vehicles, boats)
	• Restriction or suspension of licences (driver's licences, vehicle registration, marine and aviation licences, hunting and fishing licences)
	• Suspension of passport
	• Reporting of debt to credit bureaus
	• Court ordered incarceration for wilful refusal to pay
	('Family Maintenance Enforcement Act', RSBC 1996)
COL	• Prohibition to the non-resident parent to leave the country
	• Confiscation of non-resident parent's wage or property
	• Inclusion in a national registry of child support debtors
FIN	• Attachment of earnings
	• Deduction from tax refunds or distraint of assets
GER	• Wage garnishment
	• Enforcement in assets, properties, and outstanding demands
MAL	• The court may order the payment by vesting any property in trustees and pay maintenance from the income of that property (Civil court)
	• Forced payment through wage deduction from the father (sharia court)
	• The offender could be tried and jailed for defying court order for CS
NIG	• Attachment of earnings
	• Mediation
	• Intervention of extended family members and relatives
	• Public shaming
	• Public mediation through radio and television programs

KOR   • The court can order to garnish a parent's wages (transfer payment directly from the non-resident parent's employer to the resident parent) but there are significant restrictions.

                • Possible sanctions could include

                   • suspending the noncompliant parent's driver's licence

                   • suspending traveling abroad

                   • criminal penalties (one year imprisonment or a $9,000 fine)

                   • disclosure of the non-resident parent's personal information on a public website.

UK   • Collect and pay is monitored by CMS and CMS takes further action of non-payment.

                • Most common 'collection' approach is to arrange a Deduction from Earnings Order (DEO) so the maintenance is deducted automatically from the wages by employers. Deduction Order – CMS can take directly from payer's bank account.

                • Enforcement Action involves CMS seeking a 'liability order' from the Courts. Once received, CMS can take control of goods using bailiffs, and also seek powers to disqualify non-payers from seeking or holding a driving licence and/ or from holding a passport.

                • Imprisonment is also possible – though rare.

                • The receiving parent has no right to take private enforcement action through the courts.

encourage payments or punish non-compliance, respectively. They argued that the two countries, and individual states within the US, have moved along this continuum over time. However, irrespective of the approach taken, neither extreme has been terribly successful as payment rates have remained relatively unchanged.

In the countries reviewed here, we also identify the hard to soft enforcement continuum. At one extreme, Colombia, Germany, Korea, and the US were countries that could impose jail sentences for non-compliance. In Colombia, failure to pay child support could lead to prison sentences, with penalties that range from 32 to 72 months of incarceration. But such sanctions are only applied if the resident parent initiates a criminal case against the non-resident parent. Given the significant financial, judicial, and administrative barriers that unpaid, and often impoverished recipient parents face, the sanction of imprisonment is extremely unlikely. In Korea, a 12-month jail term or a $9,000 fine could be payable, but this also requires considerable evidence and effort to enact this judicial process. As such, these penalties are unlikely to be issued in all but the most egregious of cases. For the majority of unpaid child support recipients in these countries, the pursuit of arrears through the courts is not a viable option.

At the other end of the encouragement/enforcement system, Finland offers incentives to paying parents, who can claim a tax credit of up to 80 Euros (per year) for each child for whom they have paid ratified child support. In between these two poles lie the other countries, as well as other measures available in Korea, which first seek to encourage payments, but can impose penalties when payments do not eventuate. In some Canadian provinces/territories, Nigeria and the UK, fines or penalty fees can be imposed. In Australia, Korea, and the US, international travel bans can be imposed, while Korea and the US also have provisions to cancel driver's licences (in the US, also fishing and hunting licences) and listing non-compliant payers on a public register.

While these penalties and incentives are supposed to encourage payments, typically there are no penalties for late payments. If payers are later forced to comply, through the courts or other administrative means, only three countries (two Canadian provinces, Columbia, Finland) reported that interest was routinely charged. In Australia and Germany, while it was reported as possible for interest to be applied to arrears if parents pursued these through the courts, this was discretionary and was reported as almost never being applied.

CONCLUSION

This chapter has presented an overview of the technical management of child support systems across Australia, Malaysia, Nigeria, Canada, Finland, Colombia, Germany, Korea, the UK, and the USA. By describing access to the child support system, to the calculation of payment amount, through to the collection of payments, and to the enforcement of payments, the country-specific chapters (4–14) are situated in a broader context in which each system can be comparatively critiqued. The following, Chapter 2, presents the conceptual framework that furthers the critique of child support systems, internationally, as it explores the tensions embedded within parents' access to and the administration of child support. First, poverty and child support are understood through the tension between privatisation and the responsibility of the state. Second, gender and child support are in tension given the negation of gender differences and commitment to gender justice. Finally, the tensions between systems and child support are ultimately between unconnected technical solutions and coherent policy. The three tensions of child support provide a comprehensive and complex understanding of the weakness and strengths of each country's system.

REFERENCES

Brady, M. and Cook, K. (2015). The impact of welfare to work on parents and their children. *Evidence Base: A Journal of Evidence Reviews in Key Policy Areas, 3*, pp. 1–23.

Cook, K. (2021). State tactics of welfare benefit minimisation: the power of governing documents. *Critical Social Policy*. https://doi.org/10.1177/02610183211003474

Department of Human Services (2019). Child support and your Family Tax Benefit Part A, Canberra: Australian Government. Available at: https://www.servicesaustralia.gov.au/individuals/topics/child-support-and-your-family-tax-benefit-part/29646 (Accessed 26 November 2019).

DWP (2021). 'Open consultation Child Maintenance: modernising and improving our service.' 18 June.

Employment Support and Income Assistance Regulations (2019). https://novascotia.ca/just/regulations/regs/esiaregs.htm#TOC3_14

Family Law Act (SBC 2011). https://www.bclaws.gov.bc.ca/civix/document/id/complete/statreg/11025_00

Family Maintenance Enforcement Act (RSBC 1996). https://www.bclaws.gov.bc.ca/civix/document/id/complete/statreg/96127_01

Garfinkel, I., McLanahan, S.S., Meyer, D.R. and Seltzer, J.A. (eds.) (1998). *Fathers under fire: The revolution in child support enforcement*. Russell Sage Foundation.

Gorlick, C. and Brethour, G. (1998). Welfare-to-work programs in Canada: An overview. Canadian Council on Social Development.

Hakovirta, M. (2011). Child maintenance and child poverty: a comparative analysis. *Journal of Poverty and Social Justice*, *19*(3), pp. 249–262.

Hakovirta, M. and Hiilamo, H. (2012). Children's rights and parents' responsibilities: Child maintenance policies in Finland. *European Journal of Social Security*, *14*(4), 286–303.

Hakovirta, M., Skinner, C., Hiilamo, H. and Jokela, M. (2020). Child poverty, child maintenance and interactions with social assistance benefits among lone parent families: A comparative analysis. *Journal of Social Policy*, *49*(1), 19–39.

House of commons (2023). REF: https://commonslibrary.parliament.uk/research-briefings/cbp-7774/ (Accessed 12 July 2021).

Kela. (2022). Child maintenance allowance. https://www.kela.fi/web/en/child-maintenance-allowance. (Accessed 1 March 2022).

Lens, V. (2002). Welfare reform, personal narratives and the media: How welfare recipients and journalists frame the welfare debate. *Journal of Poverty*, *6*(2), pp. 1–20.

Natalier, K. (2018). State Facilitated Economic Abuse: A Structural Analysis of Men Deliberately Withholding Child Support. *Feminist Legal Studies*, *26*(2), pp. 121–140.

OECD (2011). Doing Better for Families. Paris.

Oldham, T. and Smyth, B. (2018). Child support compliance in the USA and Australia: To persuade or punish? *Family Law Quarterly*, *52*(2), pp. 325–348.

Seccombe, K., James, D. and Walters, K.B. (1998). 'They think you ain't much of nothing': The social construction of the welfare mother. *Journal of Marriage and the Family*, pp. 849–865.

Skinner, C., Bradshaw, J. and Davidson, J. (2007). *Child support policy: An international perspective*. Corporate Document Services Leeds.

Skinner, C., Meyer, D.R., Cook, K. and Fletcher, M. (2017). Child maintenance and social security interactions: The poverty reduction effects in model lone parent families across four countries. *Journal of Social Policy*, *46*(3), pp. 495–516.

Summerfield, T., Young, L., Harman, J. and Flatau, P. (2010). Child support and welfare to work reforms: The economic consequences for single-parent families. *Family Matters*, *84*, pp. 68–78.

United Nations (1989). *Convention on the Rights of the Child*. New York: United Nations.

2. The tensions embedded within parents' access to and the administration of child support: A cross-country conceptual framework

Adrienne Byrt, Kay Cook, and Thomas Meysen

INTRODUCTION

Child support is money paid by a non-resident parent to a resident parent for the purpose of supporting children following parental relationship breakdown (OECD, 2011). In the overwhelming majority of cases, payments are by a non-resident father to a resident mother, reflecting the deeply gendered distribution of work and care that exists in most countries. In doing so, child support recognises and compensates mothers for the opportunity costs incurred as a result of being a child's primary carer. As a result, across countries, child support exists in reference to other policies that shape the opportunity costs of motherhood, and then post-separation motherhood, such as parental leave, childcare, welfare, and employment policies (Hakovirta, Cook and Sinclair, 2020).

Building on the previous chapter's exploration of the distinctive and similar technical mechanisms that operationalise each country's child support systems, this chapter presents a conceptual framework that identifies the broader societal tensions across countries. The purpose of this chapter is to contextualise each of the following country reports, frame the gendered context in which child support operates, and where opportunities might exist for child support or wider policy reform to better support the work of care conducted by single parents.

Nieuwenhuis and Maldonado (2018, p.2) conceptualised the 'triple bind' of single parenthood. Characterised by 'inadequate resources, inadequate employment and inadequate policies', the triple bind highlights the constraints experienced by single parents, most often experienced by mothers. Following these binds, this chapter provides a conceptual overview of caring resources, employment opportunities and policy framings. Here, we locate the triple bind of single parenthood within the broader socio-cultural gendered expectations placed on mothers post-separation. It provides a framework through which to assess child support's role in arbitrating between such issues as private and state responsibility for children's welfare; between the negation of gender differences versus a commitment to gender justice; and between child support constructed as a series of unconnected technical solutions and versus a coherent policy solution.

THE GENDERED TRIPLE BIND OF SINGLE PARENTHOOD

All societies discussed in this collection are governed by patriarchal structures, whether neoliberal systems that revere 'homo economicus' or familial, religious systems. The dominance of the male breadwinner model remains steadfast across societies regardless of the changing nature of women's work, and the persistence of gendered wage gaps exacerbate separated mothers' economic risk (Cancian and Meyer, 2018). Separated mothers most often take on resident parenting as separated fathers are afforded choice in whether they pay child support, and how much child support they will provide (Cook and Natalier, 2013; Nieuwenhuis and Maldonado, 2018).

While child support systems across nations tend to centre broader parental responsibility, invariably, mothers are left with the burden to navigate complex systems to access, justify, and receive child support (Cook, 2022). In addition, while child support policies may set out how much money non-resident parents are required to provide for the upkeep of children, and family law may prescribe the amount of time that children spend with their parent living elsewhere, mothers must 'pick up the slack' in any shortfall in the amount of funding or time provided. As a result, women's time and resources are always contingent. Unexpected costs, such as medical bills or school requirements fall exclusively on low-income mothers. At the same time, women's ability to generate an adequate income through work may be unexpectedly curtailed at any time due to children falling ill or fathers not adhering to child contact orders. As such, mothers are inevitably and inescapably bound to being carers first and breadwinners second; while fathers are regarded in policy and practice as breadwinners first and caregivers second. The consequences of this unspoken truism are that mothers face inadequate resources to support their caring work, inadequate employment to achieve financial stability and inadequate policies to mitigate these risks. While child support is seen as a panacea to providing mothers with additional resources, it alone is not enough to overcome the gender of responsibility for caring labour.

Broadly, child support systems centre the wellbeing of children through goals to reduce poverty. Yet, amid patriarchal societal structures within which men earn more and take on less domestic responsibility than women, the negation of gender differences fails to recognise the persistence of the expectation of gendered responsibility on mothers. Subsequently, mothers face economic uncertainty and prospective poverty when the provision of child support is also uncertain. In light of the negation of gender difference, this collection highlights a commitment to gender justice as country-specific chapters elucidate the ways in which separated mothers continue to bear economic and caregiving burdens as they traverse complex child support systems.

This chapter also shows the tensions inherent in child support systems when technical solutions become detached from parents' lived reality. Access to child support systems across countries can be limited when receiving parents are in rural or remote areas, are constrained by time due to work responsibilities, or encounter language barriers. Across countries, access to affordable and available childcare also remains limited, further entrenching gendered demands on separated mothers and exacerbating the need for the provision of child support from the non-resident parent. In order to navigate complex child support systems while also contending with a lack of accessible childcare, resident parents must persist without guidance or support amid the underlying assumption that they will have sufficient legal and financial literacy to do so. Noting the first gendered tension inherent in the provision of child support – as resident parents are more likely to be mothers – the navigation of complex systems also becomes gendered. Separated mothers must contend with being both a breadwinner and a caregiver, while labouring through burdensome systems that may or may not meet the needs of the children once administrative requirements are met.

Finally, this chapter frames the tension between privatisation and the responsibility of the state in order to demonstrate how poverty remains an ongoing vulnerability in the lives of separated mothers and their children. While research shows that child support can ameliorate child poverty (Cuesta, Guarin and Eickmeyer, 2022; Cuesta and Meyer, 2014; Hakovirta, 2011; Hakovirta, Meyer and Skinner, 2022; Skinner et al., 2007), often this aim is not fulfilled. While the broad sweeping goal of the provision of child support across countries in this collection is to reduce children's poverty post separation, the triple bind of gendered burdens endured by mothers in patriarchal societies and the persistent demands to navigate complex systems both serve to entrench single mother-headed family poverty. Although child support has the potential to lift children out of poverty, the reality of withheld or unpaid contributions from the non-resident parent means this potential is rarely met (Cuesta and Meyer, 2014).

The tensions between gender, systems, and poverty with the provision of child support highlight the complexity of access to and the administration of child support to improve the economic wellbeing of the children of separated parents. These tensions occur in societies in which the nature of families is changing as parents remarry and take on responsibility for stepchildren or have second families (Meyer, Skinner, and Davidson, 2011; Nieuwenhuis and Maldonado, 2018). Furthermore, amid rising costs of living and accelerating environmental, health, and economic disruptions, emerging adults are living with their parents longer, changing the nature of what it means to have 'a dependent', and subsequently, the nature of child support provision. Furthermore, as single mothers contend with economic uncertainty and disruptions, they must remain responsible for meeting the emotional, psychological and material (for example, food, housing, security) needs of their children. The following section elucidates these issues through the lens of the gendered triple bind to demonstrate how each bind cascades into the other, complicating single parents' access to work and childcare; simultaneously making child support more pivotal yet also inadequate to meet their intractable, and often unmet, needs.

A CONCEPTUAL OVERVIEW

There are multiple, cascading binds that resident parents – typically and almost exclusively single mothers – experience when accessing child support. The first bind results from resident parents' limited resources to care for children, experienced either as a lack of childcare or a lack of time or financial ability to provide care for children directly. Second, women's employment opportunities are limited or complicated by their lack of childcare, or single mothers are underemployed due to the need to access part-time or flexible work or due to career gaps that may have occurred in the early years of their children's lives. Finally, although social security policy and child support are intended to ameliorate the impacts of limited resources and employment opportunities, both ultimately fail to recognise the role of gender (i.e., women are predominantly the resident parent) and the public/private division of responsibility therein. As a result, child support is often viewed as a private responsibility, to be dealt with privately between parents (Cook, 2022). As such, the challenges that single mothers face in accessing caring resources, employment and public support reinforce and complicate each other, resulting in cascading binds. These binds are most often endured by single mothers who bear disproportionate responsibility for navigating the public and private systems of provisioning

(Natalier, 2018) that shape women's ability to resource their families while simultaneously ensuring that children's caring needs are met.

Securing Caring Resources

The policy bridge that makes possible women's provisioning of financial and caring resources is the accessibility and affordability of formal or informal childcare (Brady, 2016). As single mothers contend with gendered demands and limitations on their working life, adequate childcare remains limited and is unaffordable in many nations. Cuesta's (2022) recent policy recommendations for UN Women highlighted the urgency and importance of reform to ensure single-mother families can access high-quality, affordable childcare, given paid work offers single mothers the most significant opportunity to secure an adequate income. Workplace policy enabling mothers to take up formal childcare and government funding to make childcare financially viable rarely meets the demands of contemporary families amid rising costs of living. The limitations of national institutions and social policies to support single-mother families make women's financial provisioning more difficult, as their employment opportunities are constrained by their privatised caring responsibilities (Craig and Churchill, 2018; Houle, Turcotte and Wendt, 2017; Md Nor, 2022; Topimin, Fabeil and Abdullah, 2019). Broadly speaking, mothers consistently face higher levels of parenting stress amid the expectation and reality that they are the child's primary carer (Craig and Churchill, 2018). Furthermore, when workplace flexibility, inadequate childcare, unpaid child support, and single parenthood collide, single mothers contend with diminished wellbeing (Nieuwenhuis and Maldonado, 2018). In familial and religious social welfare systems, as well as in liberal market regimes (Mahon et al., 2012), single mothers are dependent on private forms of care, such as extended family members – often other women with caring responsibilities (Cosson, Cook and Brady, 2021) – or informal childcare systems that exist within their local neighbourhoods (Md Nor, 2022).

As the dominance of the male breadwinner model persists across nations in this collection, it is clear that care and its associated practices are feminised and entrenched (see also Jordan, 2020). Despite efforts by feminist theorists and activists to challenge feminised caregiving expectations, and subsequently, to mobilise degendered nurturing practices, the gender of caregiving must continue to be interrogated (Jordan, 2020; Ruddick, 1980). As Jordan argues, the ways in which caregiving is feminised must also be interrogated in context. The context within which single mothers are situated often demands their interaction with complex child support systems and social policies, the negotiation of difficult relationship dynamics, and the relentless work of providing adequate care and resources to children in states that rarely, or barely, support single mothers. Across the countries included in this collection, social policies often fail to support egalitarian approaches to parenting in the domestic sphere, when limited parenting leave, inaccessible childcare, or patriarchal expectations upon women to remain at home persist. For single mothers, the limitations of social policies are experienced more acutely (Jacobs and Gerson 2016), and their difficulties heightened in the context of unpaid or unenforced child support. The tension between child support policy and the lack of recognition of such gendered oppressions highlights an institutional disregard for the lack of support mothers receive post-separation.

Employment Opportunities and Barriers

As single mothers must make themselves available to attend to their families' care needs that are unable to be met by the state, the formal or informal childcare market or their family, their capacity for sufficiently high-paying or regular employment is diminished. In addition, women must dedicate considerable time to navigating the often onerous administrative burdens that exist within the legal and social welfare systems that women must engage with in order to provide adequate material resources for their children (Cook, 2022; Herd and Moynihan, 2018). The 'work' of financial provisioning that single mothers must engage in to adequately resource their families means that their capacity for engagement with the market is diminished. Research shows that they are likely to face 'in-work poverty' due to inadequate employment (Nieuwenhuis and Maldonado, 2018). Although women's participation in the workforce has increased in the last 50 years, inadequate employment (such as underemployment or part-time employment) is more likely to be experienced by women than men (Craig and Churchill, 2018; Houle, Turcotte and Wendt, 2017; Nieuwenhuis and Maldonado, 2018; Md Nor, 2022; Topimin, Fabeil and Abdullah, 2019). At the same time that single mothers' earning capacity is diminished, structural constraints limit the value of their labour when they are able to engage in the labour market. Broader societal gendered constraints, such as the gendered wage gap and feminisation of caring occupations, ultimately contributes to lower incomes among women when they participate in paid employment. In addition, single mothers' earning capacity is often diminished due to fewer career opportunities, a need to confine employment to within school or childcare hours, or endured extended career disruptions due to childbirth and primary caregiving responsibilities (Nieuwenhuis and Maldonado, 2018).

While single mothers work to meet the material needs of their children, they may, at times, be forced to choose between work and caregiving (Lavee and Benjamin, 2016). Amid neoliberal expectations to participate as economic actors who also raise productive citizens, women often choose caregiving when the demands placed on a good mother overshadow their own economic participation. The tensions between these ideological viewpoints, the ideal worker and the good mother, result in 'caring crises' for low-income mothers (Lavee and Benjamin, 2016). Yet across the countries included in this collection, welfare safety nets vary. The capacity to be able to leave work to enact the demands and obligations of good motherhood is not a choice available in many contexts, as the 'luxury' of being a full-time care giver is often only afforded to mothers with the support of a breadwinner. The irony is that while such 'intensive mothering' (Hays, 1996) is looked upon favourably for middle class mothers, upon separation, these same women may be stigmatised as 'bad mothers' for needing support from the welfare state (Martin et al., 2022; Tyler, 2020; Wolfinger, 2014) or their ex-partners (Goodall and Cook, 2020).

Conversely, separated fathers encounter fewer administrative burdens and are often afforded a modicum of choice in the form, frequency and amount of financial support that they will provide to their children. Cook and Natalier (2013) highlighted the ways in which fathers can opt in or opt out of continuing to provide child support when institutional enforcement systems are weak or foreground private arrangements. However, normative fatherhood, through which men are granted choice and autonomy, is challenged by child support policy (Cook and Skinner, 2019; 2020). Yet it is precisely the notions of fathers' choice and autonomy that promote political debate around the enforceability of child support in countries with administrative regimes.

On the other hand, mothers are disciplined by the state more readily. As they seek state benefits to support their families, single mothers must navigate the administrative burdens imposed by child support and welfare regimes in a context in which they are not deemed capable of providing all that children need (Cook, 2021; Jordan, 2020). For example, Jordan (2020) highlights aspects of parenting that are very gendered, such as discipline. Jordan points out that single mothers are framed as 'deficient' in their capacity to discipline children. In turn, fathers are essentialised through the masculinisation of their perceived capacity to provide such discipline. Through the essentialisation of parenting skills and practices, mothers are invariably framed as ineffective, inefficient, and incapable of providing to their children emotional, psychological, and material resources.

Policy, Procedure and Privatisation: The Role of the State in Child Support Administration

While the economic welfare of children remains central to the administration of familial support, the responsibilisation of single mothers to navigate complicated systems with little assistance from the state is keenly felt across the countries in this collection. Technical management of payment calculations and transfers remains the key focus of policymakers across the countries (Cook, 2021; Garfinkel et al., 1998; Gorlick and Brethour, 1998; Lens, 2002; Seccombe, James, and Walters, 1998; Skinner, Bradshaw, and Davidson, 2007). In Chapter 1, the discussion of the ways that countries determine payment amounts shows that state intervention by way of policy framing can have significant ramifications for children's financial wellbeing. Moving to the collection of payments, across most countries, state intervention wanes as resident parents – most often sole mothers – are left with few avenues to guarantee child support payments are received from non-resident parents. In cases where payments are not made, enforcement resides on a hard-to-soft continuum (Smyth and Oldham, 2018–19), and despite the existence of penalties and incentives 'on paper', very rarely are penalties enforced.

Edwards and Magarey's (1995) early writings were on single parents' complicated relationship with provisioning through the triad of the state, market and family. The competing demands of each source of support complicates single mothers' experience of gaining adequate resources to raise their children amid often contradictory pressures imposed by neoliberal, and familial/ religious, notions of individualisation, 'good mothering'. Parental responsibility remains a clear goal of all states included in this edited collection; however, whose responsibility and responsibility for what is less well articulated or consistent within the broad suite of state parenting support. At the extremes, privatised models of funding care work result in a lack of state accountability and rest on broad assumptions that non-resident fathers can and will provide for their children. Institutionalised models, however, can further entrench assumptions about fathers as breadwinners and mothers as caregivers when they fail to recognise or intervene in the very gendered nature of the need to access child support.

Neoliberal and familial sensibilities promote private responsibility for childrearing in an effort to alleviate any burden on state expenditure (Cook and Natalier, 2013; Craig and Churchill, 2018). Navigating the tensions between work and childcare becomes an individualised exercise in parenting labour which predominantly burdens mothers. Despite the changing nature of women's work in many nations, and broader social acceptability of single mothers, the responsibility of primary care – particularly post-separation – remains gendered. Most notable, the demands on mothers to navigate complex government systems and prove their worthiness in order to access child support remain highly individualised (Cook, 2022). The state demands private responsibility and public accountability of women, yet men avoid such administrative burdens. In low-income families, the tension between the responsibility of the state and an individual's responsibility becomes more pronounced. Yet policymakers rarely favour supporting single-mother families. Welfare support in place of privately funded child support is viewed as an 'unfortunate substitute' for a deadbeat father (Cancian, Meyer and Caspar, 2008). The state continues to – often erroneously – assume a father can and will pay child support. In cases where he might not, the presumption that this is not the norm reinforces the inherent 'choice' men are granted in child support policy and the lack of choice afforded to mothers who must continue to work within and outside of state systems to ensure their families' financial and caring needs are met.

CONCLUSION

The gendered triple bind of single parenthood highlights the ways in which limited access to resources and employment, and inadequate social safety nets leave parents, specifically, single mothers, to navigate complex access to child support as they raise their children. Amid expectations that place private responsibility on parents to manage and access child support in order to alleviate state burden, gender differences are negated in policy despite the overwhelming evidence that single mothers disproportionately shoulder the load of raising and housing their children. The conceptual framework presented in this chapter builds on Nieuwenhuis and Maldonado's (2018, p.2) 'triple bind' of single parenthood by foregrounding the gendered nature of single parenthood. It is the gender of parenting that is fundamental to the arguments pursued in this collection.

This edited collection uniquely captures data from a diversity of countries, governed by neoliberal welfare-states, familial and religious social structures, and social democracies. Regardless of the political landscape contextualising the development of social safety nets and child support policy, the gendered triple bind persists across countries. Single mothers endure limited opportunities for childcare support and employment, with little help from the state. The following chapters in this collection provide insight into the societal contexts, social welfare contexts, and the current and future challenges of child support in Australia, Canada, Columbia, Germany, Malaysia, Nigeria, South Korea, the UK, and the US. The lens of the gendered triple bind brings to light the limitations of child support policy across countries and lays the groundwork for possibilities to re-imagine child support that better provides for children.

REFERENCES

Brady, M. (2016). Gluing, catching and connecting: How informal childcare strengthens single mothers' employment trajectories. *Work, Employment and Society, 30*(5), pp. 821–837. https://doi.org/10.1177/0950017016630259
Cancian, M. and Meyer, D. R. (2018). Reforming policy for single-parent families to reduce child poverty. *RSF: The Russell Sage Foundation Journal of the Social Sciences, 4*(2), pp. 91–112.

Cancian, M., Meyer, D. R. and Caspar, E. (2008). Welfare and child support: Complements, not substitutes. *The Journal of the Association for Public Policy Analysis and Management, 27*(2), pp. 354–375.

Cook, K. (2021). Gender, malice, obligation and the state: Separated mothers' experiences of administrative burdens with Australia's child support program. *Australian Journal of Public Administration.*

Cook, K. (2022). *The failure of child support: Gendered systems of inaccessibility, inaction and irresponsibility.* Bristol: Policy Press.

Cook, K. and Natalier, K. (2013). The gendered framing of Australia's child support reforms. *International Journal of Law, Policy and the Family, 27*(1), pp. 28–50.

Cook, K. and Skinner, C. (2019). Gender equality in child support policy: Fathers' rhetoric of 'fairness' in a parliamentary inquiry. *Social Politics, 26*(1), pp. 164–187.

Cook, K. and Skinner, C. (2020). Technical fixes as challenges to state legitimacy: Australian separated fathers' suggestions for child support policy reform. *Social Politics, 28*(2), pp. 510–520.

Cosson, B., Cook, K. and Brady, M. (2021). 'We ask for more than we give back': Negotiating the boundaries of informal childcare arrangements. *Journal of Family Issues, 42*(5), pp. 931–957.

Craig, L. and Churchill, B. (2018). Parenting stress and the use of formal and informal child care: Associations for fathers and mothers. *Journal of Family Issues, 39*(12), 3203–3224.

Cuesta, L. (2022). Public guarantee of child support: A key policy for improving the economic well-being of lonemother families. https://www.unwomen.org/sites/default/files/2022–08/Policy-brief-Public-guarantee-of-child-support-en.pdf. Accessed 7 September 2022.

Cuesta, L. and Meyer, D. R. (2014). The role of child support in the economic wellbeing of custodial-mother families in less developed countries: The case of Colombia. *International Journal of Law, Policy and the Family, 28*(1), pp. 60–76.

Cuesta, L., Guarin, A. and Eickmeyer, K. J. (2022). Understanding child support arrangements in Colombia: A social exchange theory perspective. *Family Relations.* https://doi.org/10.1111/fare.12779

De Vaus, D., Gray, M., Qu, L. and Stanton, D. (2017). The economic consequences of divorce in six OECD countries. *Australian Journal of Social Issues, 52*(2), pp. 180–199.

Duncan, S. and Edwards, R. (1999). *Lone mothers, paid work and gendered moral rationalities.* Springer.

Edwards, A. and Magarey, S. (1995). *Women in a restructuring Australia: Work and welfare.* Allen & Unwin.

Goodall, Z. and Cook, K. (2020). The forms and functions of child support stigma. *Social Currents,* doi: 2329496520968211.

Hakovirta, M. (2011). Child maintenance and child poverty: A comparative analysis. *Journal of Poverty and Social Justice, 19*(3), pp. 249–262.

Hakovirta, M., Cook, K. and Sinclair, S. (2020). Gender equality prior to and following separation: Nordic and liberal policy inconsistencies. *Social Politics.* https://doi.org/10.1093/sp/jxaa010

Hakovirta, M., Meyer, D. R. and Skinner, C. (2019). Does paying child support impoverish fathers in the United States, Finland, and the United Kingdom? *Children and Youth Services Review,* 106.

Hakovirta, M., Meyer, D. and Skinner, C. (2022). Child support in shared care cases: Do child support policies in thirteen countries reflect family policy models? *Social Policy and Society, 21*(4), pp. 542–559. doi:10.1017/S1474746421000300

Hakovirta, M., Skinner, C., Hiilamo, H. and Jokela, M. (2019). Child poverty, child maintenance and interactions with social assistance benefits among lone parent families. *Journal of Social Policy*, pp. 1–21.

Hays, S. (1996). *The cultural contradictions of motherhood.* Yale University Press.

Herd, P. and Moynihan, D. P. (2018). *Administrative Burden: Policymaking by Other Means.* New York: Russell Sage Foundation.

Hodges, L., Meyer, D. R. and Cancian, M. (2020). What happens when the amount of child support due is a burden? Revisiting the relationship between child support orders and child support payments. *Social Service Review, 94*(2), pp. 238–284.

Houle, P., Turcotte, M. and Wendt, M. (2017). *Changes in parents' participation in domestic tasks and care for children from 1986 to 2015.* No. 89–652. Ottawa: Statistics Canada.

Jacobs, J. A. and Gerson, K. (2016). Unpacking Americans' views of the employment of mothers and fathers using national vignette survey data: SWS presidential address. *Gender & Society, 30*(3), pp. 413–441.

Jordan, A. (2020). Masculinizing care? Gender, ethics of care, and fathers' rights groups. *Men and Masculinities, 23*(1), pp. 20–41.

Lavee, E. and Benjamin, O. (2016). "I've Got No Choice": low-income mothers' emotional management of caring crisis. *Journal of Family Issues, 37*(7), pp. 997–1021.

Lens, V. (2002). 'Welfare reform, personal narratives and the media: How welfare recipients and journalists frame the welfare debate.' *Journal of Poverty, 6*(2), pp. 1–20.

Mahon, R., Anttonen, A., Bergqvist, C., Brennan, D. and Hobson, B. (2012). Convergent care regimes? Childcare arrangements in Australia, Canada, Finland and Sweden. *Journal of European Social Policy, 22*(4), pp. 419–431. https://doi.org/10.1177/0958928712449776

Martin, S., Schofield, T. and Butterworth, P. (2022). News media representations of people receiving income support and the production of stigma power: An empirical analysis of reporting on two Australian welfare payments. *Critical Social Policy, 42*(4), pp. 648–670. https://doi.org/10.1177/02610183211073945

Md Nor, Z. (2022). Precarious employment amongst low income single mothers in Malaysia: The implications on family wellbeing. *E3S Web of Conferences 339, 10th ICMR-2nd INSAEF 2021.* https://www.e3s-conferences.org/articles/e3sconf/pdf/2022/06/e3sconf_10icmr-2insaef2022_06009.pdf

Meyer, D. R., Skinner, C. and Davidson, J. (2011). Complex families and equality in child support obligations: A comparative policy analysis. *Children and Youth Services Review, 33*(10), pp. 1804–1812.

Natalier, K. (2017). Micro-aggressions, single mothers and interactions with government workers: The case of Australia's child support bureaucracy. *Journal of Sociology, 53*(3), pp. 622–636.

Natalier, K. (2018). State facilitated economic abuse: A structural analysis of men deliberately withholding child support. *Feminist Legal Studies, 26*(2), pp. 121–140.

Nieuwenhuis, R. and Maldonado, L. (2018). *The triple bind of single-parent families: Resources, employment and policies to improve well-being.* Bristol: Policy Press.

OECD (2011). Doing Better for Families. Paris.

Pollack, S. and Rossiter, A. (2010). Neoliberalism and the entrepreneurial subject: Implications for feminism and social work. *Canadian Social Work Review*, *27*(2), pp. 155–169.

Risman, B. J. (2004). Gender as a social structure: Theory wrestling with activism. *Gender and Society*, *18*(4), pp. 429–450.

Ruddick, S. (1980). Maternal thinking. *Feminist Studies*, *6*(2), pp. 342.

Seccombe, K., James, D. and Walters, K. B. (1998). 'They think you ain't much of nothing': The social construction of the welfare mother. *Journal of Marriage and Family*, *60*(4), pp. 849–865.

Skinner, C., Bradshaw, J. and Davidson, J. (2007). Child support policy: An international perspective. Corporate Document Services Leeds.

Smyth, B. and Oldham, T. (2018–19). Child support compliance in the USA and Australia: To persuade or punish. *Family Law Quarterly*, *52*(2), pp. 325–348.

Topimin, S., Fabeil, N. and Abdullah, A. (2019). Women's business survival: Challenges and strategies for single mother entrepreneurs. *Academic Journal of Business and Social Sciences*, *3*, pp. 1–10.

Tyler, I. (2020). Stigma: The machinery of inequality. London: Zed Books.

Wolfinger, E. (2014). Australia's welfare discourse and news: Presenting Single mothers. *Global Media Journal Australia Edition*, *8*(2), pp. 1–16 https://www.hca.westernsydney.edu.au/gmjau/wp-content/uploads/2014/11/GMJAU_Australias_Welfare_Discourse_and_News.pdf

3. Australia's child support system in the context of the welfare system and demographic change

Kay Cook and Sarah Sinclair

INTRODUCTION

In this chapter, we outline the demographic and social policy conditions that frame the nature, purpose and function of the Australian child support system. We begin by setting out the social context in which the system operates, including an overview of population trends, and changing family dynamics since the introduction of no-fault divorce in 1975. We then provide an overview of patterns of parental education, employment, and the distribution of wealth and poverty over time. Next, we outline the social welfare policy context that frames the role and function of the child support system, including welfare-to-work requirements and childcare accessibility and affordability. The chapter concludes with an overview of the child support system, including an identification of ongoing challenges and future considerations.

SOCIETAL CONTEXT

Australia's population is currently over 25.5 million (compared to 13.9 in 1975), with one in four current Australian residents born overseas and 38 per cent of Australia's annual population growth due to net overseas migration. This makes Australia one of the most culturally diverse and multicultural countries in the developed world (Australian Bureau Statistics [ABS], 2021a). A far cry from the preceding, racist 'White Australia' policies of the 1900s–1960s, the Whitlam government (1972–75) established a policy of multiculturalism which has continued to date. The primary countries from which Australian migrants originated (in order of rank) for 2019–2020 include India, China, United Kingdom, Philippines, Vietnam, Nepal, New Zealand, Pakistan, South Africa and the USA, with migration shifting over time away from Europe and towards Asia (ABS, 2021f).

Families

As of June 2021, Australia recorded 7.3 million families, 83.4 per cent of which were couple families, 15 per cent were one parent families with 79.8 per cent of these being single mothers and 1.5 per cent classified as 'other families'. Moreover, 45.5 per cent of total families were families with dependants, of which 81.1 per cent were families with children under 15 (ABS, 2021a). These figures reflect changing family formation trends. In 1976, couple families with children made up nearly half of families (48 per cent). By 2016, a little over a third of families were couples with children (37 per cent) while the percentage of couples without children increased by 10 per cent. The proportion of single-parent families with dependent children also increased during this time, rising from 8.6 per cent of families in 1981, to 10.0 per cent in 2021 (AIFS, 2023) to more recent figures of 1 in 7 families being one parent families (15 per cent). Of the approximate 1 million Australian one parent households, 59.5 per cent have dependent children – 81.8 per cent of which are single mother households (AIFS, 2020a).

Despite population growth, the Total Fertility Rate (TFR) currently sits at 1.58 births per woman, down from 1.97 in 2009, although the fertility rate for Aboriginal and Torres's Straits women is currently above replacement at 2.25 births per woman (ABS, 2021b). This decline in fertility and resulting impending structural ageing of the population is perceived to be a significant economic challenge facing Australia, thus the fall in fertility is a significant backdrop to family policy development in Australia. In Australia, population policy and family policy are entwined on several levels. To provide an example, in 2004 a universal cash 'Baby Bonus' payment (AUD $3000) made to a family on the birth of a child was implemented to address falling fertility rates by reducing financial barriers to starting or expanding a family. The payment was gradually phased out between 2009 and 2014 and, although the payment was miniscule in terms of the total cost of a child, birth rates did increase significantly over the period (Sinclair et al., 2012) with the Total Fertility Rate moving closer to the desired replacement rate of 2.1 births per woman.

Despite population policy-based initiatives such as the Baby Bonus, Australians have modest access to parental leave, with 52 per cent of employers offering paid primary carer's leave and 46 per cent offering secondary carer's paid leave (WGEA, 2022). A relatively modest government funded Paid Parental Leave (PPL) scheme was introduced in 2011 as the Baby Bonus was phased out. The PPL provides 18 weeks of paid parental leave to the primary carer paid at the minimum wage equivalent of 41 per cent replacement of the average wage (Bassford and Fisher, 2020). However, given Australia's gender wage gap, the payment inadvertently reinforces women as the primary carer of young children as will be described shortly.

Marriage and Divorce Trends in Australia

In the 1950s and 1960s, marriage in Australia was early and nearly universal. The crude first marriage rate in the 1960s was 85–87 per cent, falling to 71 per cent in 1976 on the introduction of the no fault principle in 1976. Since then, antipodean trends in marriage have mirrored those found elsewhere in the developed world. In 2019, for example, 73 per cent were first marriages for both, 16 per cent a first marriage for one, and 11 per cent remarriage for both. The crude marriage rate in Australia has decreased over time, from 6 to 4.5 marriages per 1,000 estimated resident population between 2009 and 2019 (ABS, 2019). The number of marriages registered in 2019 (113,815) was lower than in 1970 (116,066). The onset of COVID resulted in the largest recorded decrease (30.6 per cent) in marriages from 2019, while same sex marriages represented 4.8 per cent of all marriages that same year. There is, however, a persistence of marriage in higher socioeconomic status groups and for educated women (Heard, 2011). Another prevailing trend is the secularisation of marriage. In 1902, 97 per cent of marriages were performed by ministers of religion. However, by 2000, for the first time, there were more marriages performed by civil celebrants than by ministers of religion increasing to 80 per cent of marriages performed by civil celebrants by 2020 (Qu, Baxter and Carroll, 2022).

In 2020, the crude divorce rate in Australia remained at 1.9 divorces per 1000 people, stable from 2019. In 2020 there were 9,355 divorces involving one child and 10,484 had two children and over 4,000 with three children or more (ABS, 2021e). The median marriage length for Australians before separation is 8.5 years while divorce is usually finalised 3–4 years later (after 12.2 years) with the median age of divorce 45.9 years for men and 43.1 years for women. Couples need to be separated for a minimum of 12 months to qualify for a divorce and need to demonstrate that proper arrangements have been made for any children. Most separating parents (97 per cent) do not go to court to decide their parent arrangements although 16 per cent use dispute resolution via mediation services or legal representatives. About 3 per cent use the courts to determine parenting arrangements and these are predominantly families affected by domestic violence, child safety concerns or other complex issues (AIFS, 2019). In both court-ordered and non-court ordered arrangements, the most common outcome is for children to spend most of their time with their mother while seeing their father regularly.

Parental Education and Employment

Research by the Australian Institute of Family Studies reports that work family arrangements in Australia are highly gendered with fathers far more likely to be working full time than mothers despite increases in mothers in paid employment between 1991–2016. Over this period the proportion of stay at home dads barely changes – sitting at 3–4 per cent (Qu and Warren, 2018).

The employment rate of the working-age Australian population (aged 15–64) has followed a general upward trend since the late 1970s with the exceptions of recessions in the early 1980s and 1990s and the global financial crisis (AIHW, 2023). However, different groups within the labour force, such as women and single parents have different employment experiences. Two of the most significant changes have been the increase in women's education and their increased labour force participation. Rates of high school completion have more than doubled for boys (36 to 81 per cent) and tripled for girls (29 to 88 per cent) over the period spanning prior to 1970s and following the introduction of no fault divorce legislation in 1975 and Australia's child support system in 1988/89 (Gray et al., 2019). While a greater proportion of girls than boys complete high school, Australian women also comprise the majority of university graduates (Norton, Cherastidham and Mackey, 2018). As of May 2021, half of all young women aged 25–34 years now hold a bachelor degree or above, compared with just over a quarter (26 per cent) twenty years ago (May 2001) (ABS, 2021g). However overall, it was more common for men (69 per cent) than women (49 per cent) to be fully engaged in work and or study, noting the proportions for young men and women were exactly the same: 90 per cent each for 15–19 year olds, and 73 per cent each for 20–24 year olds. This illustrates that gender deviations in work or study are driven by those aged 25 or older.

Women's high rates of advanced education, however, have not translated into higher wages than men, or lower unpaid labour. Rather, women tend to drop out of, or significantly reduce their hours in the labour market upon childbirth, hearkening back to a version of the 'marriage bar' of the 1900s that saw women banned from employment upon marriage. However, the employment rate for partnered mothers has increased from 30 per cent in 1984 to 63 per cent in 2019, and for single mothers with the youngest child under 5 from 19 per cent in 1984 to 39 per cent in 2019 (AIFS, 2020b).

The Australian unemployment rate (currently 4.0 per cent – July 2022) has broadly moved lower over the previous two decades; however, this belies the increasing level of underemployment (those who are willing and able to work more hours) driven by both structural and cyclical factors. The disproportionate gender effects of COVID-19 are yet to be fully understood, however data show that in the year to September 2020, total monthly hours worked fell by 5.9 per cent for males and 3.8 per cent for females. Job loss was proportionately larger amongst young people (aged 20–29) and older people. It was also disproportionately higher in female-dominated sectors such as Accommodation and Food Services. Unlike an earlier recession in 1991, when more than 9 per cent of jobs lost were previously held by males, a significant share (around 40 per cent) of the jobs lost in the 2020 recession (year to August 2020) were jobs previously held by females (Birch and Preston, 2021).

Employment data also show that part-time work and other flexible work arrangements have become more prevalent over time, with a recent survey by the WGEA (2022) identifying that nearly four in five employers have a formal flexible work policy or strategy. In 2017, one in five mothers worked at home, and two in five used flexible working hours to help juggle their work and family responsibilities (Baxter, 2019).

The Gender Wage Gap

Australian women, on average, earn considerably less than men and, although improving, there are differentials in average full-time wages of men and women. Currently, Australia's national gender pay gap (based on weekly ordinary earnings) is 13.8 per cent. which has positively been decreasing from a high of 18.5 per cent in 2014 (Workplace Gender Equality Agency, 2022). However, the total renumeration pay gap including superannuation, bonuses and additional payments puts the gender pay gap at 22.8 per cent. Full time working men still on average take home around A\$25,700 more than full time working women. Much of this difference is due to occupational segregation, the gendered prevalence of part time work and time out of the labour force to meet caring responsibilities. Women continue to dominate part-time and casual roles with only 38.1 per cent of full-time workers being women. Despite primary carers leave becoming available to both men and women, only 12 per cent of those that took it last year in Australia were men (WGEA, 2022). It is estimated that it will take another 26 years to close the total renumeration pay gap in Australia (WGEA, 2022).

Interestingly, although female employment participation rates have increased since 1995 there has been a negative trend for average weekly hours worked. This reflects a persistence of the underlying primary male breadwinner model with women expected to take the largest proportion of caring responsibilities while working to supplement household income. This gendered parental distribution of caring and labour market responsibilities persists prior to and after separation. While female employment rates have rapidly escalated, coupled with service provisions such as childcare support, no provisions have been made to allow fathers to contribute more to care (Cook, 2019). Typically, shared care sees paternal care occur 'every second weekend and half of the school holidays' that does not interfere with men's earning capacity, while placing almost all responsibility for coordinating concurrent work and care on women (Cook and Skinner, 2019). The interaction of employment and care responsibilities for one parent families is evidenced by the fact that the proportion of employed one parent families with dependants generally increased with the age of the youngest dependant. The proportion of one parent families with an employed parent was lowest when the youngest dependant was under 5 (45.3 per cent) and the highest when the youngest dependant was between 15 and 24 (72.2 per cent). Given the high proportion of female headed single parent households, this pattern was more prominent for single mothers (61.3 per cent of single mothers were employed compared with 75.8 per cent of single fathers (ABS, 2021d)).

Wealth and Poverty

In a market-based system such as that present in Australia, gendered labour market inequities inevitably flow through to gendered wealth and poverty disparities. Today poverty rates in single mother families make up a large proportion of the 18 per cent of Australian families in poverty. ACOSS reports that over a third of those living in sole parent families in which the main earner is female live in poverty (37 per cent) compared with 18 per cent in sole parent families in which the main earner is male, and 10 per cent in partnered families where the main earner is male (ACOSS, 2020). In 1972/73, prior to the introduction of no-fault divorce, 38 per cent of single mother families lived in poverty, which had increased to 50 per cent in 1980 (McClelland, 2000), despite the introduction of a range of mothers' benefits (Bryson, 1995).

At the time that the Australian child support system was introduced in 1988/89, women were likely to withdraw from the labour market upon the birth of their children, and only resume on a part-time basis thereafter. In the 1980s, 94 per cent of coupled fathers and 44 per cent of coupled mothers were employed (Gray et al., 2019) (Figure 4.1). However, typically, women's employment was part-time in nature (ABS, 1995), while women's eligibility to benefit payments remained tied to their role as carers. In 2015, around 1 in 3 single parent families (30 per cent) with dependent children under 5 years were in severe financial stress. Phillips and Narayanan (2021) report almost 1 in 4 (23 per cent) skip meals, limit heater use or rely on charities to get by (Phillips and Narayanan, 2021). Their analysis of household expenditure data indicates 31 per cent of single parent families lived in poverty in 2017 with financial stress higher for families with children under 5. This financial stress is amplified for single mothers due to continued lower labour force participation and gender pay gaps. It should also be noted that superannuation (mandatory pension savings) is typically not paid during paid parental leave ensuring mothers will continue to make up a higher proportion of those with lower pension balances and poverty rates as they age (WGEA, 2022).

Housing Affordability

A notable point of difference with Australia from other country contexts is access to and availability of affordable housing. Access to quality housing is critical to wellbeing and housing precarity is a particular concern for lower income single parents. In 2017/18 11.5 per cent of households spent 30–50 per cent of gross income on housing costs with another 5.5 per cent spending 50 per cent or more (AIHW, 2021). The social housing program in Australia increasingly focuses on those in greatest need, particularly focusing on addressing homelessness. Waiting lists are long and nationally at 30 June, 2020, there were 155,100 households awaiting a public housing allocation (AIHW, 2021). Government housing support programs are available for low/moderate incomes renting through the private market including rent assistance payments for tenants and subsidy schemes for landlords to provide below-market rental rates. However, even with these assistance packages the 2021 rental affordability index report highlights the housing stress faced by single parents in Australia. For example, a single parent working part time with one child under 5, with an estimated annual income of \$42,000, including government assistance, could not afford any two-bedroom dwelling across all metropolitan and regional areas. Single mothers also face additional cost pressures such as childcare and healthcare which confound financial stress. Affordability does improve when single parents are working full time, as Australia's social welfare policy has sought to incentivise.

SOCIAL WELFARE CONTEXT

Australia's welfare state has traditionally been described as a highly distinctive 'wage earner's welfare state' (Castles, 1985), underpinned by high minimum wages, national wage arbitration and protectionist economic and immigration policies in the early part of the 20th century. As such, a distinguishing feature of the social welfare system was the focus on wages policy (Castles, 1985) much of which got retrenched with market and industrial relations reforms of the 1980–1990s. However, feminist policy scholars have more precisely characterised Australia as a 'white, male wage earner's welfare state' (Bryson, 1992), given that transfers and unemployment benefits typically favoured temporarily unemployed male breadwinners (Marston and Zhang, 2019). The lone male-breadwinner model on which Australia's welfare state was based was generally regarded as no longer capable of delivering Australian families an adequate income (Mitchell, 1999). Over this period, sole parent poverty rates climbed from 38 per cent in 1972–3 to 50 per cent in 1981–2 (McClelland, 2000), while a Social Security Review recommended increasing family payments, putting further pressure on an already burgeoning welfare budget (Edwards, 2019).

Between 1941 and 1987 assistance to families and assistance with the costs of children were not asset or means tested. However, over the next two decades the family allowance target population narrowed significantly, with a move from a universal provision to a view of social security as a safety net. Changes to allowance eligibility resulted in a 22 per cent drop in the number of recipients, from 1978 to 1999 despite a 4 per cent increase in the dependent child population (ABS, 2000).

In later years, despite more targeted family payments to those most in need, the adequacy of payments to act as a sufficient safety net remains questionable. Before benefits were raised by $150 per fortnight in April 2021 (Services Australia, 2021), Australian welfare benefits had not increased in real terms since 1997. Rates were, and continue to be, well below the relative poverty line (60 per cent of median income and the poverty line established by the Australian inquiry into poverty in 1973 (Melbourne Institute, 2019). Drawing on OECD data, the Grattan Institute (Coates and Cowgill, 2021) show how the $50 increase moves the Australian unemployment benefit from being the lowest to the second lowest in the OCED, behind only Greece, even after the modest increase.

Welfare to Work

Since 2006, Australian single parents whose youngest child is over the age of 8 have been moved from the more generous Parenting Payment Single to the far more meagre JobSeeker Allowance (41 per cent of the minimum wage). Single parents must also satisfy part-time 'welfare-to-work' mutual obligation requirements of 30 hours per fortnight once the youngest child turns 6. As of March 2021, 1.6 million people received an unemployment or parenting payment, representing about 7.9 per cent of the population over 16, and 21 per cent of those received the parenting payment (1.6 per cent of the population over 16) (AIHW, 2021). As 'job seekers', Australian single mothers are subject to compulsory 'mutual obligations', such as job search activities, engaging with JobNetwork providers and other reporting obligations. Failure to comply can result in payment suspensions. De Gendre et al. (2021) show that disposable incomes of single-mother households were significantly reduced relative to partnered mothers when the Welfare-to-Work Act came into effect in July 2006, a trend that continued with the Global Financial Crisis and a 2013 suspension of grandfathered single parenting payment rules. The loss in income was compensated by higher reliance on Disability Support Payments, work hours, and child-care expenditures and that this loss in welfare targeted at single mothers had long term negative impacts on child skill development suggesting that Australia's welfare reform over the past two decades has negatively impacted single mother families. These negative effects were reiterated by the findings of Kiely and Butterworth (2014) who analysed the Household Income and Labour Dynamics in Australia (HILDA) survey, to examine the health consequence of the 2006 Welfare to work reforms on vulnerable populations. They find that those who transitioned to non-parenting payments after the reforms were introduced had higher rates of mental health problems compared to both pre-reform.

Childcare

During the 1970s and 1980s, a range of childcare services and programs were introduced to allow mothers more easily to engage in the labour market (Mahon et al., 2016); as such, childcare provides a further example of the entwinement of population and family policies in Australia. To support women's labour market transition, Australia has provided childcare subsidies since 2000. From 2 July 2018, the most recent iteration of the system is known as the means-tested Child Care Subsidy (CCS). For employed parents, the Child Care subsidy (CCS) is paid directly to an approved childcare provider to reduce payable fees if a parent has 14 per cent of care or more, meets residency and vaccination rules and if the child is younger than 13 (or 14–18 with a disability). The CCS payment is worked out on family income, and the hours of recognised activity (for example, work, education etc.) with an hourly rate cap depending on the type of care provided. As a result, caring parents face substantial costs, with Australia having some of the most expensive out-of-pocket childcare fees in the OECD (Brennan, 2019; Mahon et al., 2016) (on average $13,000 equivalent to a private school secondary education considered out of reach of many Australian families). From July 2022 the childcare subsidy was increased for families with multiple children under the age of 6. The subsidy increases by 30 per cent for a second child and subsequent children under 6. It also has a measure to remove the annual cap on the amount of CCS that can be paid for families with incomes above $189,390. Of relevance to this analysis is that childcare costs are excluded from the 'Costs of Children' used to calculate liabilities.

The changes to single mothers' welfare benefit eligibility over time and increasing work requirements show Australia's strong preference for single mothers to be engaged in the labour market rather than being supported by the welfare state. However, women's earning capacity is limited by their caring responsibilities. The normative shared care arrangement of fathers having children every-second weekend and half of the school holidays means that fathers can quarantine their care to weekends and periods of annual leave that leave their employment capacity unaffected. For mothers, by contrast, the high costs of childcare (among the highest in the OECD) and detrimental tax and benefit taper rates that see women's effective marginal tax rates reach almost 100 per cent in some circumstances (Stewart, 2018), means that mothers disproportionately suffer the financial consequences of children's care.

CHILD SUPPORT

The Australian child support scheme commenced a little over forty years ago, in 1988/89, in response to rapidly escalating rates of single mother family poverty and the concomitant welfare budget blowout that followed the introduction of no-fault divorce in 1975. Given the rising numbers of single parents, the burgeoning cost of providing benefits, and the growing number of children living in poverty during the 1980s, Australia's original child support scheme was designed to 'rais[e government] revenue as well as assis[t] in alleviating child poverty' (Edwards, 2019, p. 141). To achieve this balance, non-resident fathers were required to increase personal financial responsibility for their children.

The principal objects of the Australian scheme are to allow children to share in both parents' standard of living; ensure that children receive an adequate level of financial support; limit Commonwealth expenditure; and not provide a work-disincentive to parents (Daniels, 1990). There is an emphasis on aligning the level of support with the costs of children and keeping the determination of financial support outside of the court system.

In determining the amount of child support to be paid, the original Australian formula only referenced the non-resident parent's income in almost all circumstances (Edwards, 1986). This was due to the fact that prior to the introduction of the scheme, 90 per cent of single parent families were headed by mothers (Edwards, 1986), which fell to 88 per cent in 1992 (Hancock, 1998) and has continued to decline – albeit very modestly – to 81 per cent in 2021. As such, the scheme maintained the Australian benefit system's reference to the male-breadwinner and female-carer welfare model that existed at the time of the scheme's design, whereby 94 per cent of fathers, yet only 44 per cent of mothers, were employed (Gray et al., 2019) – a point which we will return to shortly.

In addition to transferring men's income directly to children, to achieve the government's aim to reduce welfare expenditure, child support was included as income in the calculation of one single mother benefit payment. As such, while fathers experience full 'pass through' of their payments to children, receiving parents experience almost 50 per cent 'claw back' of child support payments in the form of reduced benefit payments. In more than half of all child support cases, where payments are transferred privately between parents, the claw back of FTBA (Family Tax Benefit part A) occurs irrespective of whether child support payments are received, as it is the 'expected' rather than the 'received' amount of child support that is used in FTBA payment calculations.

As such, while child support payments were recently shown to reduce single parents' likelihood of being in poverty by 21 per cent (Skinner, Cook and Sinclair, 2017), the poverty-reduction benefits of child support are largely negated by mothers' low benefits and poor earnings potential (Skinner, Meyer, Cook and Fletcher, 2017). A critical assessment of Australia's child support scheme could conclude that its original poverty reduction aim has been over-shadowed by its focus on reducing welfare expenditure. At the same time, non-resident parent financial responsibility for children remains central.

CURRENT AND FUTURE CHILD SUPPORT CHALLENGES

Technical and Procedural Issues

Australia's child support formula is regarded as an advanced system whose formula takes into consideration the costs of new children in each parent's home, changes to parental income and the percentage of overnight care time provided by each parent. Child support orders can be repeatedly modified to take variations in each parent's care time and income into account. However, while the benefits of such flexibility may be seen as advantageous, the seeming responsiveness of the formula also creates expectations for accuracy and transparency that are not able to be met.

Regular fluctuations in income, driven by a more casualised workforce complicates the income-based child support system, particularly when child support received interacts with the benefits system. Receiving parents may receive child support payments in 'lump' form and have to go through a reporting process of underpayment in one time period to overpayment in another, while paying parents with fluctuating incomes may experience a lag between when income is earned and when child support payments are due. Apart from the risk of having to repay social security payments overpaid in a given month, this inconsistency in expected child support as a result of highly casualised and flexible labour markets makes budgeting for both parents challenging.

Research has indicated that government systems and existing communication technologies are not well equipped to record and report on the lived fluidity of such arrangements (Cook et al., 2015; Cook, 2021a), with recent research revealing that women are disproportionately burdened by the administration of the child support system (Cook, 2021b). Then, in Australia, like elsewhere, the number of children living apart from one parent is increasing. In addition, due to Australia's particularly multicultural society, families are increasingly likely to exist transnationally. The COVID-19 pandemic has increased the number of single parent households, with already geographically separated families further emotionally separating during this time. This is especially the case for transnational families who face ongoing border restrictions. For the children in such families, geographic barriers also pose significant risks to their financial wellbeing.

Gender and Degendering

While Australia's current child support policy is framed as being gender-neutral in design and implementation – operationalised within the child support formula through the equal treatment of both parents' share of care, proportion of costs and their capacity to pay – deeply gendered norms regarding the family organisation of work and care, as outlined above, continue to predominate. As such, the gender of child support is an ongoing challenge.

Men's enduring, individualised responsibility for children as a male bread-winner is a point that has been contested since the outset of the scheme, fought in terms of the scheme's 'fairness' to paying fathers (Edwards, 2019; Ministerial Taskforce on Child Support, 2005), and one that continues to spark controversy. In the 30-plus years since the scheme's inception, rounds of incremental reform have sought to de-gender the formula as an implicit means of dismantling this male breadwinner model. These changes have achieved the inclusion of both mothers' and fathers' incomes in the calculation of child support payments, payment discounts for father-provided overnight care, and the recognition of in-kind provisions such as private school fees in lieu of pay-ments (seeking to destabilise the link between mothers' care and payments). Each of these amendments has been championed by aggrieved payers and high-income payers (Cook and Natalier, 2016). While mothers' experiences have been actively excluded from reform processes (Cook and Natalier, 2014), the voices of non-Anglo parents, including Indigenous and migrant parents, have been almost invisible. As such, Australia's child support system can be seen to entrench westernised models of nuclear families and individual auton-omy that may not align well with contemporary, multicultural society.

The endurance of the male breadwinner model, however, continues to shape Australian child support policy reforms. The formula now provides discounts for caring costs associated with new children. Given the de-gendered formula, these discounts apply to children from both parental and maternal re-partnering but given Australia's entrenched gender wage gap and women's part-time employment status, fathers complained of the unfairness of this arrangement in evidence presented at the 2015 child support inquiry (Cook and Skinner, 2021). As Cook (2019, p. 260) again notes,

> While it is not surprising culturally, it has been a major challenge in contemporary social policy that gendered patterns of work and care persist following relationship breakdown; as these trends run counter to the de-gendered policy narrative that has been incrementally progressed.

Given the mismatch between child support's enduring male-breadwinner model and contemporary family life, questions are raised as to the purpose of child support in Australian society.

Within the child support system – which seeks to distribute the costs of children more equitably between the earning and caring parent – the costs of care borne by mothers receive little political attention. As research on the stigma experienced by separated mothers within the child support system reveal, mothers are often at pains to point out their child-centric expenditure, rather than spending money on themselves (Natalier and Hewitt, 2014). Similarly, Goodall and Cook's (2021) analysis found that child support recipients felt that they had to defend themselves against perceptions that they contravened maternal norms of child-centric expenditure, patriarchal norms regarding men's financial authority and autonomy, and familial norms related to seeking financial contributions from a male breadwinner who resided outside of the nuclear family unit. As such, the authority of fathers within the nuclear family unit is strong and imbues women's own regard for how or whether they should negotiate and receive payments. Politically, there is also a perception that separated mothers manipulate fathers and the child support, welfare and family law systems for financial gain. Indeed, the Deputy Chair of the 2019–2021 House of Representatives Standing Committee on Social Policy and Legal Affairs inquiry into Australia's family law system has repeatedly insisted that mothers fabricate claims of domestic and sexual violence in order to deny fathers care of children and ultimately increase their child support payments.

CONCLUDING REMARKS

Australian child support policy is being asked to do some heavy lifting in terms of minimising state responsibilities for children's wellbeing upon parental separation in a context of low wages, income insecurity, high childcare costs and housing unaffordability. Given structural changes to employment, households and care, child support as a policy is becoming increasing incapable of achieving this task. While government policy has sought to implement incremental 'workarounds' to solve problems to do with women's earnings, shared care, adult children's continued economic dependence, and transnational families there remain ongoing contests and Australia's child support system will face significant challenges in the years ahead. What has not featured prominently in this review, or in Australian child support research (Cook, McKenzie and Knight, 2011) or policymaking (House of Representatives Standing Committee on Family and Community Affairs, 2003; Ministerial Taskforce on Child Support, 2005; House of Representatives Standing Committee on Social Policy and Legal Affairs, 2015), are the needs and interests of children. Centring children's wellbeing could provide a pathway to balancing state, payer and recipient parent interests and smoothing administrative barriers to policy success.

REFERENCES

Australian Bureau of Statistics (ABS). (1995). *Australian Social Trends*, Catalogue No. 4102.0. Canberra: ABS.

Australian Bureau of Statistics (ABS). (2000). *Australian Social Trends*. No. 4102.0. Canberra: ABS.

Australian Bureau of Statistics (ABS). (2013). *Population Projections, Australia*, Catalogue No. 3222.0. Canberra: ABS.

Australian Bureau of Statistics (ABS). (2019). *Marriages and Divorces, Australia*. Canberra: ABS. Available:https://www.abs.gov.au/statistics/people/people-and-com munities/marriages-and-divorces-australia/latest-release Accessed 5 July 2021.

Australian Bureau of Statistics (ABS). (2021a). Population. Canberra: ABS. Available: https://www.abs.gov.au/statistics/people/population Accessed 10 January 2022.

Australian Bureau of Statistics (ABS). (2021b). National State and Territory population. Available: https://www.abs.gov.au/statistics/people/population/national-state -and-territory-population/latest-release. Accessed 10 January 2022.

Australian Bureau of Statistics (ABS). (2021c). *Births, Australia 2020*. Canberra: ABS. Available: https://www.abs.gov.au/statistics/people/population/births-australia/2020 Accessed 10 January 2022.

Australian Bureau of Statistics (ABS). (2021d). *Labour Force status of families June 2021*. Canberra: ABS. Available: https://www.abs.gov.au/statistics/labour/employm ent-and-unemployment/labour-force-status-families/latest-release Accessed 10 January 2022.

Australian Bureau of Statistics (ABS). (2021e). *Marriages and Divorces* 2020 Canberra: ABS. Available: https://www.abs.gov.au/statistics/people/people-and-commun ities/marriages-and-divorces-australia/latest-release Accessed 10 August 2022.

Australian Bureau of Statistics (ABS). (2021f). *Migration, Australia*. Canberra: ABS. Available: https://www.abs.gov.au/statistics/people/population/migration-australia/ latest-release#net-overseas-migration. Accessed 10 January 2022.

Australian Bureau of Statistics (ABS). (2012g). *Education and Work*. Canberra: ABS. Available: https://www.abs.gov.au/statistics/people/education/education-and-work -australia. Accessed 10 August 2022.

Australian Council of Social Services. (2020). *Poverty in Australia 2020: Part 2 - Who is affected?* ACOSS and The University of New South Wales.

Australian Institute of Family Studies (AIFS). (2020a). Population and households. Melbourne: AIFS. Available: https://aifs.gov.au/facts-and-figures/population-and-households. Accessed 11 January 2022.

Australian Institute of Family Studies (AIFS). (2019). Parenting arrangements after separation. Melbourne: AIFS. Available: https://aifs.gov.au/sites/default/files/publication-documents/1910_parenting_arrangements_after_separation.pdf. Accessed 11 January 2022.

Australian Institute of Family Studies (AIFS). (2020b). Families then and now: How we worked. Melbourne: AIFS. Available: https://aifs.gov.au/research/research-reports/families-then-now-how-we-worked. Accessed 11 January 2022.

Australian Institute of Health and Welfare (AIHW). (2023). Housing Affordability. Available: https://www.aihw.gov.au/reports/australias-welfare/housing-affordability. Accessed 10 January 2022.

Bassford, M., and Fisher, H. (2020). The impact of paid parental leave on fertility intentions. *Economic Record, 96*(315), 402–430.

Baxter, J. (2019). *Fathers and work: A statistical overview* (Research summary). Melbourne: Australian Institute of Family Studies. Retrieved from aifs.gov.au/aifs-conference/fathers-and-work. Accessed 10 January 2022.

Beaumont, P., Hess, B., Walker, L., and Spancken, S. (2014). *The recovery of maintenance in the EU and worldwide*. Oxford: Hart Publishing.

Birch, E., and Preston, A. (2021). The Australian labour market in 2020. *Journal of Industrial Relations, 63*(3), 303–320.

Brady, M., and Cook, K. (2015). The impact of welfare to work on parents and their children. *Evidence Base*, 2015 (*3*), 1–23 doi 10.4225/50/57C$E8591249A

Brennan, D. (2019). The good mother in Australian childcare policy. In C. Pascoe Leahy and P. Bueskens (Eds.), *Australian mothering: Historical and sociological perspectives*, 339–358. Palgrave McMillan.

Bryson, L. (1992). *Welfare and the state: Who benefits?* Palgrave.

Bryson, L. (1995). Two welfare states: One for women, one for men. *Women in a restructuring Australia: Work and welfare.* Sydney: Allen and Unwin.

Cass, B. (1995). Gender in Australia's restructuring labour market and welfare state. In A. Edwards and S. Magarey (Eds.), *Women in a restructuring Australia: Work and welfare.* Sydney: Allen and Unwin, 38–59.

Castles, F. G. (1985). *The working class and welfare: Reflections on the political development of the welfare state in Australia and New Zealand, 1890–1980.* Taylor & Francis.

Chambers, M., Chapman, B., and Rogerson, E. (2021). Underemployment in the Australian labour market. *Bulletin*, June Quarter 2021.

Coates, B., and Cowgill, M. (2021). The JobSeeker rise is not enough. *The Grattan Blog*, 24 February. Available: https://blog.grattan.edu.au/2021/02/the-jobseeker-rise-is-not-enough/ Accessed 4 March, 2021.

Cook, K. (2019). Gender, social security and poverty. In P. Saunders (Ed.), *Social security and poverty in Australia: Social policy after Henderson*, 250–267. Melbourne University Press.

Cook, K. (2020). The devaluing and disciplining of single mothers in Australian child support policy. In C. Pascoe and P. Bueskens (Eds.), *Australian mothering: Historical and sociological perspectives*, 381–402. Cham: Palgrave Macmillan.

Cook, K. (2021a). State tactics of welfare benefit minimisation: the power of governing documents. *Critical Social Policy*. https://doi.org/10.1177/02610183211003474

Cook, K. (2021b). Gender, malice, obligation and the state: Separated mothers' experiences of administrative burdens with Australia's child support program. *Australian Journal of Public Administration, 80*(4), 912–932.

Cook, K., Mckenzie, H., and Knight, T. (2011). Child support research in Australia: A critical review. *Journal of Family Studies, 17*(2), 110–125.

Cook, K., McKenzie, H., Natalier, K., and Young, L. (2015). Institutional processes and the production of gender inequalities: The case of Australian child support research and administration. *Critical Social Policy, 35*(4), 512–534.

Cook, K., and Natalier, K. (2014). Selective hearing: The gendered construction and reception of inquiry evidence. *Critical Social Policy, 34*(4), 515–537.

Cook, K., and Natalier, K. (2016). Gender and evidence in family law reform: A case study of quantification and anecdote in framing and legitimising the 'problems' with child support in Australia. *Feminist Legal Studies, 24*(2), 147–167.

Cook, K., and Skinner, C. (2019). Gender equality in child support policy: Fathers' rhetoric of 'fairness' in a parliamentary inquiry. *Social Politics: International Studies in Gender, State & Society, 26*(1), 164–187.

Costello, P. (2004). *Australian Broadcasting Corporation LateLine. Costello hands down ninth Budget [TV program transcript].* Broadcast 11 May, 2004. http://www.abc.net.au/lateline/content/2004/s1106256.htm. Accessed December 2008.

Daniels, D. (1990). *Parliamentary Research Service Background Paper: The Child Support Scheme.* Canberra: Department of the Parliamentary Library, Parliament of Australia.

de Gendre, A., Schurer, S., and Zhang, A. (2021). *Two decades of welfare reforms in Australia: How did they affect single mothers and their children?* (No. 14752). Institute of Labor Economics (IZA).

Edwards, M. (1986). Child support: Assessment, collection and enforcement issues and possible directions for reform. In *Windsor Yearbook of Access to Justice, (6),* 93–140.

Edwards, M. (2019). The child support scheme: What collaborative innovation can achieve. In J. Luetjens, M. Mintrom, and P. 't Hart (Eds.), *Successful Public Policy: Lessons from Australia and New Zealand,* 139–164. Canberra: ANU Press.

Faroque, F. (2004). 'So, will you do it for your country?' *The Age.* May 15th. Retrieved from So, will you do it for your country? (theage.com.au).

Goodall, Z., and Cook, K. (2021). The forms and functions of child support stigma. *Social Currents, 8*(2), 145–162.

Gray, M., Qu, L., Stanton, D., and Weston, R. (2019). Fifty years of changing families: Implications for income support. In P. Saunders (Ed.), *Revisiting Henderson: Poverty, social security and basic income,* 67–88. Melbourne: Melbourne University Press.

Hancock, L. (1998). Reforming the child support agenda? Who benefits? *Just Policy: A Journal of Australian Social Policy,* (12), 20–31.

Heard, G. (2011). Socioeconomic marriage differentials in Australia and New Zealand. *Population and Development Review, 37*(1), 125–160. https://doi.org/10.1111/j.1728–4457.2011.00392.x

Henderson, R. (1975). *Australian Government Commission of Inquiry into Poverty: First Main Report.* Canberra: Australian Government Publication Service.

House of Representatives Standing Committee on Family and Community Affairs. (2003). *Every Picture Tells a Story: Report on the Inquiry into Child Custody Arrangements in the Event of Family Separation.* Canberra: Commonwealth of Australia.

House of Representatives Standing Committee on Social Policy and Legal Affairs. (2015). *From conflict to cooperation: Inquiry into the child support program.* Commonwealth of Australia.

Kiely, K. M., and Butterworth, P. (2014). How has Welfare to Work reform affected the mental health of single parents in Australia? *Australian and New Zealand Journal of Public Health, 38*(6), 594–595. http:// doi.org/10.1111/1753- 6405.1230

Lesthaeghe, R. (2014). The second demographic transition: A concise overview of its development. *Proceedings of the National Academy of Sciences, 111*(51), 18112–18115.

Mahon, R., Bergqvist, C., and Brennan, D. (2016). Social Policy Change: Work–family tensions in Sweden, Australia and Canada. *Social Policy & Administration, 50*(2), 165–182.

Marston, G., and Zhang, J. (2019). Limitation of the Australian Social Security System. In P. Saunders (Ed.), *Social security and poverty in Australia: Social policy after Henderson,* 141–162. Melbourne: Melbourne University Press.

McClelland, A. (2000). *No child ... Child poverty in Australia.* Brunswick, VIC: Brotherhood of St Laurence.

Melbourne Institute (2019). *Poverty lines: Australia.* Melbourne: The University of Melbourne.

Ministerial Taskforce on Child Support. (2005). *In the best interests of children – Reforming the Child Support Scheme.* Canberra: Commonwealth of Australia.

Mitchell, D. (1999). Family policy and the state. In L. Pocock (Ed.), *Women, public policy and the state,* 73–84. Melbourne: Macmillan Education Australia.

Natalier, K., and Hewitt, B. (2014). Separated parents reproducing and undoing gender through defining legitimate uses of child support. *Gender & Society, 28*(6), 904–925.

Norton, A., Cherastidham, I., and Mackey, W. (2016). *Mapping Australian higher education 2016.* Melbourne: Grattan Institute.

OECD. (2019). *Society at a Glance 2019: OECD Social Indicators.* Paris: OECD Publishing. https://doi.org/10.1787/soc_glance-2019-en.

Phillips, B., and Narayanan, V. (2021). Financial stress and social security settings in Australia. ANU Centre for Social Research and Methods.

Qu, L., Baxter, J., and Carroll, M. (2022). *Marriages in Australia.* Australian Institute of Family Studies, https://aifs.gov.au/research/facts-and-figures/marriages-australia. Accessed 10 August 2022.

Qu, L., and Warren, D. (2018). *Work and family: Household division of labour 1991–2016.* Australian Institute of Family Studies. https://aifs.gov.au/research/facts -and-figures/work-and-family. Accessed 12 August, 2022.

Services Australia. (2021). Jobseeker payment – How much you can get. Available: https://www.servicesaustralia.gov.au/individuals/services/centrelink/jobseeker -payment/how-much-you-can-get. Accessed 22 February 2021.

Sevenhuijsen, S. (1986). Fatherhood and the political theory of rights: Theoretical perspectives of feminism. *International Journal of the Sociology of Law, 14*(3–4), 329–340.

Sinclair, S., Boymal, J., and De Silva, A. (2012). A re-appraisal of the fertility response to the Australian baby bonus. *The Economic Record, 88,* 78–87.

Skinner, C., Cook, K., and Sinclair, S. (2017). The potential of child support to reduce lone mother poverty: Comparing population survey data in Australia and the UK. *Journal of Poverty and Social Justice, 25*(1), 79–94.

Skinner, C., Meyer, D., Cook, K., and Fletcher, M. (2017). Child maintenance and social security interactions: the poverty reduction effects in model lone parent families across four countries. *Journal of Social Policy, 46*(3), 495–516.

Stewart, M. (2018). Personal income tax cuts and the new Child Care Subsidy: Do they address high effective marginal tax rates on women's work? *Tax and Transfer Policy Institute Policy Brief 1/2018*. Canberra: Australian National University.

Walker, L. (2015). *Maintenance and Child Support in Private International Law*. London: Bloomsbury.

Warren, D., Baxter, J., and Qu, L. (2020). *How we worked*. Australian Institute of Family Studies. Available from Australian Families Then & Now: How we worked (aifs.gov.au).

Wolfinger, E. (2014). Australia's welfare discourse and news: Presenting single mo-thers. *Global Media Journal Australian Edition, 8*(2): Available: https://www.hca.westernsydney.edu.au/gmjau/wp-content/uploads/2014/11/GMJAU_Australias_Welfare_Discourse_and_News.pdf . Accessed 10 January 2022.

Workplace Gender Equality Agency (WGEA). (2022). *Australia's gender pay gap statistics 2021*. Canberra: Australian Government. Available: https://www.wgea.gov.au/publications/australias-gender-pay-gap-statistics Accessed March 8, 2022.

4. The child support system in Canada: An overview

Hannah Roots and Rhonda Breitkreuz

INTRODUCTION

Child support in Canada has the social policy objective of ensuring that children do not financially suffer as a result of a separation or divorce of their parents. Broadly, this policy is based on the assumption that both parents are responsible for the financial support of the child. This is achieved through the transfer of funds from one parent (paying parent) to the other parent (receiving parent) to help meet the costs that the recipient parent incurs as a result of caring for the child. However, in the changing landscape of Canadian family life, a number of the foundational assumptions of the current child support system are no longer relevant. Families that share parenting of their children across households, families that have adult children living at home, or families that have formed second families, fall outside of the parameters of the system. Furthermore, social assistance recipients do not benefit financially from the policy as it is currently administered in many Canadian jurisdictions. Given that the guidelines for child support in Canada are nearly 25 years old, and the assumptions upon which the guidelines are based are no longer valid for a growing number of families, Canada's child support system may be characterised as outdated. As such, it is in need of reform in order to ensure that the policy is reflective of the composition of contemporary families and meets their needs.

In this chapter, we explain how child support policy operates in Canada, outline the assumptions upon which it is based, highlight the limitations and gaps of the current system, and conclude with some recommendations for child support policy reforms in Canada. To situate our review and analysis of child support policy, we start with a broad overview of the societal, social welfare, and policy contexts of Canada. We also provide a brief overview of the situation of single mothers as one family type, and briefly identify some of the challenges for single mothers within the Canadian context.

SOCIETAL CONTEXT

Overview

Canada is a diverse country with nearly 38 million people, and nearly one-fifth (7.2 million) of those are under 18 years of age (Statista, 2019). It is a nation of First Peoples and immigrants. Indigenous people comprise 4.9 per cent of the Canadian population (Statistics Canada, 2018a), and one-fifth of the population identifies as a visible minority, the highest among G8 countries (Statistics Canada, 2017a). It has two official languages, English and French. In addition to the diversity among race, ethnicity and language, Canada has considerable family diversity. Just over two-thirds (67.7 per cent) of Canadian households have a child under 18 living in them. Among families with children in Canada, 67 per cent are married, 16.7 per cent are in a co-habiting relationships and 16.3 per cent are lone parent families (Statistics Canada, 2018b). One-quarter of Canadians between the ages of 35–64 are in a second or subsequent marriage or common-law relationship (Statistics Canada, 2019). Furthermore, over half of those who married a second time had children with their current spouse (Statistics Canada, 2019). Among lone parent families, 81 per cent are headed by mothers and another nine per cent of children of divorced parents live equally between their parents' homes (Moyser, 2017; Vanier Institute, 2019). Over one-third of young adults aged 20–34 live with their parents (34.7 per cent). Some of them are students, some have returned home after living independently, and some haven't left home yet. At least some of them are financially dependent on their parents (Statistics Canada, 2017b). Given the diversity among families, a one-pronged approach to child support is unlikely to meet everyone's needs.

Gendered Expectations for Work And Care

Within this larger societal context, Canadian women and men still 'do gender' in their paid and unpaid work. Although mothers have high employment rates, their labour force attachment rates still lag behind Canadian fathers and women without children (Beeston, 2016; Moyser, 2017; OECD, 2019). The employment rate for Canadian mothers in couples was 76.2 per cent overall, compared to fathers in couples, which was 90.5 per cent (Moyser, 2017). Houle, Turcotte and Wendt (2017) show that in 2015, Canadian mothers conducted 38 per cent of the total paid work hours of parents, compared to fathers' contributions at 62 per cent of the paid work hours. Furthermore, women still earn less than men. Among all employed women between the ages of 25 and 54 (considered the core working age group in Canada), women earned an average of $26.92 per hour. In contrast, their male counterparts earned $31.05 per hour. Stated differently, women earned $.87 cents for every dollar men earned (Pelletier, Patterson and Moyser, 2019). A disproportionate number of women hold part-time work in minimum wage jobs in comparison to their male counterparts (Vosko, MacDonald and Campbell, 2009).

Similarly, there are statistically significant differences in household work (i.e. housework, yard work and household maintenance) where women in couples do 1.6 times more household domestic work than men (Milan, Keown, and Urquijo, 2011). Likewise, although fathers' participation rates in childcare have increased significantly in the past several decades, there is still a partic-ipation gap between fathers and mothers, where mothers do twice as much childcare as fathers (Houle, Turcotte and Wendt, 2017). The gendered nature of paid and unpaid work has implications for women's economic security upon relationship dissolution.

Single Mothers

After separation and divorce, women are at risk of income insecurity and poverty (Canadian Women's Foundation, 2017) due to a combination of poor quality, low-paid jobs, a gendered wage gap, fewer hours of paid work, a low net worth, and a disproportionate responsibility for unpaid care work of chil-dren. Given that single mothers comprise just over 80 per cent of lone parent families, understanding their realities is particularly important to understand the implications of child support policy for them.

Labour-force participation rates for single mothers have gone up sub-stantially in Canada in recent years and are nearly on a par with partnered mothers. Lone mothers have a labour-force participation rate of 82 per cent in comparison to the labour-force participation rate of 85.8 per cent for partnered mothers with an employed spouse and children aged 6–15 (Statistics Canada, 2021a). However, high labour-force attachment rates are not equated with income security for many single mothers. Part of the challenge, particularly for low-income, single mothers, is that women in Canada hold a disproportionate number of low-paid, part-time jobs in the service industry that do not typically include benefits, autonomy, or flexibility (Vosko, MacDonald and Campbell, 2009). In addition, single mothers have a greater burden of care and the jobs that low-income mothers are able to attain often have characteristics that are not conducive to single parenting (Breitkreuz and Williamson, 2012; Mason, 2003). As a result, many single mothers continue to struggle with inadequate income and the challenge of combining paid and unpaid work on their own (Breitkreuz, Williamson and Raine, 2010). Not surprisingly, the poverty rate for lone-mother families is four times that of two-parent families, with nearly

30 per cent of this group in poverty compared to 7 per cent of coupled families, and 10 per cent overall (Statistics Canada, 2021b).

Income discrepancies are striking when looking at average incomes and net worth according to family type. While couple families have the highest average household income of $126,000, the average annual income of lone parents is $81,700 for fathers and $63,800 for lone mothers. Furthermore, couple families have nearly three times the net worth of lone mothers ($700,000 and $240,000 respectively). Notably, lone fathers have twice the net worth of lone mothers ($530,000 and $240,000 respectively) (Fox and Moyser, 2018). Clearly, economic risk is gendered, and so the extent to which single mothers receive adequate and equitable child support has significant implications for their wellbeing and that of their children.

The Canada Child Benefit (CCB), a quasi-universal benefit, has been significant in reducing child poverty in Canada in recent years, providing up to $628/month per child to families, calculated by net family income (Government of Canada, 2021b). However, high rates of poverty among single-mother families remain. Given the persistently lower market incomes of women and the high rates of poverty among single-mother families, an effective child support policy becomes critical to ensure ongoing financial wellbeing for them and their children.

SOCIAL WELFARE CONTEXT

In addition to a diverse population, Canada has a rather complex federal system of government where provinces have jurisdiction over education, health and social services (for example, income support, family support and child welfare). Through the transfer of funds from the federal government to provinces and territories for education and healthcare, there is a universal, and somewhat consistent, provision of service offered within these programs across the country. Likewise, parental leave, offered through the federal employment insurance program, has a baseline consistent across the country, with additional variation offered depending on whether provinces and/or companies offer any top-ups. The federal baseline program offers 50 weeks of a combination of maternity (just the mother) (15 weeks) and parental benefits for either parent (35 weeks) at a replacement rate of 55 per cent of median income, or 18 months of leave at a replacement rate of 33 per cent of median income. Because replacement income is just over half of median income, this will mean a substantial loss of earnings for all women, with a greater gap for women of higher incomes. Maternity benefits are reserved for the mother, and either parent can use the parental benefits (Government of Canada, 2020). An additional five weeks are reserved for fathers only, with a 'use it or lose it' clause. While basic education, healthcare, and parental leave are somewhat uniform in Canada, there are a number of other family and social policies that lack consistency across provinces and territories, and fall short in public funding, including childcare and social assistance.

Canada's provision of childcare is characterised as patchwork, with uneven provision and uneven quality, a shortage of spaces, and a lack of affordability (Breitkreuz and Colen, 2018; Daly, 2012; Mahon, Anttonen, Bergqvist, Brennan, and Hobson, 2012). Notably, there are regulated spaces for just over one-quarter of children aged 0–5 in most Canadian provinces (Friendly, Larson, Feltham, Grady, Forer and Jones, 2018), even though the labour-force participation rate for women with children aged 0–5 is nearly 70 per cent (Moyser, 2017). Furthermore, the vast majority (over 80 per cent) of childcare costs are paid by parents (Friendly et al., 2018). However, the federal government has recently made some attempts to improve childcare. It introduced the Multilateral Early Learning and Child Care Framework (MELCCF) in 2017 to provide a guarantee of $7.5 billion over 11 years for childcare and early learning in Canada (Government of Canada, 2017). Further, COVID-19 sparked a national conversation about the importance of childcare and the strain put on mothers when it is unavailable. As a consequence, in April 2021, the federal government promised $30 billion (CAN) over five years and $9 billion after that to create a Canada-wide childcare program with $10/day childcare (Government of Canada, 2021a). To date, nine of the ten provinces and one of the three territories have signed on for this program.

Unlike childcare, which shows promise of improvement, social assistance in Canada is 'stuck in the muck'. Contemporary welfare provision offered through provincial social assistance programs in Canada is means-tested and considered a program of last resort, characterised by policy criticised as 'stingy'. To illustrate, the social assistance income for a parent and one child ranges from $18,372 in the Province of Nova Scotia to $25,409 in the Province of Quebec (Maytree, 2021). In comparison, the median after tax income in Canada in 2019 is $62,900 overall, and $56,100 for lone-parent families (Statistics Canada, 2021c). Furthermore, Canada has adopted a welfare-to-work model of social assistance for those deemed 'expected to work'. Consequently, welfare recipients must demonstrate efforts in seeking employment, participating in employability programs, or attending school in exchange for welfare benefits (Breitkreuz, 2005; Gorlick and Brethour, 1999; Vosko, 1999). Importantly, in most provinces, social assistance is clawed back when child support payments are made to a single-mother family, ensuring that for many low-income single-mother families, poverty will remain a constant. We will come back to this theme later.

CHILD SUPPORT POLICY IN CANADA

Focus of Child Support Policy

The primary focus of Canada's child support system is to ensure parental responsibility for the financial support of their children. The underlying premise of the child support guidelines is that children of intact families benefit from both parents' incomes and that should not change if their parents separate or divorce (Government of Canada, 2021c). Importantly, only the parents of a child have an obligation to support the child. A step-parent may be considered to be a parent, for the purposes of child support, if the step-parent stands in place of a parent towards the child, a concept known as *in loco parentis* (Chartier v. Chartier, 1999). This extends the obligation to support a child to those who are not biological parents but assume the role of a parent towards a child. The obligation is continuous and cannot be unilaterally terminated by the step-parent, ensuring that a child that benefitted from the support of a non-biological parent will continue to receive that support, even after the termination of the relationship between the step-parent and the other parent.

More recently, poverty reduction has become part of the discourse in child support, reflecting the prevalence of poverty in single-parent families. However, it is not yet an explicit goal for any child support system in Canada. The role of child support in poverty reduction in Canada is not well researched. Federal government statistics (Government of Canada, 2016a) refer to US studies about the role of child support in moving people out of poverty; Canadian research on this issue is difficult to find. Research from the Province of British Columbia tracks payments both to parents in receipt of income assistance, and parents that had been in receipt of income assistance but were no longer receiving income assistance benefits. In 2014/2015, 20 per cent of the funds collected were sent to families formerly in receipt of social assistance ($42 million), and just under 8 per cent of funds ($16 million) were sent to families currently in receipt of social assistance (British Columbia, 2015). To the extent that these families are some of the poorest in the province, these numbers substantiate the impact of child support for poor families. However, the fact that most provinces (not including British Columbia) claw back social assistance monies if child support is received undermines the notion that child support will meaningfully contribute to poverty reduction.

The fact that so many single parent families live in poverty also suggests that child support may not actually be effective in ensuring that the circumstances of children are not materially affected by their parents' separation or divorce, which is a key goal of the child support scheme. Whether this is due to the inability or unwillingness of parents to seek child support, the non-payment of child support, or the clawback of social assistance when child support is paid is unclear. The stark differences between the number of children living in poverty in single parent households in comparison to two-parent households indicates that parental separation does have an adverse economic effect on children, despite the best efforts of the child support system to engineer a different outcome.

CHILD SUPPORT IMPLEMENTATION

Within Canada's federal system, child support is a provincial/territorial responsibility, offered through the provincial family court system in all regions. Child support is determined using child support guidelines based on the paying parent's income and the number of children. Canada's child support system is fairly similar to the US child support system, to the extent that both systems are largely court-based and use child support guidelines. Administrative processes in Canada are only used for enforcement of child support, not for obtaining or varying child support orders, with the exception of limited provincial recalculation programs such as those in the provinces of British Columbia and Alberta. However, unlike the US with its fairly uniform Title IV-D child support agency requirements (Social Security Act, 1975), in Canada child support programs are more fragmented.

The process for child support works like this. To obtain a divorce, reasonable arrangements for the support of the children must be included in the divorce order (Divorce Act, 1985). Parents who were not married follow a similar process. All separated parents are encouraged to come to an agreement about child support. If the parents can agree, they have some flexibility in setting the child support amount, as long as reasonable arrangements have been made for the support of the children. To be enforceable, a child support order must either be made by a court order, or, if contained in an agreement made by the parties, filed with a court. Any variation of a child support order must be made or approved by a court.

Shortcomings of Canada's Child Support System

There are a number of substantial shortcomings in Canada's child support system as it is currently designed, as outlined below.

Onus on parent seeking support

The problems with the system become apparent when parents cannot agree on the child support amount. In this case, the receiving parent is responsible for securing support for the children. This is a major shortcoming of the Canadian system: unless parents are able to agree, the parent seeking child support is responsible for initiating the court process to obtain a child support order, for initiating changes to child support, and for requesting enforcement assistance, should payments not be made as ordered. This puts the responsibility and burden of securing child support on the parent with whom the children live, who is usually the mother. In addition to caring for the children, usually in combination with paid work, the onus of securing child support becomes the mother's problem. There is no equivalent obligation on the father to secure a child support order where no agreement is reached, or to voluntarily address the non-payment of child support where it is ordered. Neither is the burden on the mother seeking child support recognised or compensated in the court-based system. Parents are expected to bear their own costs for seeking a child support order unless there is exceptionally egregious conduct by the other party.

Fragmentation: lack of uniformity
Eligibility for child support (i.e., the child's right to receive child support) is consistent across all provinces and territories, and the federal Divorce Act applies to all marital breakdowns. Furthermore, provincial and territorial legislation is similar to the Divorce Act, and children of married or unmarried parents are treated equally. Children of same-sex parents are included. However, despite the similarity in the legislative framework for child support across Canada, the experience of parents who obtain, vary or enforce a child support order varies significantly. This is because the administration of the system is a provincial or territorial responsibility, and services are uneven across provincial and territorial borders.

Furthermore, instead of dealing with a single child support agency, as in the US, parents must deal with multiple agencies or programs and multiple levels of court, if they need to obtain, vary, or enforce a child support order. For example, legal aid for Court applications to obtain or vary child support orders is completely separate from other services and is rarely available unless family violence issues are present; an issue which again falls disproportionately on the mother to document and demonstrate. Social services departments provide limited government assistance for obtaining an order, but only for persons in receipt of social assistance. Limited support for other parents may be available through court-based or Ministry of Justice/Attorney General programs, but these are generally limited to mediation and assistance with preparation of documents outside the court process. Particularly for parents with limited resources, the process can be challenging and confusing.

In short, parents in some provinces and territories may experience significantly greater challenges in obtaining or varying a child support order than in others, further adding to the stress and burden of parents (usually mothers) attempting to secure child support. While the aims of the child support policy are laudable, the lack of programs to support parents through the process create significant obstacles. Because of this lack of consistency in administrative processes, Canada's system, in comparison to child support systems in other countries, may be characterised as fragmented, lacking uniformity across the provinces and territories.

Barriers to obtaining or varying child support

Like many other countries, child support guidelines are used in Canada to establish the amount of child support to be paid to the receiving parent. Although they are termed 'guidelines', by law the courts must use the guidelines in almost every case. The guidelines developed by the federal government for Divorce Act matters (an area under federal jurisdiction) have been adopted by almost all provinces and territories. The three provinces that have developed their own guidelines (Manitoba, New Brunswick and Quebec) have followed the same basic approach for calculating the support amount but have made some changes to the calculation process.

The guidelines work on the principle that both parents should share the same portion of their income with their children as if they lived together. A 'percentage of income' model is used that sets out monthly child support amounts in a table based on the paying parent's level of income, and the number of children eligible for child support. In theory, the child support payments should be responsive to changes in the paying parent's income, with modification being possible where the income increases or decreases.

However, as in other countries where the child support system is court-based, the ability to adjust a child support order based on parental income changes requires both information that the income has changed, as well as an expeditious accessible process to modify the court order. The burden rests on the receiving parent to request child support and to seek a modification where appropriate. In most cases, the receiving parent is at a significant information disadvantage, as he or she has no way of knowing whether the paying parent's income has changed, unless that information is voluntarily disclosed by the paying parent, or the receiving parent initiates a court proceeding. Advocates have noted: '... our system puts the burden of making sure the money is collected entirely on the parent with the least economic stability, the least knowledge of fluctuations in the payor parent's income and the least access to lawyers' (Mangat et al., 2020). Unlike systems where government assistance is available to access paying parent income information for the purpose of establishing or modifying child support orders, in the absence of voluntary disclosure, Canadian parents have to start costly legal proceedings simply to obtain the information necessary to initiate a request for a child support order.

Publicly funded legal assistance for parents needing to make a court application to obtain or vary a child support order is limited in all provinces, and self-represented litigants comprise the majority of litigants in family law cases in most courts across Canada. Programs for assisting parents to reach agreements outside court and programs for the recalculation of child support may be available to a limited extent in some provinces and territories, but this assistance rarely extends to assistance during court. This creates a significant barrier for parents needing to access court, as these processes can be arcane and difficult to navigate without legal representation.

The challenges faced by parents attempting to access the court to obtain or vary a child support order are reflected in the significant numbers of parents that are self-represented in Canadian family courts. Federal surveys of judges, lawyers and other family justice professionals estimate that between 50 per cent and 80 per cent of parties to civil/family actions are self-represented (Government of Canada, 2016b). In response to the growing number of self-represented litigants, most provinces have developed and published resources for litigants, as well as issuing guidelines for lawyers and the judiciary (Canadian Judicial Council, 2006), endorsed by the Supreme Court of Canada (Pintea v. Johns, 2017), on managing cases where the parties are self-represented. Despite the increased resources now available to self-represented litigants, most report 'feeling frustrated, overwhelmed, stressed and defeated by the legal process' (Scarrow et al., 2017). Moreover, the provision of 'self-help' resources ignores the reality of most single parents, who do not have the time or resources to research the law, draft and prepare documents, and attend lengthy court proceedings.

Parental usage of child support orders
Perhaps due to the complexity of the system, a significant number of parents do not obtain child support orders or agreements. A 1994–1995 research study showed that almost one-third of Canadian children whose parents have separated had no agreement regarding child support payments. The likelihood of having a child support order or agreement was greater (57 per cent) in cases where the parents had divorced, than in common-law unions (42 per cent). Of parents in the process of getting a divorce, 37 per cent had no child support order in place (Government of Canada, 2015). Whether these parents without orders find the system too challenging to navigate to obtain a child support order, or whether the parents without orders or agreements are able to amicably support the children without an order or agreement, remains unknown.

Although the research is limited, it does appear that child support is more likely to be paid where the parents have a private agreement (66 per cent received payment) than where the child support is required under a court order (43 per cent) (Government of Canada, 2015). That parents with private agreements have a better success rate shows that where effective policy is most needed (i.e., in cases where parents cannot reach an amicable and equitable agreement on their own), the system falls short, leaving mothers and children without proper support to help them attain financial support for which they are legally entitled. The lack of compliance with voluntary agreements is equally troubling, suggesting that even where parents are able to reach an agreement, in many cases those agreements are not long-lasting, putting the burden, once again, on the mother to seek redress through the courts.

Compliance with court-ordered support payments
Effective enforcement of child support is a critical part of the child support process. If child support is not paid voluntarily by a parent, the receiving parent may ask a provincial or territorial child support enforcement program to assist in collection. Although the service is cost-free, the burden of compiling the necessary documents and initiating the request falls to the mother. Enforcement of child support orders by the child support programs in all provinces and territories is largely administrative rather than court-based, and collection steps are initiated by provincial or territorial maintenance enforcement programs, without court involvement. These government programs enforce unpaid child support on behalf of receiving parents, through a variety of mechanisms such as wage garnishment and interception of government benefits.

Statistics Canada research (2011) estimated that 58 per cent of divorced or separated parents with a written child support order or agreement had registered their order or agreement with the provincial/ territorial child support enforcement program (Government of Canada, 2015). That over half of those with a written order were part of the enforcement program underscores the importance of this program functioning well.

Available evidence suggests that the enforcement program has mixed results. Data from nine jurisdictions shows that the child support enforcement programs are able to secure full payment of the regular monthly child support payment in two-thirds of their cases, and partial payment in eight per cent of cases (Statistics Canada, 2013). However, more comprehensive data from British Columbia (2019–2020) shows a different story: 32 per cent of all cases were fully paid, receiving ongoing payments each month and having no arrears. Just under 64 per cent of cases were partially paid and had some level of arrears. Only 3.96 per cent of cases had never received a payment (British Columbia, 2020). While the results from British Columbia are encouraging in comparison to those from other provinces, it is still noteworthy that only one third of cases were paid in full and on time, clearly highlighting the limitations of the child support system and confirming that simply having a child support order does not mean that the support will be paid.

Child support and social assistance payments
Perhaps the biggest problem with child support in Canada and its ability to ensure that children share in their parents' resources is not with the users or

the policy per se, but with the social assistance policies that interact with it. In most provinces, social assistance payments are clawed back by one dollar for every child support dollar received by that parent. Provinces and territories may choose to provide a reduced social assistance benefit to the receiving parent, along with the child support, or they may simply retain the child support (up to the amount of the social allowance paid) and provide the full amount of social assistance to the parent.

In either scenario, there is no net benefit to the parent that has invested time, energy and resources in acquiring a child support order, and little incentive for the paying parent to comply with the child support order, as the monies paid do not benefit the children. Whether the child support is paid or not, the amount received by the parent is the same. If the child support payments are retained by the government, and the receiving parent only receives social assistance, the receiving parent may not even be aware of whether payments are being made or not, effectively excluding the parent from the process which was intended to benefit the children in his or her care. If the receiving parent is required to pursue a child support order as a condition of entitlement to social assistance benefits, the parent is then faced with the unenviable option of choosing to expend time and resources obtaining a child support order that will only benefit the government or forgoing social assistance.

Even after the receiving parent stops receiving social assistance, unpaid child support for the period the parent was in receipt of benefits will be retained by the government. The rationale for this policy is explained by the Province of New Brunswick:

> This policy recognizes that parents have the main responsibility for the financial support of their children. Parents who do not have custody should have to support their children if they can. Taxpayers should not be required to take on this financial duty. Family support payments are deducted dollar for dollar from social assistance cheques (New Brunswick, 2021b).

While promoting the objective of parental responsibility for children, this policy does nothing to improve the situation of children living in poverty. To address this, four provinces (British Columbia, Nova Scotia, Prince Edward Island, and Ontario) have made legislative changes to allow receiving parents to retain the full amount of any child support payments made. New Brunswick has recently announced similar changes (New Brunswick, 2021a). There are increasing calls for other provincial and territorial governments to end the practice of deducting child support from income assistance (Newfoundland and Labrador, 2018). Allowing single parents to retain all the child support paid, without impacting the flow of social assistance payments to the family, is a very simple means of increasing the resources of some of Canada's most vulnerable families.

To add insult to injury, welfare recipients are further penalised and stigmatised because, in almost all provinces, parents that are in receipt of social assistance benefits from the government must collect their child support through the provincial/territorial child support program. In contrast, parents that are not receiving social assistance may choose to receive payments directly from the maintenance payor, or they may choose to have payments collected through the child support enforcement program. By creating this distinction, the policy implies that welfare recipients cannot be trusted, and need a mediating body for their payments. While the intervention of a government enforcement program may reduce conflict between the parents, the policy also forces poor women to use scarce resources to engage with a program, when the benefit of that engagement will flow entirely to the government as long as they are in receipt of government benefits.

If a goal of child support is to reduce child poverty in Canada, it must make a meaningful contribution to the standard of living experienced by the single-parent household. For many parents in receipt of social or income assistance in Canada, some of the poorest families in Canada, the payment of child support provides no material benefit to the family.

GAPS IN CURRENT CHILD SUPPORT POLICY

In broad terms, the child support system in Canada sets out a reasonably predictable framework for separated parents to share the economic consequences of a family breakup. Yet, as we have shown above, there are a number of key problems with it. In addition to these problems, a key area of concern in the Canadian child support system is the relevance of the underlying child support model to Canadian families today. There has been no substantive guideline review since the introduction of the guidelines in 1997, and in the intervening years, the structure of Canadian families has changed, as have attitudes to parenting, support of children, and the payment of child support.

The underlying model, which uses the percentage of the paying parent's income as the basis for the guidelines, has not been reviewed to determine whether it continues to be an appropriate model for Canadian families, particularly given the changes in participation of women in the workforce. In the US, where guideline reviews are required by federal legislation, most states have moved from the percentage of paying parent income model, used in Canada, to an Income Shares model. Only twelve states continue to use the percentage of paying parent's income model (Venohr, 2013). Like the model used in Canada, the Income Shares model is also based on the underlying principle that children should be entitled to a similar level of support as they would have received had the parents never separated or divorced, but the model uses the income of both the paying and receiving parent in calculating the guideline amount. Given that there are undoubtedly some separated families that have a resident parent earning more than the non-resident parent, there is merit to using a model that better reflects the composition of separated families in Canada.

In addition to not easily accommodating families with this type of income differential, the guidelines also fall short in how they deal with changing family forms in Canada. Although the Government of Canada has characterised the guidelines as flexible (Government of Canada, 2015), in practice there are a number of reasonably common family situations that cannot be easily accommodated within the guidelines. These include: (i) situations where children continue to be dependent upon their parents as young adults; (ii) child support in situations of remarriage with second families; and (iii) the increased likelihood that children live across households. Deviation from the guidelines is permitted in these circumstances but no guidance is provided as to how the child support should be set (Divorce Act, 1985). Families in these situations are left to determine by themselves, or with the assistance of the Court, the amount of child support to be paid. All of these gaps point to the problem that the guidelines are out of date and in need of reform in order to provide parents with a framework for determining child support without the necessity of initiating costly or prolonged litigation.

Children Over Age of Majority

In Canada, a significant percentage of children over the age of majority continue to live with, and be dependent upon, their parents. Under Canadian law, the obligation to support these children does not automatically terminate when the child reaches the age of majority. Child support will continue to be owed for as long as the child continues to be a child of the marriage (Divorce Act) or a child as defined under the provincial/territorial legislation. Whether a particular child continues to be entitled to child support will depend upon a combination of factors, including whether the child continues to be in school, whether the child is working, and whether the receiving parent continues to support the child. The determination is case specific.

Once a determination has been made that a child continues to be entitled to child support, the uncertainty continues as the child support guidelines do not necessarily apply to determine the quantum of child support. Thus, unlike other facets of child support where the introduction of child support guidelines brought certainty and predictability, determination of the entitlement of children over the age of majority for child support remains an area where there is uncertainty. Whether a court will award child support for an adult child depends upon the 'socially contentious issue of when economic childhood ends, and when and how the adult obligation of self-support begins' (Bala, 2008).

Families with children over the age of majority make up a significant percentage of the child support enforcement program caseloads. In 2019, children over age 19 (the age of majority in British Columbia and the age at which a child is legally considered an adult) comprised thirty per cent of the children enrolled in the province's child support enforcement program (British Columbia, 2020). The uncertainty around the duration of child support for these children is one of the most significant shortcomings of the child support guidelines.

Parents With Second Families

Remarriage or re-partnering of one or both of the former spouses creates another area of uncertainty (and potential litigation) for separated parents. If a paying parent is able to establish that paying the guideline table amount would create an 'undue hardship' (section 10 child support guidelines) as a result of their legal obligation to support another child, the court may order a different amount to be paid. How the amount to be paid is determined in this scenario is not set out in the guidelines, making it difficult for parents to agree without taking the matter to court. One-quarter of Canadians between the ages of 35–64 were in a second or subsequent marriage or common-law relationship (Statistics Canada, 2019). Furthermore, over half of those who married a second time had children with their current spouse (Statistics Canada, 2019). Given the frequency of remarriage and the formation of second families, if the Child Support Guidelines are to provide a useable framework for parents for child support, additional guidance needs to be provided to assist parents and avoid the need for litigation where parents remarry and form second families.

Shared Parenting (Formerly Called Shared Custody)

A similar gap exists in situations where parents share the custody or parenting of children, defined in Canada as a situation where the child spends at least 40 per cent of the time with each parent. In these cases of shared parenting, deviation from the guidelines is permitted, but no guidance is given to parents to facilitate an out-of-court settlement. For parents that are attempting to reach an amicable settlement of parenting and child support, arguably the ones most likely to enter a shared parenting arrangement, the lack of guidance on the issue of child support undermines the overall objective of supporting parents to reach an agreement without resorting to the legal process (Palmer, 2013). If shared custody trends are increasing, child support approaches will have to be adapted to reflect this change. Unfortunately, the Canadian Census uses households as their unit of analysis rather than families, so it is currently unable to track children living across households.

CONCLUSIONS AND RECOMMENDATIONS

Child support has the potential to play a meaningful role in contributing to income security for Canadian children whose parents live in different households. And, for families who fit within the child support system's parameters (often middle-class, financially stable formerly married couples with children who divorce amicably), it generally works well. Paying parents provide payment to receiving parents, and children's financial needs are met. Unfortunately, for families whose realities don't fit into the assumptions upon which this policy is based, the system falls short and fails to meet its key objective of ensuring that children's financial needs are met. This is particularly true for families who are typically poor and marginalised, in part because the current system lacks agility, and is unable to adapt to changing conditions in the paying parents' income, and in part, because of how it interacts with social assistance policies.

As we have shown, due to the changing landscape of Canadian family life, a number of foundational assumptions of the current child support system are no longer relevant. Families that have adult children living at home, families that have formed second families, and families that share parenting of their children across households, fall outside of the parameters of the system. Furthermore, in many provinces, families on social assistance experience a dollar-for-dollar claw back, therefore not contributing to improving the financial wellbeing of these families. As such, in many provinces and territories, child support policy on its own and in combination with social assistance policy, is in need of substantial reform.

With the benefit of over twenty years of experience with the guidelines, it should be possible to provide more assistance to parents in these circumstances. There are some useful examples that could be followed to address some of these issues. The development of Advisory Guidelines (Government of Canada, 2008) for spousal support might provide a model for creating consistency and certainty in an area where individual circumstances can vary. The spousal support guidelines were developed by two family law professors with funding from the federal government to make spousal support more consistent and predictable. They are not law, but many judges in Canada base their decisions about spousal support on the Advisory Guidelines. Similar 'advisory guidelines' for parents who have children over the age of majority, who are supporting children from multiple relationships, or who share the parenting of a child across households would provide a basis for parents to reach agreement where these situations arise.

The challenges of changing the child support guideline model should not be underestimated. As child support is determined under the federal child support guidelines for married parents who are divorcing, and under provincial or territorial guidelines for parents who were never married to ensure that children of married and non-married relationships are treated equally, the same child support tables are used. Changes to the guidelines would require a coordinated federal/provincial/territorial effort but would bring Canada into line with the guideline models used elsewhere and might better reflect the current income differentials between spouses. At a minimum, a comprehensive review of the existing child support guidelines model and its relevance to today's Canadian families would ensure that the amount of child support being paid by parents is being fairly and accurately determined. Making some reforms to these policies would work toward ensuring that the policy is reflective of the composition of contemporary families. In addition, it would meet the overall child support policy goal of ensuring that children whose parents are no longer together still experience the same standard of living as they did prior to the separation of their parents.

REFERENCES

Bala, N. (2008). *Child support for adult children: When does economic childhood end?* Queen's University Faculty of Law Legal Studies Working Paper No. 08–01. https://ssrn.com/abstract=1123979

Beeston, L. (2016). *Fewer Canadian mothers work than those in many rich countries. Toronto Star.* Retrieved from https://www.thestar.com/news/canada/2016/08/03/fewer-canadian-mothers-work-than-those-in-many-rich-countries.html.

Breitkreuz, R. S. (2005). Engendering citizenship - A critical feminist analysis of Canadian welfare-to-work policies and the employment experiences of lone mothers. *J. Soc. & Soc. Welfare, 32,* 147–166.

Breitkreuz, R. and Colen, K. (2018). Who cares? Motivations for unregulated child care use. *Journal of Family Issues, 39*(17), 4066–4088.

Breitkreuz, R. and Williamson, D. (2012). The self-sufficiency trap: A critical examination of welfare-to-work. *Social Service Review, 86*(4), 660–689.

Breitkreuz, R., Williamson, D., and Raine, K. (2010). Disintegrated policy: Welfare-to-Work participants' experiences of integrating paid work and unpaid family work. *Community, Work, and Family, 13,* 43–68.

British Columbia. (2015). *2014 – 2015 Family Maintenance Enforcement Program Annual Report.* Retrieved from https://www.fmep.gov.bc.ca/assets/uploads/2015/01/BCFMEP-Annual-Report-2014–2015.pdf.

British Columbia. (2020). *2019–2020 Family Maintenance Enforcement Program Annual Report.* Retrieved from https://www.fmep.gov.bc.ca/assets/uploads/2021/04/BCFMEP-Annual-Report-2019–2020.pdf.

Canadian Judicial Council. (2006). *Canadian Judicial Council Issues Statement of Principles on Self-Represented Litigants and Accused Persons* https://cjc-ccm.ca/en/news/canadian-judicial-council-issues-statement-principles-self-represented-litigants-and-accused.

Canadian Women's Foundation. (2017). *Fact Sheet: Women and Poverty in Canada.* Toronto: Canadian Women's Foundation. Available at: https://www.canadianwomen .org/the-facts/womenspoverty/.

Chartier v. Chartier. (1999). 1 S.C.R. 242 (Supreme Court of Canada 1999).

Daly, M. (2012). Making policy for care: Experience in Europe and its implications in Asia. *International Journal of Sociology and Social Policy, 32,* 623–635.

Divorce Act (R.S.C., 1985, c. 3 (2nd Supp.)). https://laws-lois.justice.gc.ca/eng/acts/d -3.4/

Fox, D. and Moyser, M. (2018). The economic well-being of women in Canada. Catalogue No. 89–503-X. Ottawa: Statistics Canada.

Friendly, M., Larson, E., Feltham, L., Grady, B., Forer, B., and Jones, M. (2018). *Early childhood education and care in Canada, 2016.* Toronto: Child Care Resource and Research Unit.

Gorlick, C. and Brethour, G. (1999). *Welfare-to-Work program summaries.* Ottawa: Canadian Council on Social Development.

Government of Canada. (2008). *Spousal Support Advisory Guidelines July 2008.* Retrieved from https://www.justice.gc.ca/eng/rp-pr/fl-lf/spousal-epoux/spag/index .html.

Government of Canada. (2015). *Selected Statistics on Canadian Families and Family Law:Second Edition.* Retrieved from https://www.justice.gc.ca/eng/rp-pr/fl-lf/famil/ stat2000/p5.html#NPP.

Government of Canada. (2016a). *Compliance with Family Support Obligations.* Retrieved from https://www.justice.gc.ca/eng/rp-pr/fl-lf/divorce/jf-pf/cfso-ooaf.html.

Government of Canada. (2016b). *Self-Represented Litigants in Family Law.* Retrieved from https://www.justice.gc.ca/eng/rp-pr/fl-lf/divorce/jf-pf/srl-pnr.html.

Government of Canada. (2017). *Multilateral early learning and child care framework.* Retrieved from https://www.canada.ca/en/employment-social-development/ programs/early-learning- child-care/reports/2017-multilateral-framework.html.

Government of Canada. (2020). *Employment insurance maternity and parental benefits.* Retrieved from https://www.canada.ca/en/employment-social-development/pro grams/ei/ei-list/reports/maternity-parental.html.

Government of Canada. (2021a). Budget 2021: *A Canada wide early learning and childcare plan.* Ottawa: GOC. Available at: https://www.canada.ca/en/department -finance/news/2021/04/budget-2021-a-canada-wide-early-learning-and-child-care- plan.html.

Government of Canada. (2021b). *Canada child benefit.* Retrieved from http://www.cra -arc.gc.ca/bnfts/ccb/menu-eng.html.

Government of Canada. (2021c). *About child support.* Retrieved from https://www .justice.gc.ca/eng/fl-df/child-enfant/acs-cae.html.

Houle, P., Turcotte, M., and Wendt, M. (2017). *Changes in parents' participation in domestic tasks and care for children from 1986 to 2015.* No. 89–652-x Ottawa: Statistics Canada.

Mahon, R., Anttonen, A., Bergqvist, C., Brennan, D., and Hobson, B. (2012). Convergent care regimes? Childcare arrangements in Australia, Canada, Finland and Sweden. *Journal of European Social Policy, 22*(4), 419–431.

Mangat, R., Klinck, J., and Sealy-Harrington, J. (2020). *New ruling is the first step in helping mothers collect much needed child support.* Globe and Mail. Retrieved September 1, 2021, from https://www.theglobeandmail.com/opinion/article-new -ruling-is-the-first-step-in-helping-mothers-collect-much-needed child support/.

Mason, R. (2003). Listening to lone mothers: Paid work, family life, and childcare in Canada. *Journal of Children & Poverty, 9*(1), 41–54.

Maytree (2021). *Welfare incomes in 2019.* Available at: https://maytree.com/welfare -in-Canada/.

Milan, A., Keown, L., and Urquijo, C. (2011). *Families, living arrangements and unpaid work.* Ottawa: Statistics Canada. Catalogue no: 89–503-X.

Moyser, M. (2017). *Women and paid work.* Ottawa: Statistics Canada. Catalogue No: 89–503-X.

New Brunswick. (2021a). *Changes to social assistance programs increase financial support to social assistance recipients.* Retrieved from https://www2.gnb.ca/content/ gnb/en/departments/social_development/news/news_release.2021.09.0666.html.

New Brunswick. (2021b). *Social Assistance Program.* Retrieved from https:// www2.gnb.ca/content/gnb/en/services/services_renderer.10295.social_assistance _program.html.

Newfoundland and Labrador. (2018). *Making Waves: Ensuring children benefit from child support payments.* Retrieved from https://www.childandyouthadvocate.nl.ca/ files/OCYA-InvestigativeReportMakingWaves.pdf.

OECD. (2019). Labour force participation rate. https://data.oecd.org/emp/labour-force -participation-rate.htm.

Palmer, C. (2013). Child support and shared parenting in Canada: A 'reality cheque'. *Dalhousie Journal of Legal Studies, 22,* 127.

Pelletier, R., Patterson, M., and Moyser, M. (2019). The gender wage gap in Canada: 1998 to 2018. Statistics Canada. https://www150.statcan.gc.ca/n1/pub/75–004-m/ 75–004-m2019004-eng.htm#:~:text=In%20Canada%2C%20women%20in%20the ,every%20dollar%20earned%20by%20men.

Pintea v. Johns (2017). SCC 23 (Supreme Court of Canada 2017).

Scarrow, K., Robinet, B., and Macfarlane, J. (2017). *Tracking the trends of the self-represented litigant phenomenon: Data from the national self-represented litigants project, 2017.* https://representingyourselfcanada.com/wp-content/uploads/2018/04/ Intake-Report-2017-FINAL.pdf.

Social Security Act, § 310–1305 (1975).

Statista (2019). Resident population of Canada in 2020, by gender and age group. https://www.statista.com/statistics/444858/canada-resident-population-by-gender -and-age-group.

Statistics Canada. (2013). *Payment patterns of child and spousal support.* Retrieved from https://www150.statcan.gc.ca/n1/pub/85–002-x/2013001/article/11780-eng.htm.

Statistics Canada. (2017a). *Ethnic and cultural origins of Canadians: Portrait of a rich heritage.* https://www12.statcan.gc.ca/census-recensement/2016/as-sa/98–200-x/20 16016/98–200-x2016016-eng.cfm.

Statistics Canada. (2017b). *Young adults living with their parents in Canada in 2016.* Available at: https://www12.statcan.gc.ca/census-recensement/2016/as-sa/98–200-x /2016008/98–200-x2016008-eng.cfm.

Statistics Canada. (2018a). *National Indigenous day, by the numbers.* Available at: htt ps://www.statcan.gc.ca/eng/dai/smr08/2018/smr08_225_2018.

Statistics Canada. (2018b). Labour Force survey, December 2018. Available at: https:// www150.statcan.gc.ca/n1/daily-quotidien/190104/dq190104a-eng.htm.

Statistics Canada. (2019). Family matters: New relationships after separation or divorce. *The Daily,* May 15, 2019.

Statistics Canada. (2021a). Labour force characteristics by sex and detailed age group. Annual, Table 14–10–0327–01. https://www150.statcan.gc.ca/t1/tbl1/en/tv.action ?pid=1410032701.

Statistics Canada. (2021b). *Low income statistics by age, sex, and economic family type.* Table 11–10–0135–01. DOI: https://doi.org/10.25318/1110013501-eng.

Statistics Canada. (2021c). *Table2 Median after-tax income, Canada and provinces, 2015 to 2019.* Available at: https://www150.statcan.gc.ca/n1/daily-quotidien/ 210323/t002a--eng.html.

Vanier Institute. (2019). Lone mothers and their families in Canada: Diverse, resilient and strong. Available at: https://vanierinstitute.ca/lone-mothers-families-canada -diverse- resilient-strong/.

Venohr, J. (2013). Child support guidelines and guidelines reviews: State differences and common issues. *Family Law Quarterly, 47*(3), 327–352.

Vosko, L. (1999). Workfare temporaries: Workfare and the rise of the temporary employment relationship in Ontario. In D. Broad and W. Antony (Eds.), *Citizens or consumers: Social policy in a market society,* 184–204. Halifax: Fernwood Books.

Vosko, L., MacDonald, M., and Campbell, I. (Eds.) (2009). *Gender and the contours of precarious employment.* Routledge.

5. The Colombian child support system: A hybrid approach in a challenging social and economic context

Laura Cuesta[1] and Angela Guarin

INTRODUCTION

Over the last few decades, Colombian families have undergone a wide range of social, economic, and demographic transformations (Flórez and Sanchez-Cespedes, 2013; Institute for Family Studies and Wheatley Institution, 2019; Ministerio de Salud y Protección Social [MinSalud] and Profamilia, 2017). One change deserves special attention, which is the growth in the proportion of children living with only one parent, typically their mother. In this chapter we examine the Colombian policy scheme designed to prevent the potential decline in the wellbeing of children following the divorce or separation of their parents. We draw from prior research and new empirical evidence from our analysis of the 1997, 2008, and 2016 Colombian Quality of Life Survey (QLS). We describe the context in which Colombian parents work and care for their children, the policies and programs available to them, how single-parent families compare to families in which both parents co-reside with their children, and how the Colombian child support system aspires to guarantee the wellbeing of children living with only one parent.

THE SOCIAL CONTEXT

While Colombia is categorised as an upper middle-income country (The World Bank, 2022), income inequality and poverty remain pressing issues (see Table 5.1). The country's Gini coefficient ranks among the highest in Latin America (51.3 in 2019), and over 40 per cent of the population lives in poverty (Departamento Administrativo Nacional de Estadística [DANE], 2021e; The World Bank, 2019b). Addressing these issues through the labour

---

[1]   Corresponding author.

market alone poses a challenge for policymakers because most Colombians do not have quality jobs: approximately two thirds of the total employment in Colombia is informal (Elgin et al., 2021). Colombia also lags behind in terms of gender equality: compared to men, women hold more years of education (The World Bank, 2019c) but have higher unemployment rates (6.4 percentage points higher in May 2021) and lower earnings (a gender wage gap of 4 per cent in 2019) (Organisation for Economic Cooperation and Development [OECD], 2022a). Moreover, women's participation in unpaid work is higher than that of men's: the proportion of women 10 years or older doing unpaid direct care work[2] in the household (29 per cent) is twice that performed by men (14 per cent) of the same age (DANE and ONU Mujeres, 2020). Many Colombian women also experience gender-based violence: about two-thirds of women aged 13–49 reported being victims of intimate partner violence in 2015 (MinSalud and Profamilia, 2017). These issues were exacerbated by the COVID-19 pandemic (Cárdenas and Martínez B., 2020), although a recent study argues that the country is on its way to recovery (OECD, 2022b).

Table 5.1   *Socioeconomic indicators*

Socioeconomic indicators	Colombia
GDP per capita (2017 PPP $)[a]	14,731 (2019)
Gini coefficient[b]	51.3 (2019)
Poverty rate (monetary)[c]	42.5% (2020)
Poverty rate (multidimensional)[d]	17.5% (2019)
Mean years of schooling[e]	8.5 (2019)
Mean years of schooling men[e]	8.3 (2019)
Mean years of schooling women[e]	8.6 (2019)
Unemployment rate[f]	15.6 (May 2021)
	21.4 (May 2020)
Unemployment rate men[f]	13.0 (May 2021)
	18.6 (May 2020)
Unemployment rate women[f]	19.4 (May 2021)
	25.4 (May 2020)
Informal employment[g] (% of total employment)	62.4 (2018)
Minimum wage[h] (2019 PPP $)	671.7 (2019)

---

[2]   Unpaid direct care work is defined as the direct care of persons such as children and the elderly (DANE and ONU Mujeres, 2020).

Socioeconomic indicators	Colombia
Monthly labour income (men)[i] (2019 PPP)	997.7 (2019)
Monthly labour income (women)[i] (2019 PPP)	867.9 (2019)

Notes: [a](UNDP, 2020) [b](The World Bank, 2019b) [c](DANE, 2021e) [d](DANE, 2021f) [e](The World Bank, 2019c) [f](DANE, 2021d) [g](Elgin et al., 2021) [h](Banco de la República, 2021) [i](OECD, 2021b) [j](DANE, 2020a).

Some factors that have slowed the progress in reducing income and gender inequality and poverty include the internal displacement of millions of Colombians – many of whom are women – and the recent influx of Venezuelan migrants as a result of political turmoil in the neighbouring country. Colombia has both one of the largest populations of internally displaced persons (IDPs) worldwide, and the largest number of Venezuelan refugees and migrants (Oficina del Alto Comisionado de las Naciones Unidas para los Refugiados [ACNUR], 2020; Plataforma de Coordinación para Refugiados y Migrantes de Venezuela [R4V], 2020). As of June 2021, 8.1 million people were registered as IDPs in the Registro Único de Victimas, or RUV ('Colombian Government's Victims' Registry'). Likewise, as of April 2020, there were approximately 1.8 million Venezuelan migrants, half of which did not have legal immigration status (Migración Colombia, 2021; Plataforma de Coordinación para Refugiados y Migrantes de Venezuela [R4V], 2020) (see Table 5.2).

Colombia also exhibits trends typically associated with the second demographic transition (SDT), including sustained sub-replacement fertility, a decline in marriages, and a rise in cohabiting unions and nonmarital births (Esteve et al., 2012; Flórez and Sanchez-Cespedes, 2013; Institute for Family Studies and Wheatley Institution, 2019). In 2019, the fertility rate was 1.8, well below the level of replacement of 2.1 live births per women (OECD, 2021a). Changes in fertility rates have also led to changes in the age-specific population structure, with a relative reduction in the population aged 0–15 and aged 65 years old or older, and an increase in the working-age population aged 15 to 64 (MinSalud and Profamilia, 2017).

Table 5.2   Demographic, family, and household characteristics

	Colombia
Demographic characteristics	
Population[a]	48.3 million (2018)
Fertility rate[b]	1.8 children (2019)
International migrant stock as % of total population[c]	2.3% (2019)
Internally displaced persons (Officially registered)[d]	8.1 million (2021)
Venezuelan migrants[e]	1.8 million (2021)

	Colombia
Structure by age[f]	
0-17	27.75% (2018)
18-64	63.12%
65+	9.12%
Life expectancy at birth[g]	77 years (2020)
Family characteristics	
Family size (average)[h]	3.1 persons
Household structure[i]	
Two-parent nuclear household	43.44% (2018)
Single-parent household	15.42% (2018)
Extended household	16.55% (2018)
Single-person household	18.56% (2018)
Other households	6.03% (2018)
Children's living arrangements[j]	
Children living with two parents	53% (2015)
Children living with one parent	37% (2015)
Children living with no parent	9% (2015)
Rate of non-marital births[j]	82%
Remarriage[k]	
Women 15-39 years old with two or more marriages	22.6% (2015)
Men 15-39 years old with three or more marriages	25.5% (2015)
Multiple partner fertility for people with at least two children[l]	
Women	36.1
Men	35.3
Provision of direct unpaid care in the household[m]	
Women providing direct care	28.8% (2016-2017)
Men providing direct care	14.4% (2016-2017)
Gender-based violence[k]	
Women 13-49 years old who experienced intimate partner violence	66.7% (2015)

Notes: [a](DANE, 2021c) [b](The World Bank, 2019a) [c](United Nations Department of Economic and Social Affairs, 2019) [d](Unidad para la Atención y Reparación Integral a las Víctimas, 2021) [e](Migración Colombia, 2021) [f](DANE, 2021a) [g](DANE, 2020b) [h](DANE, 2021b) [i](Observatorio de Familias, 2020) [j](Institute for Family Studies and Wheatley Institution, 2019) [k](Ministerio de Salud y Protección Social and Profamilia, 2017) [l](Cuesta and Mogollon, 2019) [m](DANE and ONU Mujeres, 2020).

The well-documented retreat from marriage taking place in other countries (Institute for Family Studies and Wheatley Institution, 2019; Schoen and Cheng, 2006) is also occurring among Colombian couples: nearly twice as many adults are in cohabiting relationships (33 per cent) rather than marriages

(17 per cent) (Institute for Family Studies and Wheatley Institution, 2019). Relatedly, Colombia has the highest percentage of children born to unmarried parents worldwide (82 per cent) (Institute for Family Studies and Wheatley Institution, 2019), and many of these children live in cohabiting-couple families (Cuesta et al., 2017). In addition, union instability has reached historic highs: the share of divorced and separated women aged 25 to 29 increased by 65 per cent over the past twenty years (Arriagada, 2004; Flórez and Sanchez-Cespedes, 2013; MinSalud and Profamilia, 2017). Repartnering is also common, particularly through cohabitation (MinSalud and Profamilia, 2017).

Given these changes in fertility, union formation, and union dissolution, it is not surprising that the structure and composition of Colombian households has also changed: single-parent households, households without children, and single-person households have increased while the proportion of nuclear two-parent households and extended family households has declined (Observatorio de Familias, 2020). While the nuclear two-parent family is still the most common type of family (43.4 per cent), many children live with one parent only (37 per cent) (Flórez, 2004; Flórez and Sanchez-Cespedes, 2013), who is usually a single and unmarried mother (Cuesta and Meyer, 2014). Multiple-partner fertility (MPF) is also common: approximately one in three women with at least two children has had children with multiple fathers (Cuesta and Mogollon, 2019).

Taken together, these trends show that the social and economic context in which Colombian parents work and care for their children is challenging. The disproportionate burden of unpaid care work borne by Colombian women can be particularly difficult for mothers who have divorced or separated. These mothers, who are left to be both caregivers and providers for their families, face limited access to childcare (OECD, 2016), low earning capacity (MinSalud and Profamilia, 2017), and discrimination in the workplace (García-Rojas et al., 2020). These conditions expose single-mother families to poverty and material hardship. The country's social welfare system could help narrow the gap between the resources that mothers need to care and provide for their children and their limited earnings. However, as we discuss in the next section, the current policies and programs for families with children in Colombia have limited coverage and benefits.

THE SOCIAL WELFARE SYSTEM

Social welfare systems across Latin America and the Caribbean (LAC) are still underdeveloped (Economic Commission for Latin America and the Caribbean [ECLAC], 2018) and many citizens are unable to access social welfare services and programs (ECLAC, 2021; Martínez Franzoni, 2008; United Nations

Development Programme [UNDP], 2021). The resources allocated for the Colombian system are lower than the average of OECD countries. In 2018, public social spending[3] for the operation of the Colombian social welfare system, also known as the social protection system (SPS), was 13.1 per cent of the GDP, well below the 20 per cent average observed among OECD countries (OECD, 2020).

The Colombian SPS has two main components: social security and social assistance. The first component is contributory and includes health, pension, unemployment insurance and occupational risk coverage. The second component is non-contributory and includes subsidised health, a small pension scheme, cash transfers (conditional and unconditional) aimed at protecting poor families, vocational and professional training through the Servicio Nacional de Aprendizaje or SENA ('National Training Institution'), and services provided through the Instituto Colombiano de Bienestar Familiar or ICBF ('National Institute of Family Wellbeing or NIFW') (OECD, 2022c). The policies and programs aimed at supporting families with children fall under the social assistance component and are a key source of support for single-mother families (Cuesta et al., 2018).

Más Familias en Acción ('More Families in Action') is a conditional cash transfer program for poor families with children[4]. Program participants collect monthly subsidies if children in the family receive medical check-ups and attend school on a regular basis (Medellín and Sánchez Prada, 2015). The average subsidy for medical check-ups ranges from US $25 to US $30 per month while the average education subsidy ranges from US $4 to US $24 per month per child (ECLAC, 2020). These transfers were temporarily increased as a response to the COVID-19 pandemic (Prosperidad Social, 2020a). Additionally, at the beginning of the pandemic, the Colombian government implemented two unconditional cash transfer programs: Compensación del IVA ('Value Added Tax Reimbursement, VAT'[5]) and Ingreso Solidario ('Solidarity Income'). In 2020, about one million families received five payments of approximately US $20 per payment as part of the VAT program (Blofield et al., 2021; Prosperidad Social, 2020b). Ingreso Solidario is an

---

[3]   Includes old age, survivors, incapacity-related benefits, health, family, active labour market programs, unemployment, housing, and other social policy areas (OECD, 2020).

[4]   Very few migrants receive this transfer since budget constraints have limited enrollment of eligible families.

[5]   The VAT is a fixed amount and does not depend on an individual's consumption (Ham et al., 2022). Additionally, regarding taxes in Colombia, only 5 per cent of income earners pay personal income taxes; as a consequence, most people do not file income tax returns (OECD, 2022c).

unconditional cash transfer of approximately US $40 per month. This program targets poor, informal workers and households that are not beneficiaries of other social programs, including migrant families (Blofield et al., 2021; Cárdenas and Martínez B., 2020). As of 2022, these social assistance programs are ongoing.

Colombian families with children may also participate in programs offered by the NIFW, the main government agency responsible for the protection and wellbeing of children and adolescents, particularly the most vulnerable (Instituto Colombiano de Bienestar Familiar [ICBF], 2021). One key component of the NIFW's programming is childcare and child development services. The agency offers a wide range of childcare settings, some of them targeted at the poorest families in the country (i.e., hogares comunitarios: 'community homes'). Nevertheless, only half (48.4 per cent) of Colombian children below 6 years old attend childcare programs (both privately and publicly operated), with a lower coverage in rural vs urban areas (43.5 vs 50.3 per cent) (MinSalud and Profamilia, 2017).

Prior empirical work evaluating these programs, particularly Más Familias en Acción (Departamento Nacional de Planeación [DNP], 2008), Compensación del IVA (Londoño Vélez and Querubín, 2017), and Ingreso Solidario (Gallego et al., 2021), suggest that these programs have contributed to improving the wellbeing of Colombian families. However, due to fiscal constraints, the coverage and amount of these benefits remains inadequate: 52 per cent of poor households do not receive support from the government (OECD, 2022c). Additionally, the SPS does not have benefits aimed exclusively at mothers who are separated or divorced. Single mothers may benefit from these policies and programs if they are living in poverty and means tests determine they are eligible. At the local level there have been some efforts to provide additional assistance to single parents (i.e., preferential access to credit and housing programs), but these programs are still very limited.

The current configuration of the SPS leaves some Colombians unable to access the social welfare system (ECLAC, 2021; Martínez Franzoni, 2008; UNDP, 2021), making their family arrangements a key safety net for them (Martínez Franzoni, 2008). Estimates with Census data show this is the case for the majority of Colombian mothers who are divorced or separated: between 2000 and 2007, 72.7 per cent of single mothers were co-residing with extended family (Esteve et al., 2012). However, the support that families provide to single mothers may also be limited. In the next section we present new empirical evidence on how single-parent families, more broadly defined as custodial-parent families (i.e., families in which the child lives with only one parent, including those in which the child lives with a parent and step-parent), compare to families in which both parents co-reside with their children.

CUSTODIAL MOTHERS IN COLOMBIAN SOCIETY

The proportion of custodial-parent families among all families with children has increased substantially over the past few decades. Our estimates using the Colombian Quality of Life Survey (QLS) show that approximately two in five families with children were custodial-parent families in 2008 (41 per cent) compared to one in three in 1997 (32 per cent). The increase in the share of custodial-parent families among families with children seems primarily driven by the rise in the proportion of repartnered-mother families: whereas the share of single-mother families increased by 11 per cent, the proportion of repartnered-mothers rose by 63 per cent between 1997 and 2008. Conversely, custodial-father families, whether repartnered or single, are still rare in Colombia: between 1997 and 2016, the proportion of single-father families remained around 3 per cent while the proportion of repartnered-father families hovered around 1 per cent. Blended families, or families who include two custodial parents and their children, became as prevalent as repartnered-father families in 2016. Between 2008 and 2016, however, the growth in the share of custodial-parent families among all families with children had slowed (Figure 5.1).

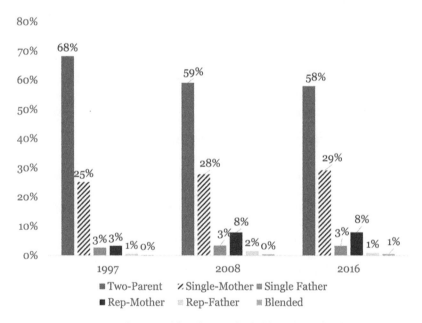

Figure 5.1   *Distribution of families with children by type of family in 1997, 2008, and 2016*

Prior research has shown that children in custodial-parent families – overwhelmingly comprised of single-mother families – are more likely to live in poverty than children in two-parent families (Cuesta et al., 2018). Our new estimates show that this socioeconomic disadvantage has persisted for years (see Table 5.3): in the two decades examined between 1997 and 2016, the poverty rate among custodial-parent families was at least 17 percentage points higher than that observed among two-parent families. While we find a significant increase in the proportion of mothers and fathers with high school education or more across family types, parents in two-parent families are still more educated than mothers and fathers in custodial-parent families. Our descriptive analyses also demonstrate that in all years, mothers in custodial-parent families are more likely to work for pay than mothers in two-parent families.

Custodial-mother families, which represent approximately 90 per cent of all custodial-parent families in Colombia, are not a homogeneous group. A significant proportion of these families include mothers who have new partners: in 2016, one in five custodial mothers were repartnered mothers. Repartnered mothers have higher family incomes and are less likely to live in poverty than single mothers. On the other hand, single mothers are more likely to receive child support than repartnered mothers, and the average annual amount received is at least half of their average annual family income. Notably, between 2008 and 2016 the proportion of single mothers receiving child support declined from 31.9 per cent to 26.1 per cent while the share of repartnered mothers that received child support increased from 12.9 per cent to 15.2 per cent.

That the vast majority of custodial mothers do not receive child support is a significant and pressing issue that needs further attention from Colombian policymakers. In the next section we describe the current child support system.

THE COLOMBIAN CHILD SUPPORT SYSTEM

The Colombian child support system has evolved from a court-based regime to a structure in which several institutions share responsibility in the determination and enforcement of child support obligations (Cuesta and Meyer, 2012). This type of system is also known in the literature as a hybrid scheme (Skinner and Davidson, 2009). Our review of the legal framework indicates that the Colombian system has two main goals. The first goal is to guarantee that the children living in custodial-parent families are provided with everything that is considered essential for their development (Ley 1098, 2006; Constitución Política de Colombia, 1991; Decreto 2737, 1989). While current laws do not provide a comprehensive list of items deemed as essential, they include examples of broad categories such as food, housing, clothing, medical assistance, recreation, and education. The second goal is to promote parental

Table 5.3   Socioeconomic characteristics of two-parent and custodial-parent families in 1997, 2008, and 2016

	1997		2008			2016		
	Two-parent family	Custodial-parent family	Two-parent family	Custodial-parent family		Two-parent family	Custodial-parent family	
Family characteristics								
Custodial-mother family		89.9		87.9			89.5	
Number of children	2.2	1.8	1.9	1.8	***	1.7	1.6	***
Age of youngest child								
0-5 years old	53.8	46.4	47.9	46.3	***	47.8	43.4	*
6-11 years old	28.1	29.5	30.3	30.9	**	30.4	33.8	
12-17 years old	18.0	24.1	21.9	22.7	***	21.7	22.8	
Annual family income in PPP	22193.5	9268.5	16386.6	9050.7	***	16414.8	8259.8	***
Family lives in poverty	38.3	55.6	33.4	50.3	***	30.9	49.0	***
Family lives in urban area	81.2	87.1	80.5	88.5	***	82.5	88.8	***
Parents' characteristics								
Mother's age								
18-29 years old	31.0	30.8	30.0	32.6	***	31.5	32.4	**
30-39 years old	40.0	31.9	35.5	32.6	***	36.4	36.2	
40-49 years old	21.4	19.9	26.4	19.9	+	24.5	17.4	***
50-59 years old	7.7	8.1	6.6	5.0	***	7.6	4.9	***
Age is missing	0.0	9.3	1.5	9.9	***	0.0	9.1	***
Mother's education								
Less than high school education	71.7	69.3	53.9	53.6	***	37.8	38.2	***

	1997			2008			2016		
	Two-parent family	Custodial-parent family		Two-parent family	Custodial-parent family		Two-parent family	Custodial-parent family	
High school education	14.8	15.4	+	21.4	22.2	*	28.4	28.9	
More than high school education	9.5	8.2		16.1	14.4		27.1	23.5	
Education is missing	4.0	7.1	***	8.6	9.8	*	6.7	9.5	***
Mother's employment									
Employed	40.7	55.2	***	48.6	53.8	***	47.9	57.6	***
Not employed	59.3	35.5	***	49.9	36.3	***	52.1	33.3	***
Employment status is missing	0.0	9.3	***	1.5	9.9	***	0.0	9.1	***
Father's education									
Less than high school education	71.4	57.2	***	60.2	52.3	***	45.3	43.3	***
High school education	13.4	17.7	***	19.1	20.4	***	28.6	28.4	*
More than high school education	12.5	8.4	*	15.2	13.9	*	22.8	13.4	***
Education is missing	2.7	16.7	***	5.5	13.5	***	3.3	14.9	***
N(Families)	4567	2049		5023	3759		6607	5268	

Source: Authors' calculations based on Colombian QLS of 1997, 2008, and 2016.

Notes: Weighted proportions and means presented. Statistical significance of bivariate tests for differences by type of custodial-mother family: + p<0.10, * p<0.05, **p<0.01, ***p<0.001. All amounts are converted to purchasing power parities (PPP) U.S. dollars of each year (World Bank PPP conversion factor for 1997: 574.11 Colombian pesos=1 U.S. dollar; for 2008: 1057.88 Colombian pesos=1 U.S. dollar; and for 2016: 1298.14 Colombian pesos=1 U.S. dollar) and then converted to 2019 U.S. dollars. To estimate poverty rates we assigned the equivalised family income (i.e., family income divided by the square root of family size) to each family and compared this amount with the poverty threshold. We used a poverty threshold based on 50 per cent of the median family income in Colombia. The median family income was also adjusted for economies of scale using the square root of family size.

Table 5.4   Socioeconomic characteristics of custodial-mother families by type of family in 1997, 2008 and 2016

	1997				2008				2016			
	CM	SM	RM		CM	SM	RM		CM	SM	RM	
Custodial-mother families		88.4	11.6			77.9	22.1			78.6	21.4	
Family characteristics												
Number of children	1.8	1.7	2.4	***	1.8	1.6	2.4	***	1.6	1.5	2.1	***
Age of youngest child												
0-5 years old	48.3	47.6	53.5	*	48.0	45.1	58.1	***	45.3	43.9	50.6	***
6-11 years old	28.4	27.5	35.4		30.3	30.8	28.6		33.3	33.7	32.1	+
12-17 years old	23.3	24.9	11.0	***	21.7	24.1	13.3	***	21.3	22.4	17.3	**
Annual family income in PPP	9224.9	8284.4	16378.4	***	8721.5	7453.6	13208.9	***	8063.7	6568.3	13561.4	***
Family receives child support	21.6	23.1	10.3	***	27.7	31.9	12.9	***	23.8	26.1	15.2	***
Annual child support income in PPP (All)	886.1	963.0	301.3	**	1136.0	1386.7	248.8	**	663.8	767.3	283.4	***
Annual child support income in PPP (Recipients)	4096.2	4164.6	2926.8		4099.6	4346.3	1934.0	**	2788.3	2935.2	1861.2	*
Family lives in poverty	55.4	57.0	43.2	***	51.4	54.8	39.2	***	50.3	55.1	32.4	***
Family lives in urban area	88.3	89.3	80.0	***	89.5	91.0	84.2	***	89.4	90.7	84.6	***
Parents' characteristics												
Mother's age												
18-29 years old	33.8	34.7	26.4	*	35.9	36.13	34.9	*	35.2	36.4	30.9	***
30-39 years old	35.3	33.5	49.3	***	36.1	32.42	49.1	***	40.0	36.4	53.3	***
40-49 years old	22.0	22.3	20.2	+	22.4	24.83	13.9	***	19.3	20.7	13.8	***

	1997				2008				2016			
	CM	SM	RM		CM	SM	RM		CM	SM	RM	
50 years old or more	8.9	9.5	4.1	*	5.6	6.62	2.1	***	5.5	6.5	2.0	***
Mother's education												
Less than high school education	70.1	68.5	82.0	***	53.1	49.4	66.1	***	37.0	33.7	49.0	***
High school education	15.7	16.4	10.7	**	22.7	24.3	17.4	***	29.1	29.0	29.5	
More than high school education	8.6	9.0	5.3	+	15.4	16.9	10.2	***	25.0	27.6	15.4	***
Education is missing	5.6	6.1	2.0	*	8.7	9.4	6.3	**	9.0	9.7	6.2	***
Mother is employed	61.0	62.8	47.1	***	60.0	63.9	46.3	***	63.6	67.1	51.0	***
Father's education												
Less than high school education	54.5	54.6	53.9		50.7	49.6	54.2	**	42.9	42.0	46.3	**
High school education	18.7	19.3	14.2		20.7	21.7	17.2	***	28.3	29.3	24.4	***
More than high school education	8.7	9.1	5.5		14.1	15.3	9.9	***	12.7	13.7	8.8	***
Education is missing	18.1	17.0	26.4	+	14.5	13.4	18.7	**	16.1	15.0	20.5	**
N(Families)	1827	1591	236		3359	2616	743		4756	3780	976	

Source: Authors' calculations based on Colombian QLS of 1997, 2008, and 2016.

Notes: Results within columns are for CM: All custodial mothers, SM: Single mothers, and RM: Repartnered mothers. Weighted proportions and means presented. Statistical significance of bivariate tests for differences by type of custodial-mother family: + p<0.10, * p<0.05, **p<0.01, ***p<0.001. All amounts are converted to purchasing power parities (PPP) U.S. dollars of each year (World Bank PPP conversion factor for 1997: 574.11 Colombian pesos=1 U.S. dollar; for 2008: 1057.88 Colombian pesos=1 U.S. dollar; and for 2016: 1298.14 Colombian pesos=1 U.S. dollar) and then converted to 2019 U.S. dollars. To estimate poverty rates we assigned the equivalized family income (i.e., family income divided by the square root of family size) to each family and compared this amount with the poverty threshold. We used a poverty threshold based on 50% of the median family income in Colombia. The median family income was also adjusted for economies of scale using the square root of family size.

responsibility. However, parents are not the only ones expected to play a role in children's development. As stated in the legal framework, guaranteeing children's wellbeing is a shared responsibility between families, society, and the Colombian State (Ley 1098, 2006; Constitución Política de Colombia, 1991; Decreto 2737, 1989).

Four main institutions are involved in the operation of the Colombian child support system: the judicial system; the 213 NIFW ('National Institute of Family Wellbeing') local agencies spread across the country; the family commissioners, local government authorities with presence in each of the 1,103 municipalities of Colombia; and the conciliation centres, a group of public and private agencies that assist separated parents with extrajudicial conciliation services. The judicial system, the NIFW, and the family commissioners are all authorised to establish child support obligations while conciliation centres may only assist parents with making a child support arrangement themselves. All separated parents, regardless of their marital status, may make a private arrangement themselves or seek the assistance of the child support system to establish an institutional arrangement. A private arrangement is enforceable if it meets three conditions: 1) it is stated (i.e., all elements of the child support obligation are written: amount, mode[6], frequency, and method of payment), 2) it is clear (i.e., there is no uncertainty regarding the elements of the obligation), and 3) it is enforceable (i.e., the requisites to pursue it have been met; for instance, paternity has been established or can be presumed).

Whether parents make a private or institutional arrangement may depend on factors such as parents' marital status and ability to pay for costs associated with seeking a particular type of arrangement. If the parents are married or have a registered cohabiting union[7], a child support arrangement must be reached for the union to be legally dissolved, meaning that these parents are very likely to reach a child support agreement. However, the costs of reaching these agreements can still be high. The NIFW, family commissioners, and conciliation centres run by non-profit institutions provide services at no cost, but parents seeking assistance from these agencies may incur transportation costs and may also lose earnings if they must take time off from work to gather proof of their case. In Colombia, expenditures associated with divorce proceedings include a $222 (2019 PPP) fee and legal representation costs, which may range between $1,346 (2019 PPP) and $2,018 (2019 PPP). There are also legal barriers to setting a child support arrangement for unmarried and non-cohabiting parents. If the parents never lived together, paternity must be established first.

---

[6]   Whether it is in cash, in-kind, or both.
[7]   In Colombia, law 54 of 1990 legally recognised cohabiting unions of two years or more as de facto marital unions.

A paternity establishment case may be initiated by either parent. Although the government usually covers the cost of DNA testing, a judge can decide that the father has to pay for the test after paternity is confirmed.

Child support obligations are determined on a case-by-case basis. There are some rules, but those individuals authorised to establish a child support order – including parents themselves through private arrangements – are accorded a great deal of discretion. When parents seek assistance from the NIFW or the family commissioners, they are first encouraged to reach an agreement themselves. Parents' decision regarding the amount, mode, frequency, and method of payment is then typically approved by the agency staff. When parents cannot reach an agreement, NIFW staff or a family commissioner are responsible for making a determination, mainly considering the needs of the children living with the custodial parent, the income of both parents, and the number of noncustodial parent's children (from current and prior unions). If the information of the noncustodial parent's income is not available, minimum wage can be imputed. In any case, child support orders cannot be higher than 50 per cent of the noncustodial parent's income. Parents who seek assistance from conciliation centers are also encouraged to make an agreement themselves. If parents do not reach an agreement at these agencies, they may seek assistance from the NIFW, the family commissioners or take the case to court. Parents may request an order modification when a substantial change of circumstances occurs, but overall order modifications are rare.

Child support can be paid in cash, in-kind, or both. However, Colombia does not have a public agency that is responsible for collecting and distributing child support payments. This means that how child support is transferred from the noncustodial parent to the custodial parent is ultimately determined in the child support arrangement. Noncustodial parents may use different payment methods such as cash, checks, mobile payments, and electronic bank transfers. Wage-withholding only occurs if the custodial parent has sued the noncustodial parent and a judge determines that payments would be made through this mechanism. Some examples of in-kind payments include groceries, clothing, school tuition and fees, and health insurance premiums. Colombia does not have a public guaranteed child support program to ensure that custodial parents receive child support when noncustodial parents are unemployed, have low earnings, or are unwilling to provide financial support to their children. However, custodial parents who are eligible for government assistance may receive both child support and public benefits. Child support income may impact parents' eligibility for social programs if parents report this income in SISBEN[8], an instrument to determine who is eligible for means-tested programs in Colombia.

Colombia does not have a child support enforcement program. Enforcement of child support obligations only occurs if the custodial parent sues the noncustodial parent. Examples of enforcement measures include barring the noncustodial parent from leaving the country and the confiscation of the noncustodial parent's wages and/or property. A law sanctioned on July 2nd, 2021 created a national registry of child support debtors. A custodial parent may request the inclusion of the noncustodial parent in this registry when the noncustodial parent has failed to pay child support for 3 months (Ley 2097, 2021). This law establishes that the judge or agency staff who was assigned to the case will decide whether the noncustodial parent should be included in this registry. Custodial parents may also pursue a criminal case against the noncustodial parent. This type of measure is purely punitive, however: prison sentences for failure to pay child support range from 32 to 72 months of incarceration (Ley 1098, 2006; Constitución Política de Colombia, 1991; Decreto 2737, 1989).

CONCLUSION

While child support policy in Colombia has the potential to improve the wellbeing of children living with only one parent, the vast majority of custodial-parent families do not receive financial support from a noncustodial parent. Two characteristics of the social and economic context of Colombia are likely to exacerbate this issue: the high prevalence of multiple-partner fertility (MPF) and a labour market that struggles to offer quality jobs to most Colombians. Parents' rights and responsibilities toward their children are more difficult to establish and enforce when they have children with multiple partners. The child support system has not yet adjusted to the growing complexity of families, including the high prevalence of MPF. Colombians also face a job market with high informality (Elgin et al., 2021), few employment opportunities for less-skilled workers, and a general dearth of quality jobs (Carranza et al., 2021). These issues make child support policies that rely on a strong and thriving job market (for example, determining child support orders based on parents' income and payment through automatic wage withdrawal) less successful. Some countries have addressed these challenges with public guaranteed child support programs (Hakovirta et al., 2013; Hakovirta and Eydal, 2020) but this policy is not financially viable in the short term: the COVID-19 pandemic left Colombia with approximately 40 per cent of its people living

---

[8]   Spanish acronym for *Sistema de Identificación de Potenciales Beneficiarios de Programas Sociales.*

in poverty (DANE, 2022) adding yet another burden on an extraordinarily pressured social welfare system.

Nevertheless, the Colombian child support system does provide several options to arrange how much each parent should contribute to their children's expenditures following union dissolution. Unlike other policy schemes, Colombian parents may make child support arrangements outside a family court or child support agency, and these private arrangements, like those arrangements made within family court, are enforceable. Why most custodial parents end up not benefitting from this policy is still puzzling. Prior research sheds some light on this issue showing that individual characteristics such as mother's low education are a barrier to child support receipt. Designing and implementing interventions to better serve this population is important. Two proposals to consider include: 1) creating outreach programs to improve parents' knowledge about child support services; and 2) connecting custodial parents receiving cash welfare – a group overwhelmingly comprised of women with low education – with child support agencies. Both efforts could be led by the government agency in charge of cash welfare programs.

Individual socioeconomic disadvantage is not the only contributor to the low rate of child support receipt in Colombia. Barriers to child support receipt may also stem from features of the child support system itself. For instance, our analysis of the current scheme suggests that the bulk of work required to establish and enforce a child support arrangement is borne by custodial parents alone. It may be that for the women who make up most of these parents, the costs associated with pursuing and enforcing a child support arrangement may outweigh the benefits of child support receipt. An important task for policy-makers and scholars alike will be to examine how current policies support or hinder access to child support in Colombia. A research partnership between academia and the child support system is ideal to be able to leverage the unique expertise and skills of scholars and those in the agencies operating the system. Because a low rate of child support receipt is a core issue across a wide range of countries, expanding comparative child support research will be instrumental in improving the effectiveness of child support systems worldwide.

REFERENCES

Arriagada, I. (2004). Transformaciones sociales y demográficas de las familias latino-americanas. *Papeles de Población*, *10*(40), 71–95.

Banco de la República. (2021). Legal minimum wage in Colombia. https://www.banrep.gov.co/en/wage-index.

Blofield, M., Lustig, N., and Trasberg, M. (2021). Social protection during the pandemic: Argentina, Brazil, Colombia, and Mexico (pp. 11). Center for Global Development.

Cárdenas, M., and Martínez, B. H. (2020). Covid-19 in Colombia: Impact and policy responses (p. 19). Center for Global Development.

Carranza, E., Wiseman, W., Eberhard-Ruiz, A., and Cardenas, A. L. (2021). *Jobs Diagnostic Colombia*. The World Bank.

Constitución Política de Colombia. (1991).

Cuesta, L., Hakovirta, M., and Jokela, M. (2018). The antipoverty effectiveness of child support: Empirical evidence for Latin American countries. *Social Policy & Administration, 52,* 1233–1251. https://doi.org/10.1111/spol.12437.

Cuesta, L., and Meyer, D. R. (2012). Child support receipt: Does context matter? A comparative analysis of Colombia and the United States. *Children and Youth Services Review, 34,* 1876–1883. https://doi.org/10.1016/j.childyouth.2012.05.023.

Cuesta, L., and Meyer, D. R. (2014). The role of child support in the economic wellbeing of custodial-mother families in less developed countries: The case of Colombia. *International Journal of Law, Policy and the Family, 28,* 60–76. https://doi.org/10.1093/lawfam/ebt016.

Cuesta, L., and Mogollon, M. (2019). Trends, prevalence, and correlates of multiple-partner fertility in Colombia [Paper presentation]. Population Association of America (PAA) Annual Conference.

Cuesta, L., Ríos-Salas, V., and Meyer, D. R. (2017). The impact of family change on income poverty in Colombia and Peru. *Journal of Comparative Family Studies, 48*(1), 67–96. https://doi.org/10.3138/jcfs.48.1.67.

Decreto 2737. (1989). (Testimony of Presidencia de la República).

DANE: Departamento Administrativo Nacional de Estadística. (2020a). Brecha salarial de género en Colombia. https://www.dane.gov.co/files/investigaciones/notas-estadisticas/nov-2020-brecha-salarial-de-genero-colombia.pdf.

DANE: Departamento Administrativo Nacional de Estadística. (2020b). Estimaciones del cambio demográfico: Esperanza de vida al nacer. https://www.dane.gov.co/index.php/estadisticas-por-tema/demografia-y-poblacion/estimaciones-del-cambio-demografico

DANE: Departamento Administrativo Nacional de Estadística. (2021a). Censo nacional de población y vivienda 2018: Edad. Censo Nacional de Población y Vivienda. http://systema59.dane.gov.co/bincol/RpWebEngine.exe/Portal?BASE=CNPVBASE4V2&lang=esp

DANE: Departamento Administrativo Nacional de Estadística. (2021b). Censo nacional de población y vivienda Colombia 2018: Cómo vivimos? https://www.dane.gov.co/index.php/estadisticas-por-tema/demografia-y-poblacion/censo-nacional-de-poblacion-y-vivenda-2018/como-vivimos.

DANE: Departamento Administrativo Nacional de Estadística. (2021c). Censo nacional de población y vivienda Colombia 2018: Cuántos somos? Censo Nacional de población y vivienda Colombia 2018. https://www.dane.gov.co/index.php/estadisticas-por-tema/demografia-y-poblacion/censo-nacional-de-poblacion-y-vivenda-2018/cuantos-somos.

DANE: Departamento Administrativo Nacional de Estadística. (2021d). Mercado laboral principales resultados: Mayo 2021 y marzo-mayo 2021. https://www.dane.gov.co/index.php/estadisticas-por-tema/mercado-laboral/empleo-y-desempleo.

DANE: Departamento Administrativo Nacional de Estadística. (2021e). Comunicado de prensa: Pobreza monetaria 2020. https://www.dane.gov.co/files/investigaciones/condiciones_vida/pobreza/2020/Comunicado-pobreza-monetaria_2020.pdf.

DANE: Departamento Administrativo Nacional de Estadística. (2021f). Comunicado de prensa: Pobreza multidimensional en Colombia 2018 y 2019. https://www

.dane.gov.co/files/investigaciones/condiciones_vida/pobreza/2019/cp_pobreza
_multidimensional_19.pdf.

DANE: Departamento Administrativo Nacional de Estadística. (2022). Pobreza monetaria y grupos de ingreso en Colombia. Resultados 2021. https://www.dane.go
v.co/files/investigaciones/condiciones_vida/pobreza/2021/Presentacion-pobreza
-monetaria_2021.pdf.

DANE: Departamento Administrativo Nacional de Estadística and ONU Mujeres. (2020). Tiempo de cuidado: Las cifras de la desigualdad. https://www.dane.gov.co/
files/investigaciones/genero/publicaciones/tiempo-de-cuidados-cifras-desigualdad
-informe.pdf.

Departamento Nacional de Planeación. (2008). Evaluación de políticas públicas. Programa Familias en Acción: Impactos en capital humano y evaluación beneficio-costo del programa. https://colaboracion.dnp.gov.co/CDT/Prensa/Publicaciones/Evaluaci
on-politicas-publicas-6.pdf.

Economic Commission for Latin America and the Caribbean. (2018). Expenditure on social protection. Base de Datos de Inversión Social En América Latina y El Caribe. https://observatoriosocial.cepal.org/inversion/en/indicator/expenditure
-social-protection.

Economic Commission for Latin America and the Caribbean. (2020). Más Familias en Acción (More Families in Action). Social Protection. https://socialprotection
.org/discover/programmes/m%C3%A1s-familias-en-acci%C3%B3n-more-families
-action.

Economic Commission for Latin America and the Caribbean. (2021). Social Panorama of Latin America 2020. CEPAL. https://www.cepal.org/en/publications/46688-soc
ial-panorama-latin-america-2020.

Elgin, C., Kose, M. A., Ohnsorge, F., and Yu, S. (2021). Understanding informality (MPRA Paper No. 109490; Munich Personal RePEc Archive). https://mpra.ub.uni
-muenchen.de/109490/1/MPRA_paper_109490.pdf.

Esteve, A., García-Román, J., and Lesthaeghe, R. (2012). The family context of cohabitation and single motherhood in Latin America. *Population and Development Review*, *38*(4), 707–727. https://doi.org/10.1111/j.1728-4457.2012.00533.x.

Flórez, C. E. (2004). La transformación de los hogares: Una visión de largo plazo. *Coyuntura Social*, 30. https://www.repository.fedesarrollo.org.co/bitstream/handle/
11445/1078/Co_So_Junio_2004_Florez.pdf?sequence=2.

Flórez, C. E., and Sanchez-Cespedes, L. (2013). Fecundidad y familia en Colombia: hacia una segunda transición demográfica? Bogotá: Serie Estudio a Profundidad (Basado En Las Encuestas Nacionales de Demografía y Salud-ENDS-1990/2010). https://
profamilia.org.co/wp-content/uploads/2018/12/2-FECUNDIDAD-Y-FAMILIA-EN
-COLOMBIA-HACIA-UNA-SEGUNDA-TRANSICION-DEMOGRAFICA-final
.pdf.

Gallego, J., Hoffmann, B., Ibarrarán, P., Medina, M. P., Pecha, C., Romero, O., Stampini, M., Vargas, D., and Vera-Cossio, D. A. (2021). Impactos del programa Ingreso Solidario frente a la crisis del COVID-19 en Colombia. Inter-American Development Bank. https://doi.org/10.18235/0003261.

García-Rojas, K., Herrera-Idárraga, P., Morales, L. F., Ramírez-Bustamante, N., and Tribín-Uribe, A. M. (2020). (She)cession: The Colombian female staircase fall (No. 1140; Borradores de Economía). Banco de la República. https://doi.org/10.32468/
be.1140.

Hakovirta, M., and Eydal, G. B. (2020). Shared care and child maintenance policies in Nordic countries. *International Journal of Law, Policy and the Family, 34*(1), 43–59. https://doi.org/10.1093/lawfam/ebz016.

Hakovirta, M., Kuivalainen, S., and Rantalaiho, M. (2013). Welfare state support of lone parents – Nordic approaches to a complex and ambiguous policy field. In *Changing social risks and social policy response in the Nordic welfare states.*

Ham, A., García, S., Dedios, M. C., Guarín, Á., Gómez, M. M., and Pizano, C. C. (2022). Social protection responses to forced displacement in Colombia (p. 82). ODI.

Instituto Colombiano de Bienestar Familiar. (2021). Qué es el ICBF? Instituto Colombiano de Bienestar Familiar. https://www.icbf.gov.co/instituto.

Institute for Family Studies, and Wheatley Institution. (2019). World family map 2019 mapping family change and child wellbeing outcomes. https://ifstudies.org/reports/world-family-map/2019/executive-summary.

Ley 1098. (2006). (Testimony of Congreso de la República de Colombia).

Ley 2097, (2021). (Testimony of Congreso de la República de Colombia).

Londoño Vélez, J., and Querubín, P. (2017). El impacto de transferencias en efectivo para asistencia de emergencia durante la pandemia de COVID-19 en Colombia (pp. 1–200). https://www.poverty-action.org/sites/default/files/publications/El-imp acto-de-transferencias-en-efectivo-para-asistencia-de-emergencia-durante-la-pande mia-de-COVID-19-en-Colombia.pdf.

Martínez Franzoni, J. (2008). Welfare regimes in Latin America: Capturing constellations of markets, families, and policies. *Latin American Politics and Society, 50*(02), 67–100. https://doi.org/10.1111/j.1548-2456.2008.00013.x.

Medellín, N., and Sánchez Prada, F. (2015). How Does Más Familias en Acción Work? (p. 50). https://publications.iadb.org/publications/english/document/How-does-Más -Familias-en-Acción-Work-Best-Practices-in-the-Implementation-of-Conditional -Cash-Transfer-Programs-in-Latin-America-and-the-Caribbean.pdf.

Migración Colombia. (2021). Más de un millón 742 mil Venezolanos se encontraría en Colombia para el 31 de enero de 2021 y podrían acogerse al Estatuto Temporal de Protección. Migración Colombia. https://migracioncolombia.gov.co/noticias/mas-de -un-millon-742-mil-venezolanos-se-encontrarian-en-colombia-para-el-31-de-enero -de-2021-y-podrian-acogerse-al-estatuto-temporal-de-proteccion.

Ministerio de Salud y Protección Social and Profamilia. (2017). Encuesta nacional de demografía y salud 2015. https://profamilia.org.co/investigaciones/ends/.

Observatorio de Familias. (2020). Censo de población y familia 2018 (No. 14). Departamento Nacional de Planeación (DNP). https://observatoriodefamilia.dnp .gov.co/Documents/Boletines/BOLETIN%20No.14.pdf.

Oficina del Alto Comisionado de las Naciones Unidas para los Refugiados. (2020). Los conflictos provocan cifras récord de desplazamiento interno. https://www.acnur .org/noticias/historia/2020/4/5ea864674/los-conflictos-provocan-cifras-record-de -desplazamiento-interno.html.

Organisation for Economic Cooperation and Development. (2016). Early childhood education and care in Colombia. In Education in Colombia (OECD Publishing). https://doi.org/10.1787/9789264250604-5-en.

Organisation for Economic Cooperation and Development. (2020). Social expenditure (SOCX) update 2020. https://www.oecd.org/els/soc/OECD2020-Social-Expenditure -SOCX-Update.pdf.

Organisation for Economic Cooperation and Development. (2021a). Fertility rates. Organisation for Economic Co-Operation and Development. https://doi.org/10.17 87/8272fb01.

Organisation for Economic Cooperation and Development. (2021b). Purchasing power parities (PPP). Organisation for Economic Co-Operation and Development. https://data.oecd.org/conversion/purchasing-power-parities-ppp.htm.

Organisation for Economic Cooperation and Development. (2022a). Gender wage gap (indicator). https://data.oecd.org/earnwage/gender-wage-gap.htm.

Organisation for Economic Cooperation and Development. (2022b). OECD economic outlook (preliminary version) (No. 1). https://www.oecd-ilibrary.org/sites/62d0ca31-en/index.html?itemId=/content/publication/62d0ca31-en.

Organisation for Economic Cooperation and Development. (2022c). OECD Economic Surveys: Colombia 2022. OECD Publishing. https://www.oecd.org/colombia/oecd-economic-surveys-colombia-25222961.htm.

Plataforma de Coordinación para Refugiados y Migrantes de Venezuela. (2020). Refugiados y migrantes venezolanos en América Latina y el Caribe. https://www.refworld.org.es/publisher,R4V,STATISTICS,VEN,5ed1cbc64,0.html.

Prosperidad Social. (2020a). Beneficiarios de Familias en Acción y Jóvenes en Acción recibirán nuevo pago ordinario y extraordinario en septiembre. Prosperidad Social. https://prosperidadsocial.gov.co/Noticias/beneficiarios-de-familias-en-accion-y-jovenes-en-accion-recibiran-nuevo-pago-ordinario-y-extraordinario-en-septiembre/.

Prosperidad Social. (2020b). Pago de Ingreso Solidario, previo al día sin IVA. Proseridad Social. https://prosperidadsocial.gov.co/Noticias/pago-de-ingreso-so lidario-previo-al-dia-sin-iva/.

Schoen, R., and Cheng, Y. A. (2006). Partner choice and the differential retreat from marriage. *Journal of Marriage and Family*, *68*(1), 1–10. JSTOR.

Skinner, C., and Davidson, J. (2009). Recent trends in child maintenance schemes in 14 countries. *International Journal of Law, Policy and the Family*, *23*(1), 25–52. https://doi.org/10.1093/lawfam/ebn017.

The World Bank. (2019a). Fertility rate, total (births per woman) Colombia. https://data.worldbank.org/indicator/SP.DYN.TFRT.IN?locations=CO.

The World Bank. (2019b). Gini index (World Bank estimate) Colombia. https://data.worldbank.org/indicator/SI.POV.GINI?locations=CO.

The World Bank. (2019c). World economic forum global competitiveness index: Mean years of schooling. The World Bank. https://tcdata360.worldbank.org/indicators/h22a4bb2b?country=COL&indicator=41393&countries=LCA,DMA,VCT,DOM,PER,ECU,CUB,GRD,JAM,SUR,MEX,BLZ,BRA,PRY,GUY,SLV,CRI,GTM,BOL,VEN,PAN,HND,NIC,ARG,ATG&viz=bar_chart&years=2019&compareBy=region.

Unidad para la Atención y Reparación Integral a las Víctimas. (2021). Víctimas conflicto armado. https://www.unidadvictimas.gov.co/es/registro-unico-de-victimas-ruv/37394.

United Nations Department of Economic and Social Affairs. (2019). International migrant stock 2019: Country profile Colombia. https://www.un.org/en/development/desa/population/migration/data/estimates2/countryprofiles.asp.

United Nations Development Programme. (2020). GDP per capita (2017 pp $). Human Development Reports. http://hdr.undp.org/en/indicators/194906.

United Nations Development Programme. (2021). Regional Human Development Report 2021 Trapped: High inequality and low growth in Latin America and the Caribbean—World. https://reliefweb.int/report/world/regional-human-development-report-2021-trapped-high-inequality-and-low-growth-latin.

The World Bank. (2022). World Bank Country and Lending Groups. Data. https://data
helpdesk.worldbank.org/knowledgebase/articles/906519-world-bank-country-and
-lending-groups.

6. Single mothers and the child support system in Finland

Mari Haapanen and Mia Hakovirta

INTRODUCTION

Divorces, separations and births outside of marriage have become more common and thus, it has increased the proportion of single parent families. Indeed, women head most of these families (Nieuwenhuis, 2020). As in most countries, in Finland, single mothers are among the most economically disadvantaged group. They have high poverty rates, a high risk of unemployment, and 'in-work' poverty (Chzhen and Bradshaw, 2012; Bradshaw et al., 2018; Nieuwenhuis, 2020).

Additionally, single mothers also face challenges in reconciling work and family life (for example, Moilanen, 2019). Lack of employment, low labour market incomes and inadequate policies are key contributors to the economic disadvantage of single mothers (Nieuwenhuis and Maldonado, 2018). In order to improve the economic stability of separated parents with children, child support is a key policy strategy paid as a financial contribution from one parent (non-resident) to the other (resident). This payment is ensured to financially help the children, post-separation (Hakovirta, Cuesta et al., 2022).

In this chapter, we describe the situation of single mothers and child support policies in Finland. Finland is often regarded as belonging to a dual-earner-dual carer family policy model where the explicit policy goal is to promote gender equality in care for children and paid work (Korpi, 2000; Eydal et al., 2015). When both parents are expected to be earners and governmental family benefits provide single parents with relatively generous resources, child support forms a small amount of their income sources (Hakovirta and Jokela, 2019). This makes Finland an interesting case to study child support and single mothers. We begin by describing family demography and welfare state context and set out the position of single mothers in Finland. Second, we provide a brief overview of the child support policy: policy goals and institutional arrangements, receipt rates and level of child support, and an overview of the guaranteed (advance) child support scheme. Finally, we discuss the policy challenges and consider how the family policy and child support system can address challenges for co-parenting post-separation, as well as implications for child poverty and gender equality.

FAMILY DEMOGRAPHY AND SINGLE PARENTS IN FINLAND

In recent times, family demographic patterns have substantially changed in most high-income countries (Lesthaeghe, 2020). In Finland, fertility and marriage rates have decreased considerably over approximately a decade, whereby consensual unions and out-of-wedlock births are an established family pattern (Hellstrand et al., 2020; Jalovaara and Kreyenfeld, 2020). Table 6.1 shows the trend in family characteristics in Finland from 1990–2020. In 2020, 37 per cent of the population lived in a family with children. The most common type of families with children was a family formed by an opposite-sex married couple, making up 56 per cent of families with children, and one-fifth of families with children were families of cohabiting couples. The share of single mother families has been at around 17–19 per cent of all families with children. Even though the number of single parent families consisting of a father with children has grown, their share was still very low, at four per cent of all single parent families in 2020. The proportion of reconstituted families (per cent of families with children) has increased since the early 1990s; however, the share of reconstituted families has remained at 9 per cent since 2004 (OSF, 2021).

Table 6.1   Family characteristics in Finland

	Proportion of opposite-sex married couple families	Proportion of cohabiting couple families	Share of births outside marriage (% of all births)	Proportion of single mother families	Proportion of reconstituted families
1990	76.6	9.4	25.2	12.3	6.8
2000	65.1	15.5	39.2	17.0	7.7
2010	61.3	18.4	41.1	17.5	9.1
2020	56.4	20.1	-	19.8	9.0

Note: Per cent of families with children if not otherwise determined.
Sources: OSF, 2020a, OSF, 2020b, OECD, 2022.

The number of divorces has remained stable throughout the decades, with the crude divorce rate[1] being 2.4 per cent in 2019 (OECD, 2022). The probability

---

[1]   The crude divorce rate refers to the number of divorces during a given year per 1000 people (OECD, 2022).

that a woman's first marriage ended in divorce was 38 per cent (OSF, 2020). Statistical data on separations of consensual unions are lacking, but it is estimated that they end in separation more often than marriages, even if there are children (Jalovaara and Kulu, 2018).

Jalovaara and Andersson (2018) have shown that of all children born in a union, 41 per cent had seen their original family dissolved by fifteen years of age. Furthermore, according to the research, structural factors, namely strong socioeconomic disparities, play a very important function in a child's lived experience of their family structure and potential transitions. Children of mothers with low levels of education are more likely to experience parental separation than children of mothers with higher levels of educational acquisition. According to Jalovaara and Andersson (2018), children of mothers with a low level of educational attainment, spend roughly half of their childhood living with both parents, whereas, in contrast, children of high-educated mothers spend approximately four fifths of their childhood living with both parents.

Children's Living Arrangements Post-Separation

When parents separate or do not live together, they have to decide the child's custody and living arrangements. In the 1980s, a new child custody and visiting rights law (HTL 361/1983) was enacted in Finland. This law made it possible for parents to share legal custody of their children, which is referred to as joint parental custody. When the new law came into effect, people began to view parental responsibilities differently, and the concept of joint parental responsibility gained widespread acceptance (Kurki-Suonio, 2000; Hakovirta and Hiilamo, 2012). Since then, Social Welfare offices have approved nearly 90 per cent of contracts for joint custody, 6 per cent for the mother to have full custody, and 1 per cent for the father to have single custody (THL, 2021).

An agreement on joint legal custody for children does not presuppose children's living arrangements. In Finland, parents are free to make private arrangements regarding the child's living and contact arrangements. The best interests of the child is the guiding principle behind these decisions. Parents can have their agreement formalised in a social welfare board (SWB) and if parents disagree or are unsatisfied with the formalised agreement, the court will make a decision. Although family law is designed to support both parents to share the care of children in post-separation (Kurki-Suonio, 2000; Hakovirta and Hiilamo, 2012) children's living arrangements in post-separation families are still gendered. The vast majority of children have legal residency (permanent address) with the mother, with the fathers as non-resident parents often afforded visiting rights. However, during the recent decade, there has been a change in post-separation parenting, and shared care arrangements – where a child lives almost equal time with each parent in post-separation – have become increasingly common.[2]

Figure 6.1 below presents formally approved agreements of children's living arrangements set out by the municipal social welfare board (SWB) in 2010–2020. The most common arrangement is that children live with the mother, and these figures have remained almost the same over the last decade. However, the number of parents agreeing on shared care has steadily increased over the years. For example, in 2020 there was an increase of 25 per cent in shared care agreements from the previous year (THL, 2021).

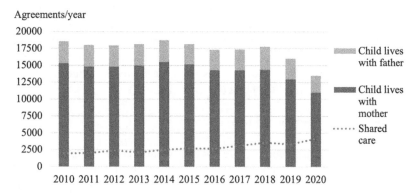

Source: THL, 2021.

Figure 6.1   Distribution of families with children by type of family in 2010–2020

The numbers presented in Figure 6.1 include only cases that had their agreement formalised by the SWB. A survey conducted in 2019 on separated parents shows that only about two thirds of the parents had officially ratified the child's living agreement (Miettinen et al., 2020). Survey data instead reveals the 'real' child-parent contact patterns. In 2002 weekly or fortnightly contact arrangements (often including half of school holidays) were the most common pattern of care where father-child contact occurred (Hakovirta and Broberg, 2007). As already seen in Figure 6.1, more children have a shared care agreement. The most recent survey data shows that in 2019, the proportion of children with a shared care arrangement was 30 per cent in Finland.

---

[2]   In Finland, shared care is defined as an arrangement where the child lives at least 40 per cent of the time with each parent (Miettinen et al., 2020).

Moreover, in Finland, as in many other countries, shared care is more common among socioeconomically advantaged families (Miettinen et al., 2020).

In late 2019, Finland established legislative changes in regards to child custody and access rights legislation, and shared care was acknowledged for the first time in the law. The legislative change means that parents can now agree on the shared care arrangement, as prior to this new law shared care was practiced through visitation or access rights. No legal presumption on a child's living arrangements was set, and the main principle is the best interests of the child (Koulu, 2019; Tolonen et al., 2019). The legislative change can affect the ways that the social norm shifts towards promoting more equal care time between separated parents, which might lead to increases in shared care arrangements in the future (Tolonen et al., 2019). Whether parents are satisfied with the child's living arrangement may also play a role how popular shared care arrangement is. There is some evidence that mothers in Finland with shared care of the child are more satisfied with the living arrangement than mothers with sole care of the child (Riser et al., 2022).

Single Parents' Position in Finland

In the Anglo-American context, the policy discourse around single mothers is very much shaped by the image of the 'welfare queen' (Duncan and Edwards, 1999; Goodall and Cook, 2021; Sheely and Maldonando, 2020). The term is less used today, but it refers to single mothers who allegedly misuse welfare payments to avoid paid work. In Nordic countries, moving away from the male breadwinner model towards a dual earner care model has meant that single mothers are not conceptualised as a social problem (Lewis and Hobson, 1997). In other words, single mothers are not seen as 'welfare queens' who are dependent on welfare benefit, but rather, they work (Forssen and Hakovirta, 1999). Hakovirta and her colleagues (2021) reported that people in countries with more gender equality hold the most positive attitudes toward single parents. However, among Nordic countries, Finland was an exception. Although attitudes toward single motherhood in Finland in general were positive, still, in 2012 more than one third of Finnish people have concerns about the ability of single parents to raise their children compared to two parent families (Hakovirta et al., 2021).

The negative discourse around single motherhood might be a result of economic vulnerabilities. The recession of the late 1980s and early 1990s was severe and families with children experienced cutbacks in social benefits, whereby single mothers were especially affected by the economic recession (Skevik, 2006). Single mother employment rates declined dramatically and since then have been eight to ten percentage points lower than that of partnered mothers between 1987 and 2011 (Härkönen et al., 2016). The labour force position of single mothers and partnered mothers in the 2010s is shown in Figure 6.2. The share of single mothers in employment was almost as high as that of partnered mothers in 2019 (76 per cent). The share of unemployed single mothers has remained slightly above that of partnered mothers.

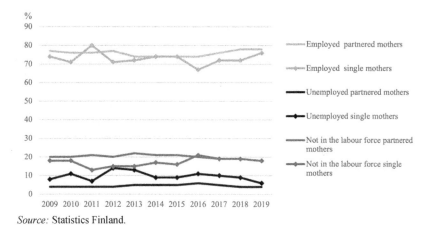

Source: Statistics Finland.

Figure 6.2   *Labour force position of single mothers and partnered mothers aged 20 to 59 in Finland in 2009–2019*

Financial strain and poverty faced by single mother families have been reported extensively in research and continue to be significant risks for single mother families also in Finland. The poverty risk among children under 18 has increased in Finland during the 2000s especially among children in single-parent families where there has been a climbing trend in child poverty. The data shows that the child poverty rate for children in single mother families was 22 per cent in 2000 and 24 per cent in 2018 (Hakovirta and Nygård, 2021). The poverty rate was more than three times higher than the poverty rate for children in families with two adults. In 2016, over two-thirds of single mothers found it difficult to make ends meet (Salmi, 2020). They are also over-represented among social assistance receipts. Every fourth single mother household received social assistance in 2017 (Ylikännö and Hakovirta, 2020). It seems that employment alone cannot provide adequate standard of living for single mothers as they still have high poverty rates despite relatively high employment rates (Nieuwenhuis, 2020). One explanation for this is that single mothers are likely to have a low level of education compared to parents in a coupled family. This pattern of an 'educational gradient' also helps to explain single mothers' elevated poverty risks in Finland (Härkönen, 2018).

In addition to difficulties in employment and inadequate income, single mothers also face work–family conflicts. Single mothers are responsible for the family breadwinner role and many single mothers are managing the requirements attached to their work and family roles (Nieuwenhuis and Maldonado, 2018). Single mothers have far greater challenges to reconcile paid work and family commitments, particularly if they work non-standard hours. Moilanen (2019) for instance, found out that working non-standard work hours is associated with time-based work-to-family conflict among single mothers indicating that the more the mother works during non-standard hours, the more she experiences time-based work-to-family conflict. Single mothers also perceive that their work during non-standard hours interferes with time for family responsibilities (Moilanen, 2019). Furthermore, single mothers often face care poverty as their informal and formal resources do not adequately meet their childcare needs (Kröger, 2010).

FAMILY POLICY AND SINGLE PARENTS

Finland is often regarded as belonging to a dual-earner-dual carer family policy model where the explicit policy goal is to promote gender equality in care for children and paid work (Korpi, 2000; Eydal et al., 2015). The family policy system aims to guarantee the well-being of families with children and thus the welfare state supports families with children in various ways. Finland has a long history of supporting shared and equal parenthood, including promoting women's participation in the labour force and encouraging fathers to take responsibility for childcare (Eydal et al., 2015; Lammi-Taskula, 2017). Family leave, early childhood education and the care system support a mother's employment. Finland was also a pioneer in encouraging fathers' care rights as it introduced birth-related paternity leave and shared parental leave in the mid-1970s and early 1980s. Paternal leave has been implemented in Finland since the 1990s (Saarikallio and Miettinen, 2021; Eydal et al., 2015).

The high labour market participation rate among mothers goes hand in hand with large investments in publicly provided childcare for preschool children (for example, Datta Gupta et al., 2008; Eydal et al., 2015). Finland has been seen to have the strongest rights for public childcare within the Nordic welfare regime (Repo, 2010). All children under school-age (zero to six years) are entitled to early childhood education and care (ECEC), either through municipality-provided care or by a carer at home, supported by the home childcare allowance regardless of parental employment status (Eerola et al., 2019) The fee for childcare is based on the family's gross income. For low income families, ECEC is free of charge. Furthermore, early childhood education for 5-year-olds and pre-primary education for 6-year-olds is free of charge for 4 hours per day. In Finland, 98 per cent of all children attend ECEC at some point before starting school at age seven (OECD, 2022).

Finland has also protected the income of families with children through different income transfers, of which the universal child allowance (or family allowance) for all children is of foremost importance. Single parents are supported within the universal social transfer system and there are no specific benefits for single parents. This way social policies have attempted to minimise any inequalities that may have existed between children from different family backgrounds (Hiilamo, 2002). However, family benefits and services targeted for families with children were developed during an era when divorce proceedings usually granted legal custody of children to mothers, and granting legal custody to fathers only occurred in rare cases. Nowadays, parents increasingly share care of their children in post-separation (Miettinen et al., 2020). However, this societal change toward more equal parenting is not supported by family policies since very often only one of the parents can receive family policy benefits and parents sharing care of their children face challenges within the social security system (Hakovirta and Rantalaiho, 2011). The increases in shared care arrangements have raised questions on whether these benefits should be shared between the parents (Miettinen et al., 2020).

In Finland, since the economic crisis in 2010, the government has pursued cuts to family benefits and services, significantly affecting the consensus surrounding universal support for families with children (Nyby et al., 2018). Furthermore, during the 2000s, policies advocating children's development as well as gender equality have become more stressed in the Nordic countries, while 'family-friendly' income strategies have lost ground. This suggests a gradual shift in accentuation away from a 'transfer-based' income protection strategy towards a 'service-based' family policy. This shift has increased child poverty, particularly among single parent families (Hakovirta and Nygård, 2021).

Single Parents and Child Support Policy

Throughout history, some children have lived apart from one of their parents and one mechanism that has protected children from the economic loss of the parent has been a private child support policy, which is a financial transfer between separated parents. All high-income countries have child support policies, as the legal duty to provide for children rests with both parents. Article 27 of the United Nations Convention on the Rights of the Child (UNCRC) outlines a legal requirement for parents / care givers to fulfill their financial obligations to their children and for nation states to make sure their children obtain financial support from their separated parents (Hakovirta, Cuesta et al., 2022).

Over the past several decades, child support has become an important part of the response both to the economic disadvantage experienced by children in single parent families and to the growing costs of state support to such families (see Skinner et al., 2007; Hakovirta et al., 2022). Child support is an important source of income for many single mothers across countries (Hakovirta and Jokela, 2019).

In Finland, the first piece of child support legislation, the Marriage Law of 1929, emphasised the responsibility of non-resident fathers towards their children born out of wedlock and the aim of child support was to ensure children the financial support of their biological parents (Kurki-Suonio, 2000; Hakovirta and Hiilamo, 2012). Throughout the 20th century, the key principles of child support policy were that liable parents – usually fathers – should pay according to their ability, and that children would be taken care of by their mothers. In Finland high levels of poverty paved the way for the first government interventions to support families economically (Gauthier, 1996). Starting in the 1970s, Finland witnessed the rapid development of family policies and the objective of family policies shifted from poverty alleviation to encouraging parents to share parental responsibilities and to ensuring that both parents had the opportunity to integrate into the labour market. This objective was emphasised in the organisation of child support policies (Hakovirta and Hiilamo, 2012). Parents' equal economic responsibility for children according to their means became the main policy principle that operates in child support policy (Skinner and Hakovirta, 2021).

Institutional arrangements and child support obligations

As noted in Chapter 2, countries organise their child support policy in various ways. According to Skinner et al. (2007) three main types occur: court-based systems, agency based systems, and hybrid systems. Finland represents the hybrid scheme in which parents, social welfare boards and the courts are involved in determining child support obligations. The Social Insurance Institution of Finland is responsible for the guaranteed child support scheme and its enforcement.

The key feature of the Finnish child support scheme is that in most cases parents have the freedom to choose how they organise child support post-separation. Parents can make private arrangements, request assistance from the Social Welfare Board (SWB) to assist with their private negotiations or if disagreements go to the court. In order to claim guaranteed child support, the agreement has to be ratified by another body to be binding (Hakovirta and Hiilamo, 2012). In 2019, 68 per cent of separated parents had a ratified child support agreement of which 58 per cent were ratified by SWB and 10 per cent by the courts. Although a greater share of parents have ratified agreements, private arrangements are quite common since over a quarter of parents do not have a ratified agreement at all. This is explicitly prominent when a child has a shared care arrangement, as 64 per cent of parents with a shared care arrangement did not have a ratified agreement on child support in 2019 (Miettinen et al., 2020).

The determination of the amount of financial obligations is based on discretion. There are calculation guidelines, however, they are not legally binding. Regardless of the guidelines, final determination of the amount of child support is made on an individual basis, and a high degree of discretion still remains. Factors that determine the level of child support include the needs of the child, economic resources of both parents, obligations to other children and the child's care time (Hakovirta and Hiilamo, 2012).

Child support receipt and poverty
In Finland, the number of single mothers receiving child support is relatively high. It is estimated that in 2013 roughly 80 per cent of non-widowed single mother households received child support, either from the state, from non-resident parents, or from both sources (Hakovirta and Jokela, 2019). If only private child support is considered, 46 per cent of single mothers received child support from the child's other parent in 2017–2018 (Hakovirta and Mesiäislehto, 2022).

Although a high proportion of single mothers in Finland receive child support either from the other parent or guaranteed child support, the amounts are relatively low. Child support comprises under 10 per cent of the single mothers' total incomes, while income from employment is the main source of income (Hakovirta and Jokela, 2019). The Luxembourg Income Study data from 2013 shows that in Finland mean annual child support was $2820, including guaranteed child support (Hakovirta and Jokela, 2019). According to the European Survey on Income and Living Standards (EU-SILC) from the year 2017–2018 mean annual child support that single mothers received from the non-resident fathers was €3224 euros per year (Hakovirta and Mesiäislehto, 2022). When considering only guaranteed support, it is estimated that it comprises 8–10 per cent of single mothers' income (Ahola, 2016).

As a relatively large proportion of single mothers in Finland are receiving child support, it has reduced poverty among single mothers and their children. Before consideration of child support, in 2013, over half of single mother households receiving child support fell below the poverty line. After consideration of the child support receipt, the child poverty rate was 33 per cent (Hakovirta and Jokela, 2019). An examination of the antipoverty effectiveness of child support among single mothers shows that child support has reduced child poverty in absolute terms by 7.9 percentage points, and this translates into a 38.9 per cent decline in child poverty. Considering only those single mothers who receive child support, the antipoverty effectiveness is substantially larger

(Hakovirta and Jokela, 2019). However, if a single mother is receiving social assistance, the amount of child support is counted as income. Accordingly, social assistance is reduced by the same amount as the child support amount paid, leaving single mother families no better off as their incomes are plugged at the level of social assistance. In this way, the potential of child support to alleviate poverty is not fully realised in the families who are also in receipt of social assistance benefits (Hakovirta et al., 2020).

Non-compliance and guaranteed child support scheme

Countries have various mechanisms to enforce compliance with child support obligations (Hakovirta, Cuesta et al., 2022). In Finland, the amount owed can be withheld from the other parent's income and then forwarded to the single parent. Currently, there is no study on the frequency or efficacy of these enforcement measures. Instead, since the late 1970s, Finland has approached nonpayment by providing a public guarantee of a minimum amount of child support, a system through which the government, under certain conditions, guarantees child support if the non-resident parent does not pay the full amount (guaranteed maintenance) (Hakovirta and Hiilamo, 2012). This flows from a principle in which every child has a right to be adequately provided for and child support is the right of the child. Most European countries now have a guaranteed child support scheme, but outside Europe these schemes are rare (Nieuwenhuis, 2020; Hakovirta, Cuesta et al., 2022).

Under the guaranteed child support scheme the state ensures minimum financial child support: a) when the parent who was required to pay child support does not pay; b) when the payment is too low because the liable parent was not able to pay more; or c) when no one person is liable for the provision of support. The purpose of guaranteed child support is to compensate for, or supplement, the parental support to which the child is otherwise entitled to, and to guarantee a minimum level of support to the parent with custody of the child or with whom the child resides (Hakovirta and Hiilamo, 2012). If the level of child support the non-resident parent is paying is sufficiently high and is paid regularly, no guaranteed maintenance is paid. If the child support paid by the non-resident parent is less than the guaranteed level, the remainder is paid as a guaranteed payment by the state.

The receipt of state guaranteed child support is common. In 2010, half of single mother families received it. The majority (59 per cent) of those single mothers who received the guaranteed support did so because the non-resident parent did not pay the obligated amount (Ahola, 2016). Guaranteed child support is a standard rate benefit and the full amount in 2022 was 172.59 euros per month. Thus, it does not consider the individual needs of a child, and the level of the guaranteed amount is about 70 per cent of the child support ordered for a typical couple in Finland (Hakovirta, Cuesta et al., 2022). Still, guaranteed child support is an important instrument to secure at least some child support for children in single parent families.

SINGLE MOTHERS AND FUTURE CHALLENGES FOR CHILD SUPPORT POLICY

The Nordic countries are known for having extensive family policies with low poverty rates and a high level of well-being among families with children (for example, Hiilamo, 2002; Eydal et al., 2015). However, during the past twenty-five years Finland has experienced financial crisis, whereby Finnish governments have cut family benefits and services. Together with welfare benefit cuts and an unstable and precarious labour market, the economic position of single mothers has weakened.

As poverty among single mother families has increased, child support has become an important income source for those single mothers receiving it. However, low receipt rate of child support is a core issue in Finland, as in many other countries (Hakovirta and Mesiäislehto, 2022). Moreover, of the low-income single mothers who need the support most receive child support less often than their needs (Hakovirta and Jokela, 2019). The increasing precariousness and instability of job markets is likely to exacerbate low receipt rates of child support and make it more difficult for the other parent to pay support. Finland, however, has a guaranteed child support scheme, to address nonpayment or irregular payment to ensure some child support for children. A stable amount of child support eases budgeting in a single parent family, and children are not harmed by nonpayment. The government ensures collection, and single mothers can use a given amount of regular child support in a way that best supports the child (Hakovirta, Cuesta et al., 2022). This may also help single mothers who experience economic abuse, as child support can keep them tied to the abuser (see for example, Royal, 2022; Kaittila et al., 2022). Furthermore, private child support negotiations and agreements made without assistance may not be ideal in the context of family violence as there are power differentials between the parties involved (Patrick at al., 2008).

Another critical issue for low income single mothers is the way in which child support is treated in determining social assistance benefits. In Finland, single mothers receiving social assistance are likely to be no better off financially irrespective of whether any child support is paid by the other parent, minimising its value to single mothers (Hakovirta et al., 2020). For example, the OECD has called for policy changes so that countries should consider passing on at least some of the child support that is paid (OECD, 2011).

Cases involving low-income parents are not the only situations in which child support policies are facing challenges. Shared care is becoming an increasingly common post-separation living arrangement for children, which might also explain the low receipt rate of child support. In shared care, fewer parents share the financial obligation of supporting their child through child support payments (Miettinen et al., 2020). While in the Finnish child support scheme there is freedom for parents to decide on how to share the economic responsibility of the child, research is needed on how parents in shared care arrangements share the economic responsibility, and how it affects the position of single mothers in Finland. If parents are sharing the financial obligation of supporting their child through child support payments the amounts owed when children move from spending time primarily with one parent to spending approximately equal time is only slightly lower (Hakovirta, Meyer and Skinner, 2022). Thus, it has been shown that the Finnish child support system prioritises lessening single mother poverty rather than achieving gender equality by encouraging fathers' sharing of care and acknowledging care time in child support guidelines. Finnish family policies and family laws generally boost shared parenting but this aim to support gender equality does not correspond well with child support policy. Child support policy is providing less incentive for the father to care for children post-separation, treating fathers and mothers in gendered ways as 'earners' and 'carers' (Hakovirta, Cook and Sinclair, 2019). Consistent with other countries (see Hakovirta et al., 2021), shared care should be embedded to a greater extent in the child support scheme, entitling the other parent to a larger deduction in child support if the child spends almost equal time with both parents.

REFERENCES

Ahola, E. (2016) Elatustuen merkitys yksinhuoltajaperheiden toimeentulolle [The Importance of Guaranteed Child Support to Lone Parent's Income] in Haataja, A., Airio, I., Saarikallio-Torp., M., and Valaste, M. (eds) *Laulu 573 566 perheestä. Lapsiperheet ja perhepolitiikka 2000-luvulla* [Families with Children and Family Policy in the 21st Century]. Helsinki: Kela. pp. 288–306.

Bradshaw, J., Keung, A., and Chzhen, Y. (2018) Cash benefits and poverty in single-parent families in Nieuwenhuis, R., and Maldonado L.C. (eds) *The triple bind of single-parent families: Resources, employment and policies to improve wellbeing.* Bristol: Bristol University Press, pp. 337–358.

Chzhen, Y., and Bradshaw, J. (2012) Lone parents, poverty and policy in the European Union. *Journal of European Social Policy, 22*(5), pp. 487–506.

Datta Gupta, N., Smith, N., and Verner, M. (2008) PERSPECTIVE ARTICLE: The impact of Nordic countries' family friendly policies on employment, wages, and children. *Review of Economics of the Household, 6*, 65–89.

Duncan, S., and Edwards, R. (1999) *Lone mothers, paid work and gendered moral rationalities.* London: Palgrave Macmillan.

Eerola, P., Lammi-Taskula, J., O'Brien, M., Hietamäki, J., and Räikkönen, E. (2019) Fathers' leave take-up in Finland: Motivations and barriers in a complex Nordic leave scheme. *SAGE Open, 9*(4), pp. 1–14.

Eydal, G.B., Rostgaard, T., and Hiilamo, H. (2015) Family policies in the Nordic countries: Aiming at equality in Guðný Björk Eydal and Tine Rostgaard (eds) *Handbook of family policy*. Cheltenham, UK and Northampton, MA, USA: Edward Elgar Publishing, pp 195–208.

Forssén, K., and Hakovirta, M. (1999) Work incentives in single parent families, in Ringen, S., and de Jong, P. (eds) *Fighting poverty: Caring for children, parents, the elderly and health*. Aldershot: Ashgate Publishing, pp.117–145.

Gauthier, A. (1996) *The State and the family*. Oxford: Clarendon Press.

Goodall, Z., and Cook, K. (2021) The forms and functions of child support stigma. *Social Currents*, *8*(2), pp. 145–162.

Hakovirta, M., and Broberg, M. (2007) Parenting from a distance: The factors connected to the contact between children and a non-resident parent. *Nordisk Sosialt Arbeid*, *27*(1), pp. 19–33.

Hakovirta, M., and Hiilamo, H. (2012) Children's rights and parents responsibilities: Child maintenance policies in Finland. *European Journal of Social Security*, *14*(4), pp. 286–303.

Hakovirta, M., and Jokela, M. (2019) Contribution of child maintenance to lone mothers' income in five countries. *Journal of European Social Policy*, *29*(2), pp. 257–272.

Hakovirta, M., and Mesiäislehto, M. (2022) Lone mothers and child support receipt in 21 European countries. *Journal of International and Comparative Social Policy*, *38*(1), pp. 36–56.

Hakovirta, M., and Nygård, M. (2021) Nordic Family Policy in the 2000s: From a 'Transfer-Based' towards a 'Service Based' Family Policy, in Aidukaite, J., Hort, S., and Kuhnle, S. (eds) *Challenges to the welfare state: Family and pension policies in the Baltic and Nordic countries*. Cheltenham, UK and Northampton, MA, USA: Edward Elgar Publishing, pp. 52–71.

Hakovirta, M., and Rantalaiho, M. (2011) Nordic family policy and shared parenthood. *European Journal of Social* Security, *13*(2), pp. 247–266.

Hakovirta, M., Cook, K., and Sinclair, S. (2019) Gender equality prior to and following separation: Nordic and liberal policy inconsistencies. *Social Politics: International Studies in Gender, State and Society*, *28*(4), pp. 1115–1136.

Hakovirta, M., Cuesta, L., Haapanen, M., and Meyer, D.R. (2022) Child support policy in high income countries: Similar problems, different approaches. *The ANNALS of the American Academy of Political and Social Science*, *702*(1), pp. 97–111.

Hakovirta, M., Kallio, J., and Salin, M. (2021) Is it possible for single parents to successfully raise children? Multilevel analysis of attitudes toward single parents in 22 welfare states. *International Journal of Comparative Family Studies*, *52*(1), pp. 117–144.

Hakovirta, M., Meyer, D.R., and Skinner, C. (2019) Does paying child support impoverish fathers in the United States, Finland, and the United Kingdom? *Children and Youth Services Review*, *106*, pp. 104485.

Hakovirta, M., Skinner, C., Hiilamo, H., and Jokela, M. (2020) Child poverty, child maintenance and interactions with social assistance benefits among lone parent families: A comparative analysis. *Journal of Social Policy*, *49*(1), pp. 19–39.

Härkönen, J. (2018) Single-mother poverty: How much do educational differences in single motherhood matter? in Nieuwenhuis, R., and Maldonado, L. (eds) *The triple bind of single-parent families: Resources, employment and policies to improve well-being*. Bristol: Policy Press.

Härkönen J., Lappalainen E., and Jalovaara, M. (2016) Double disadvantage in a Nordic welfare state: A demographic analysis of the single mother employment gap in Finland, 1987–2011. Stockholm Research Reports in Demography, 11 (2016).

Hellstrand, J., Nisén, J., and Myrskylä. M. (2020) All-time low period fertility in Finland: Demographic drivers, tempo effects, and cohort implications. *Population Studies*, *74*(3), pp. 315–329.

Hiilamo, H. (2002) *The rise and fall of Nordic Family Policy. Historical development and changes during the 1990s in Sweden and Finland.* Stakes Research Report 125. Helsinki: Stakes.

Jalovaara, M., and Andersson, G. (2018) Disparities in children's family experiences by mother's socioeconomic status: The case of Finland. *Population Research and Policy Review*, *37*(5), pp. 751–768.

Jalovaara, M., and Kreyenfeld, M. (2020) Childbearing across partnerships in Finland and Germany. Mortelmans, Dimitri (ed.) *Divorce in Europe: New insights in trends, causes and consequences of relation break-ups.* Cham: Springer.

Jalovaara, M., and Kulu, H. (2018) Separation risk over union duration: An immediate itch? *European Sociological Review*, *34*(5), pp. 486–500.

Kaittila, A., Hakovirta, M., and Kainulainen, H. (2022) Types of economic abuse in post-separation lives of women experiencing IPV: A qualitative study from Finland. *Violence Against Women*, *0*(0), pp. 1–19.

Korpi, W. (2000) Faces of inequality: Gender, class, and patterns of inequalities in different types of welfare states. *Social Politics: International Studies in Gender, State & Society*, *7*(2), pp. 127–191.

Koulu, S. (2019) Lapsen huoltolain uudistus ja ymmärrys perheestä. [Reform of the Child Custody and Access Act and Understanding of the Family]. *Janus sosiaali-ipolitiikan ja sosiaalityön tutkimuksen aikakausilehti*, *27*(4), pp. 413–421.

Kröger, T. (2010) Lone mothers and the puzzles of daily life: Do care regimes really matter? *International Journal of Social Welfare*, *19*(4), pp. 390–401.

Kurki-Suonio, K. (2000) Joint custody as an interpretation of the best interests of the child in critical and comparative perspective. *International Journal of Law, Policy and Family*, *14*(3), pp. 183–205.

Lammi-Taskula, J. (2017) Fathers on leave alone in Finland: Negotiations and lived experiences in O'Brien., M., and Wall., K. (eds) *Comparative perspectives on work–life balance and gender equality: Fathers on leave alone.* London: Springer, pp. 89–106.

Lesthaeghe, R. (2020) The second demographic transition, 1986–2020: Sub-replacement fertility and rising cohabitation— a global update. *Genus*, *76*(10), pp. 179–218.

Lewis, J., and Hobson, B. (1997) 'Introduction', in Lewis, J., (ed.) *Lone mothers in European welfare regimes: Shifting policy logics.* London: Jessica Kingsley.

Miettinen, A., Hakovirta, M., Saarikallio-Torp, M., Haapanen, M., Kalliomaa-Puha, L., Kurki, P., Sihvonen, E., Heinonen, H.M., and Kivistö, N. (2020) Lasten vuoroasuminen ja sosiaaliturva: vuoroasumisen nykytila ja merkitys etuus- ja palvelujärjestelmän kannalta. [Children's shared residence and social security]. Publications of the Government´s analysis, assessment and research activities 2020: *51*. Helsinki: Prime Minister's Office.

Moilanen, S. (2019) *Managing the 'triple demand': Lone mothers' nonstandard work hours and work–family reconciliation.* JYU Dissertations No. 112. Jyväskylä: University of Jyväskylä.

Nieuwenhuis, R. (2020) *The Situation of Single Parents in the EU*. European Parliament. Available at www.europarl.europa.eu/thinktank/en/document.html?reference=IPOL_STU(2020)659870. Accessed on 24.09.2022.

Nieuwenhuis, R., and Maldonado, L. (2018) *The triple bind of single-parent families: Resources, employment and policies to improve well-being*. Bristol: Policy Press.

Nyby, J., Nygård, M., and Blum, S. (2018) Radical Reform Or Piecemeal Adjustments? The Case of Finnish Family Policy Reforms. *European Policy Analysis*, *4*(2), pp. 190–213.

OECD (2011) *Doing Better for Families*. Available at https://www.oecd.org/social/soc/doingbetterforfamilies.htm. Accessed on 23.10.2022.

OECD (2022) *Family Database*. Available at https://www.oecd.org/els/family/database.htm. Accessed on 15.8.2020.

Official Statistics of Finland (OSF) (2020) Changes in Marital Status 2019. Available at http://www.stat.fi/til/ssaaty/2019/02/ssaaty_2019_02_2020–11–12_tie_001_en.html. Accessed on 20.05.2021.

Official Statistics of Finland (OSF) (2020a) Families. 2020, Appendix table 3. Families with underage children by type in 1950–2020. Available at http://www.stat.fi/til/perh/2020/perh_2020_2021–05–28_tau_003_en.html. Helsinki: Statistics Finland. Accessed on 24.10.2022.

Official Statistics of Finland (OSF) (2020b) Families. 2020, Appendix table 4. Reconstituted families 1990–2020. Available at http://www.stat.fi/til/perh/2020/perh_20 20_2021–05–28_tau_004_en.html. Helsinki: Statistics Finland. Accessed on 24.10.2022.

Official Statistics of Finland (OSF) (2021) Families 2020. Available at https://www.stat.fi/til/perh/2020/perh_2020_2021–05–28_tie_001_en.html. Accessed on 17.08.2021.

Patrick, R., Cook, K., and McKenzie, H. (2008) Domestic violence and the exemption from seeking child support: Providing safety or legitimizing ongoing poverty and fear. *Social Policy & Administration*, *42*(7), pp. 749–767.

Repo, K. (2010) Families, work and home care. Assessing Finnish child home care allowance. *BARN – Forskning om barn og barndom i Norden*, *28*(1), pp. 43–61.

Riser, Q.H., Haapanen, M., Bartfeld, J., Berger, L., Hakovirta, M., Meyer, D., and Miettinen, A. (2022) Maternal satisfaction with joint and sole child physical placement arrangements following separation in Wisconsin and Finland. *Family Process*, *00*, pp. 1–21.

Rotkirch A., and Miettinen A. (2017) Childlessness in Finland, in Kreyenfeld M., and Konietzka D. (eds) *Childlessness in Europe: Contexts, causes, and consequences*. Demographic Research Monographs. Springer Open, pp. 139–158.

Royal, K. (2022) Coronavirus has been the perfect excuse for him to just stop paying: Child maintenance and economic abuse in the UK during the COVID-19 outbreak. *Journal of Gender-Based Violence*, *6*(2), pp. 261–277.

Saarikallio-Torp, M., and Miettinen, A. (2021) Family leaves for fathers: Non-users as a test for parental leave reforms. *Journal of European Social Policy*, *31*(2), pp. 161–174.

Salmi, M. (2020) Lapsiperheiden köyhyys pitää yllä köyhyyden kierrettä [Child Poverty Maintains the Cycle of Poverty], in Kallio, J., and Hakovirta, M. (eds) *Lapsiperheiden köyhyys ja huono-osaisuus [Child Poverty and Disadvantage]*. Tampere: Vastapaino, pp. 37–72.

Sheely, A., and Maldonando, L. (2020) *What US Policymakers Can Learn from How the EU Tackles Poverty among Single Parent Families?* Available at https://blogs.lse.ac.uk/usappblog/2020/12/10/what-us-policymakers-can-learn-from-how-the-eu-tackles-poverty-among-single-parent-families. Accessed on 14.08.2022.

Skevik, A. (2006) Lone motherhood in the Nordic countries: Sole providers in dual-breadwinner regimes in Ellingsaeter, A.L., and Leira, A. (eds) *Politicising Parenthood in Scandinavia: Gender Relations and the Welfare States*. Bristol: Policy Press, pp. 241–264.

Skinner, C., Bradshaw, J., and Davidson, J. (2007) *Child Support Policy: An International Perspective*. Department for Work and Pensions Research Report, Leeds: Corporate Document Services.

THL (2021) *Lapsen elatus ja huolto sekä vanhemmuuden selvittäminen 2020*. [Custody and maintenance of the child and determination of parenthood 2020] Available at https://www.julkari.fi/handle/10024/143118?show=full. Helsinki: Finnish Institute for Health and Welfare. Accessed on: 23.10.2022.

Tolonen, H., Koulu, S., and Hakalehto, S. (2019) Best interests of the child in Finnish legislation and doctrine: What has changed and what remains the same? In Haugli, T., Nylund, A., Sigurdsen, R., and Bendiksen, L. (eds) *Children's constitutional rights in the Nordic countries*. Leiden, The Netherlands: Brill, pp. 159–184.

Ylikännö M., and Hakovirta M. (2020) Lapsiperheet toimeentulotuen asiakkaina [Families with children as social assistance recipients] in Korpela, T. (ed.) *Ojista allikkoon? Toimeentulotukiuudistuksen ensi metrit [The First Steps of Social Assistance Reform]*. Helsinki: Social Insurance Institution of Finland, pp. 278–301.

7. Child support as part of a multifaceted but fragmented system in Germany

Christina Boll and Thomas Meysen

SINGLE PARENTS AND THEIR CHILDREN IN GERMAN SOCIETY

Major Trends in Family Lives in Germany

During the last couple of decades, societal, economic, and demographic transitions, indicated for example by a rising age at first birth, a change in work preferences, and constantly high separation rates have led to a notable change in family prevalence and composition in Germany. In a population of 83.2 million, a total of 13.7 million (16.4 per cent) were children under 18 in 2020 (Statistisches Bundesamt, n.d.a). Between 1996 and 2019, the population share of people living in families with minor children decreased from 56.6 per cent to 48.31 per cent in 2019 (Statistisches Bundesamt, 2020a). The number of families declined too: While in 1996, the number of families with minor children stood at 9,429,000, it was only 8,189,000 in 2019. Of the latter, 3,197,000 (39 per cent) have a migration background: at least one family member or one parent did not acquire German citizenship at birth (Statistisches Bundesamt, 2020a). The birth rate stood at 1.54 children per woman and 1.43 per man in 2020, which matches the average in Europe while for women with a foreign nationality the rate was 2.0. At the time of first birth, mothers' average age was at 30.2 years, fathers' at 33.2 (Statistisches Bundesamt, 2021a). Compared to countries such as France or Sweden, birth rates in Germany are quite modest. The reasons are multifaceted, but most researchers agree on increasingly demanding parenting norms (Doepke and Zilibotti, 2019; Gerlach, 2017), still quite traditional gender roles (particularly in the western part of Germany (Zoch, 2021)) and a shortage of institutional childcare facilities for toddlers (Jähnert and Ziesmann, 2021, p.50).

Family forms are also becoming more and more diverse: today, childlessness is widely accepted (Dorbritz, 2005; Kreyenfeld and Konietzka, 2017), while homosexual couples are becoming increasingly accepted (de

Vries, 2020, p. 20), and the institution of marriage has lost its binding force (Schneider, 2012; Hoffmann-Nowotny, 1996). From 1950 to 2020, the incidence of marriages per 1,000 inhabitants more than halved (from 11.0 to 4.5; Statistisches Bundesamt, n.d.b). Thus, although married couples still dominate among families with minor children, their share decreased from 81 per cent (1996) to 70 per cent (2019) while the share of unmarried couple families more than doubled during this time (from 4.8 to 11.5 per cent). Moreover, the decreasing role of marriage coincides with changes in separation behavior. As unmarried couples are more likely to separate (Radenacker, 2018, p.8), separation dynamics are constantly high. Since the early 1990s, the share of divorces that involve minor children has remained consistent at about 50 per cent (Radenacker, 2018, p. 8).

Increasing role of single parents
The flipside of the downturn of couple families is the rising importance of single parents. In 2019, there were 2.18 million children living in 1.52 million single parent families in Germany. Sixteen per cent of Germany's minors live in a single parent household. The proportion is higher in the eastern part than in the western part of the country. In 2018, almost 9 out of 10 single parents were females (Statistisches Bundesamt, 2020a). Forty-two per cent of single parents are unmarried, 37 per cent divorced, 5 per cent widowed and 16 per cent are married but live apart from their partner (BMFSFJ 2021b: p. 8). The share of the unmarried is higher among single mothers compared to single fathers. However, being unmarried does not necessarily mean being unpartnered. For single mothers, Bastin (2016) shows in an investigation based on data from the German Family Panel (pairfam) that 13 years after transition into single parenthood, only 10 per cent remain unpartnered. After five years, half of single mothers live together with a new partner.

Due to both a higher number and lower age of children living with them, single mothers more often struggle to adhere to the labour market. Compared to couple families and single mothers, single fathers are more likely to live with only one child which is less often at preschool age (BMFSFJ, 2021a, p.56). Therefore, closing demand gaps in institutional childcare for toddlers is a promising political strategy to foster employment of single mothers with young children.

Single parents have on average lower levels of educational achievement than parents in couple families, whereby the difference is more pronounced for women (Statistisches Bundesamt, 2018, p.22). One fifth (22 per cent) of single mothers are lowly educated and another fifth (21 per cent) have a tertiary degree, whereas the shares are 15 per cent and 30 per cent, respectively, for mothers living in couple households (BMFSFJ, 2021b, p.8). A poor qualification makes it even more difficult to remain in the labour market. However, the

73 per cent employment rate of single mothers is higher than for mothers living in couple households (69 per cent); single mothers' weekly hours of work are higher, too (BMFSFJ, 2021b, p.8). This reflects the higher need to provide that single mothers are confronted with.

SINGLE PARENTS' HOUSEHOLDS ECONOMICALLY UNDER PRESSURE

At-Risk-of-Poverty Rates

Despite their higher average earnings, net monthly household incomes of single parents lag behind those of couple families. Whereas 68 per cent of the latter have more than 3,200 euros at their disposal, 57 per cent of the former have to cope with 2,000 euros at maximum. More than one fifth (22 per cent) of single mothers have less than 1,300 euros per month (BMFSFJ, 2021b, p.38). Overall in Germany, the average monthly income of full-time employees was at 3,975 euros in 2020 (Statistisches Bundesamt, 2021b).

Single parents suffer, as in most countries, from above-average poverty risks. Although figures somewhat depend on the underlying data set, the percentage share of being under the poverty threshold ranges from 41.6 (Microcensus, 2018) to 36.8 (Socio-economic Panel (SOEP), 2017) to 33.8 per cent (EU-SILC, 2017). The respective poverty thresholds for a single parent with one child below age 14 are 1,346, 1,518, and 1,419 euros, respectively (BMFSFJ, 2021a, p.448; Stichnoth, 2020). The official poverty level calculated by the Federal Ministry of Finance was at 824 euros a month for single adults and 455 euros per child in 2022 (BMF, 2020). The poverty threshold reflects 60 per cent of the median value of means-adjusted net household income (BMFSFJ, 2021a, p.446). As investigations for the period 2005–2017 show, single parents exhibited higher poverty rates throughout, compared to couple households with one child or two children and also compared to families with three or more children. Couple households with up to two children face below-average risks, but those with at least three children also face above-average risk, which makes the outstanding risks of single parents even more remarkable. However, the average masks a notable heterogeneity among single mothers. While poverty rates of formerly married single mothers decreased, the rate for formerly cohabiting mothers almost doubled in the four decades around the turn of the millennium. Mothers who became single mothers by birth of their child faced the sharpest risk increase in poverty: from 33 per cent (1984–1997) to 61 per cent (2007–2016). The different evolution of poverty risk is driven by a different social composition: formerly cohabiting mothers became increasingly inactive in the period of labour market reforms (1998–2006), the same holds true for mothers who became single mothers and who are additionally disadvantaged by their below average qualification (Hübgen, 2020a, pp. 188–198).

The concept of material deprivation spotlights poverty from a different perspective. Rather than being compared against an income benchmark, deprived families are unable to pay for unexpected expenses or to 'afford some items considered by most people to be desirable or even necessary to lead an adequate life' (Eurostat, n.d.). In Germany, among single parents at risk of poverty, every second (50 per cent) cannot afford to go on holiday for one week a year, compared to 29 per cent of couple households with one child. Further, one quarter (24 per cent) of single parents cannot afford a car, whereas this holds for only 13 per cent of one-child-couple households (BMFSFJ, 2021a, p. 453). A third measure indicating poverty is social transfer receipt. More than one in three single parent-households (35 per cent) relies on basic security benefits (BMFSFJ, 2021a, p. 455).

Intense Employment Mitigates Poverty Risks

Gainful employment significantly reduces poverty risks. As maternal employment became more widespread in recent decades, the number of dual earner households continuously increased, which is why single earner households fall further and further behind (Grabka and Goebel, 2017). Nine in ten (90 per cent) employed single mothers earn a living wage, compared to only 73 per cent of mothers in couple households (BMFSFJ, 2021b, p. 41). In families with no earners, the at-risk-of-poverty rate is 64 per cent, which decreases to 30 per cent for single parent households with a part-time and 15 per cent with a full-time earner (BMAS, 2017, p. 252). Weekly working hours are identified as a key driver of economic independence. Logistic regressions based on SOEP data underscore the decisive role of qualification and labour market experience and point to above-average risks for migrants (Hübgen, 2020b). Due to tax-breaks (see below: relief amount), higher employment probability and hours, single parents exhibit higher average net earnings, compared to mothers in couple households (BMFSFJ, 2021b, p. 40).

Income Evolution of Single Mothers after Separation

A recent study based on SOEP data shows that among mothers with whom all the children live and where the father is not involved in childcare on weekdays (the 'most traditional' group), neither mothers' equivalised net household income nor their earnings improve up to five years after separation. This also applies to sole resident-mothers with caring ex-partners; 2 per cent of those mothers have a new partner in the year after separation. The only group where equivalised household income, but not maternal earnings, recover during that time are mothers where at least one child lives with the father and where the father spends above-zero childcare minutes during weekdays (i.e., the 'most egalitarian' group) (Boll and Schüller, 2021). Moreover, the authors explored the gender gap in economic well-being around separation and find that mothers sustained deeper drops than did fathers – a result that echoes previous evidence based on German data (Bröckel and Andreß, 2015; Leopold and Kalmijn, 2016).

Although exploiting a rich set of socio-demographics, investigations in this field have been unable to infer causal relationships (Boll and Schüller, 2021). Though, there is some evidence for the notion that for mothers who entered single parenthood by childbirth or after separation from a formerly cohabiting partner, financial conditions began to worsen some time before (Geis-Thöne, 2019; Hübgen, 2020a). This could hint at single mothers as a negatively selected group. Results from a new study based on SOEP data lend support to this notion (Birkeneder and Boll, 2021). Separated mothers increase their working hours in anticipation of the separation event and afterwards. Accounting for this and other behavioural adjustments, the positive selection into separation turns negative. This means that already in the pre-separation phase, women who later separated differed in some unobserved characteristics from their peers who did not separate. Mothers' selection into these traits did not only impact the separation event but also its economic consequences. More research will be necessary to uncover these mechanisms to be able to infer political conclusions.

CHILD SUPPORT AND CARE AS TWO SIDES OF THE SAME COIN

Child Support Agencies: Support to Realise an Unreliable Income Source

Irrespective of labour market performance and potentially underlying factors, child support payments for child(ren) or alimony payments for the single parent her-/himself constitute a relevant portion of single parents' household income. According to a survey of 899 single parents with minor children living in Germany in 2020, 87 per cent of single parents report those claims for themselves or for their children, whereby single mothers report them more often than single fathers (90 per cent vs. 61 per cent) (BMFSFJ, 2021b, p. 41; IfD, 2020). However, 17 per cent do not receive the full amount or report irregular receipt and a further 35 per cent do not receive any payments. The rates of fully, partially and not fulfilled child support obligations remain unchanged over the recent two decades (forsa, 2002; Hartmann, 2014; BMFSFJ, 2021b, p. 23; IfD, 2020). The reason for absent or insufficient payments of child support are in

64 per cent of cases the poor economic capacity of the debtor. Forty eight per cent of single parents say that the debtor refuses to pay, and 35 per cent of the single parents who do not receive full payments for their child renounce them voluntarily in order not to strain the relationship (Hubert et al., 2020).

To assert and enforce child support and alimony claims, Germany provides for a hybrid system with administrative and judicial support. Single parents can make use of administrative services at the local level within the child and youth welfare agencies (*Jugendamt*). 505,809 children received the services of a representation in the establishment of paternity and to collect child support in 2018 (*Beistandschaft*) (Statistisches Bundesamt, 2019). Child support and alimony can be, and in most cases are, notarised free of cost as enforceable authentic instruments by the local authorities. If no amicable solution can be achieved and notarised by administrative services or notaries, then the courts come into play (Knittel, 2017; Boehm et al., 2016). Here, means tested legal aid is provided.

In a paternalistic tradition within the German speaking countries in Central Europe, children do not receive advice and support but the local administrations represent the children as special curators at the request of the single parent. Unlike the child support agency services provided elsewhere (e.g. Takayesu, 2013; Saue et al., 2013), the German services are characterised by partiality. This results in an approach that does not address the child support debtors as receivers of services. It does not include their empowerment, does not address the barriers for payments, and does not systematically differentiate between the reasons why child support is not paid (Beinkinstadt, 2004).

Shared Parenting Arrangements and Care after Separation

The difficulties of single mothers to recover from financial struggles around separation originate in a widely unchanged labour division between parents after separation, although for divorced parents, joint legal custody is today's norm (Köppen et al., 2018). Shared parenting arrangements with a more active role for fathers remain uncommon, though (Steinbach et al., 2021). Mothers still bear the lion's share of childcare – not only before but also after separation and divorce (Walper, 2018; Walper et al., 2016). So far, separation has hardly changed the well-known traditional intra-couple division of childcare tasks (Boll and Schüller, 2021). An investigation based on SOEP data, which traces real couples' time use for childcare and paid work before and after separation, reveals that this holds true even if at least one child lives with the father and the father is involved in childcare during the workweek. Even in those settings, mothers stay highly involved in childcare and/or fail to redirect released childcare time to the labour market (Boll and Schüller, 2021). Analyses based on the German Family Panel (pairfam) and the German Time Use Survey 2012/13 stress the well-known gender gap in childcare time, irrespective of with whom the child resides. They suggest that regarding childcare time, residing with the children makes a greater difference for fathers than mothers. This points to the importance of policies that support a more gender-equal share of child residency upon separation. Demand-adequate institutional childcare is a key issue in this regard (ibid).

Family Policies in the 15 Years after the Turn of the Millennium Address Societal Change

Germany has often been classified as a country that favours a modernised male breadwinner model, which is characterised by men as the main economic providers and women as part-time workers and mothers as carers (Köppen et al., 2018, p. 1165). However, the outlined demographic transitions have questioned the functioning of the old-fashioned family model and the traditional gender division of labour. Addressing societal change, major policy reforms have been enacted in the 15 years after the turn of the millennium to ease compatibility of work and family, boost gender equality and stimulate a stronger post-separation involvement of fathers (Adler and Lenz, 2016). The parental leave reform, which came into effect in 2007 incentivised paternal involvement with the provision of exclusive daddy months. As empirical evidence suggests, the reform has effectively strengthened paternal child involvement (Tamm, 2019). The reform was succeeded by an amendment in 2015, which introduced a financial gratification for parents' simultaneous uptake of part-time work and leave (*Partnerschaftsbonus*).

Apart from policies targeting families as a whole, specific policies have focused on post-separation families. In particular, the legal custody reform (*Kindschaftsrechtsreformgesetz*) enacted in 1998 has strengthened the rights of separated formerly unmarried fathers towards their children (Dethloff, 2015). It did not grant those fathers with joint legal custody but with the right to apply for it during pregnancy or later. To date, joint legal custody of formerly unmarried parents requires them to make a joint custody declaration or to apply for joint legal custody at the family courts. A working group at the Ministry of Justice suggests a legal custody reform that replaces this declaration by a mother's agreement to the father's acknowledgement of paternity (BMJV, 2019; Scholz and Wilke, 2020).

Corresponding legislative reforms: child support and day-care
In its 16th legislative period the federal parliament (*Bundestag*) passed two major reforms: a maintenance law reform (*Unterhaltsrechtsänderungsgesetz*) and a day-care facilities expansion for children (*Kinderförderungsgesetz*). Both came into force in 2008. While the explanatory memorandum of the

latter focused on improvements in respect to the compatibility of family and work, the establishment of equivalent living conditions throughout Germany and the preservation of legal or economic unity (Deutscher Bundestag, 2008), the explanatory memorandum to the maintenance law reform claimed a 'strengthening of the children's best interests' (Deutscher Bundestag, 2006). A clarification has been incorporated that child support for minor children is prioritised in the hierarchy of maintenance claims (sec. 1609 Civil Code). Further, it levelled out the differences between formerly cohabiting and formerly married with respect to caregiver maintenance, which compensates the foregone labour income of the mother (or theoretically the father) and reflects traditional gender roles that still prevail in Germany. Until the end of 2007, caregiver maintenance after divorce was paid to the parent who cared for the common child until the child's eighth birthday, while formerly unmarried caregivers were forced to work from the child's third birthday on. Since the 2008 reform, the latter applies irrespective of the former family status of the caregiving parent (Deutscher Bundestag, 2007a). But still, nation-wide child support regulations assume that children will mainly reside with one parent after separation (Dethloff, 2015). The parent with whom under-age, unmarried children live generally fulfils his/her maintenance obligation by caring for and bringing up the children, while the other parent is obliged to contribute to child maintenance by money payments, which are referred to as cash maintenance.

Further, institutional childcare facilities have been continuously expanded during that time (Deutscher Bundestag, 2008). To date, divergences between East and West are paradigmatic to the cultural clashes after the German reunification: in 2006, 39.3 per cent of the children under the age of 3 went to childcare facilities in East Germany but only 7.9 per cent in West Germany (13.6 per cent overall). The rates of toddlers in day-care went up to 51.5 per cent, respectively 29.4 per cent in 2018 (33.6 per cent overall), hence, significant differences remain (BMFSFJ, 2019, p.10). However, depending on the study and presumably related methodological differences, 13.7 per cent or 27 per cent of the parents of children under the age of 3 and 3.9 per cent or 2 per cent from the age of 3 to school enrollment claimed an unmet demand for a day-care slot (BMFSFJ, 2021a; Anton et al., 2021). Day-care for children is a task for child and youth welfare, not the education system. It is provided by local communities and NGOs. Structural quality is set by federal and regional law and guidelines while compliance is monitored by regional supervisory authorities. Another reform gave children a justiciable right to enrollment in day-care from August 1st, 2013 on and forced the local child and youth welfare offices to plan day-care centres according to the parents' wishes (Meysen and Beckmann, 2013). All children are addressed similarly. Compared to toddlers (children below age three) who live with coupled parents, toddlers of single parents are less often enrolled in day-care. In the age group from 3 until school enrollment, single parents significantly more often (+8 percentage points) have a need for a full-day place (35 hours a week) than children of parents living in couple households (Anton et al., 2021). During primary school age single parents more often make use of day-care for their children than coupled parents (Hüsken et al., 2021, p.19). The shift to childcare use after the age of 3 correlates with the insufficient employment services provided to single parents before the child is aged 3 (see below).

FINANCIAL SUPPORT IN A FRAGMENTED SOCIAL SECURITY NET

Welfare Benefits for Single Parent Households

A notable share of single parents, particularly those with low education, poor employment experience and/or young children, receive welfare benefits. As noted above, one third (34.6 per cent) of single parent households, but only 7.0 per cent of couple households with minor children, received the means-tested guaranteed basic security benefits for job seekers, which falls under the Social Code Book II (BMFSFJ, 2021b, p. 45). Transfer receipt increases with the number of children. Among single parents with two or more children, almost half (45.4 per cent) of single parents receive this benefit. Single mothers in welfare benefit receipt who enter employment mostly assume a so-called *Minijob* (in 2022, the income limit is 6,240 euros p.a., or 520 euros as a monthly average). In contrast to female earners in couple households who can count on their partners' income, single mothers usually remain tied to benefit receipt in this situation (Lietzmann, 2014). The minimum wage amounts to 9.60 euros as of July 1st, 2021. The marginally employed (*Minijobber*) are entitled to the minimum wage, too. Average monthly earnings exceeding 520 euros are subject to taxes and social insurance contributions. These can be circumvented by a maximum 46 hours a month (Knappschaft Bahn-See and Minijobzentrale, 2021), but avoiding being taxed can go hand in hand with the risk of remaining trapped in poverty. Moreover, households with more than one child prove unable to escape welfare receipt even with a full-time income at minimum wage (Bundesagentur für Arbeit, 2020). That a full-time job does not shield against poverty and welfare receipt is particularly true for single mothers (Müller and Lien, 2017). As a result, this group often depends on basic security benefits even if employed (Achatz et al., 2013) and they often stick longer with receipt of those benefits than mothers in couple households (Lietzmann, 2014). If children grow up and reach school age, single mothers in welfare receipt resume work more often and more quickly than their female counterparts in couple households. The opposite holds true for preschool-aged children. This relates to the legal base that sets mothers free of the obligation to actively search for work until the third birthday of their child which leads to case workers' strategy not to offer employment services to single parents during that time (BMFSFJ, 2021a, p. 454). That is, particularly in the child's first three years, single mothers are very vulnerable regarding unmet child support obligations from the side of their ex-spouses.

Advance Payments and Struggles to Get Out of Poverty Despite Child Support

If a child does not receive any or less than the so-called minimum child support s/he has a right to advance payments (*Unterhaltsvorschuss*). The legally secured claim depends on the child's age and ranges from 174 euros per month for children until the age of 6, 232 euros until the age of 12 to 309 euros until majority in 2021. Since the reform in 2017, the eligibility period for advanced payments has been unlimited ending with majority at the latest (BMFSFJ, 2021b, p. 42). The fact that more than one third (36 per cent) of single parents are currently receiving advance payments for their children and that a further 20 per cent received it in the past, impressively illustrates the importance of this policy and the failures of the child support system to provide for regular, reliable payments (ibid.).

Child support, caregiver maintenance payments and advance payments together make up a significant part of single parents' household incomes. Single parents in non-employment, with a low income or a low educational level are particularly likely to receive advance payments (BMFSFJ, 2021b). But still, among single parents receiving advance payments, the net household income share of these payments is roughly one fourth (25.2 per cent; BMFSFJ, 2021b). However, the actually paid amount is deducted from the benefits accordingly and the single parent households financially remain in poverty.

Moreover, tax law also provides for a contribution to the enhancement of the financial situation in single parent households. Since 2004, single parents benefit from a relief amount that can be deducted from taxable income, if a child at minor age lives with them, and for whom they are entitled to child benefit or child allowance (BMFSFJ, 2021b). Due to the progressive income tax, parents with higher incomes benefit more. This is why this measure barely reduces poverty risks, neither among the total of single parents nor among recipients. Note that this is not the primary goal of the relief measure, which aims at easing the financial burden associated with lone parenthood and house-keeping. To address the specific burden single parents underwent during the COVID-19 pandemic, the German government significantly raised the relief amount, which further increases with every additional child (BMFSFJ, 2021b)

Family Policies Partly Cushion Single Parents' Poverty Risks

There are different statistical measures of poverty risks. An internationally established measure of monetary poverty is the at-risk-of-poverty rate that depicts the share of people with an equivalised disposable income (after social transfers) that is below 60 per cent of this value's national median. Cash transfers and tax-breaks effectively cushion single parents' poverty risks. Simulations based on pre-reform data show that, regarding the total of families, the advance payment of maintenance decreases the at-risk-of-poverty rate among recipients by 5.8 per cent. The rate would be notably higher if the payment did not reduce the basic security benefits by the exact amount, which leads to a zero-sum situation (Bonin et al. 2013, p. 97). Neither child support nor advance payments increase the income of single parent households which receive benefits. The child-related part of the unemployment supplement under Social Code Book II (*Arbeitslosengeld II*) turned out to be the most effective in terms of mitigating poverty risks. The reduction is about 18.1 per cent among recipients (Prognos, 2014, p. 202). This results from the fact that 80 per cent of the fiscal expenses relating to this measure reach families below the poverty threshold (BMFSFJ, 2021a, p.465). The child supplement (*Kinderzuschlag*) and the parental benefit (*Elterngeld*) are second and third, reducing poverty risks by 16.5 per cent and 9.7 per cent, respectively. The child-related portion of the housing allowance comes fourth with 5.9 per cent, followed by advance payments (Prognos, 2014, p. 202; Bonin et al., 2013). Measures are effective in reducing poverty, if (1) they are sufficiently targeted to population subgroups facing poverty risks and (2) make a difference for these groups' monthly disposable income. Single parents are likely to be in this subgroup and although they may benefit from the aforenamed benefits, too, advance payments has an extra impact in this regard. Note that apart from monetary support, institutional day-care has an important leverage on family poverty. By easing parents' labour market involvement, day-care facilities decrease poverty risks by 11.9 percentage points (pp) among couple households and by 19.1 pp among single parents (Bonin et al., 2013. p. 72). Taken together, if single parents received none of the mentioned or other family policies, their at-risk-of-poverty rate would be 13.5 pp higher (BMFSFJ, 2021a, p. 466; Stichnoth, 2020). This means that child-related cash transfers as well as childcare services are effective measures to combat single parents' poverty. Cash transfers increase family income directly, childcare facilities provide earnings opportunities as parents can spend the released childcare time on the labour market. Germany pursues a combination of both policies.

In 2015, Germany spent 3.06 per cent of its gross domestic product (GDP) on family benefits, whereby 1.09 pp refer to cash transfers and 1.13 per cent to services. Less than 1 per cent (0.84) refers to tax-breaks (OECD Social Expenditure Database; Boll, 2021).

POST-SEPARATION CONFLICT RESOLUTION IN A BINDING SETTING

Another reform that has shaped post-separation conflict resolution is the act on family court proceedings of 2009. In the explanatory memorandum of the legislator's core solutions, amongst others, there was a focus on an acceleration of contact and custody proceedings, avoidance of longer contact discontinuities, and encouragement of parents' amicable solutions (Deutscher Bundestag, 2007b, p. 2). If a family conflict on contact and custody, not child support, reaches the court an 'early hearing' shall be held not later than a month after the motion for judgement has been filed. The intention is to decelerate and de-escalate the family conflict dynamics through acceleration of proceedings (Heinke et al., 2021; Wegener, 2020, p.1012). Courts shall encourage parental agreements at every phase of the proceedings. The procedural goal is to help parents to regain independence in the ability to make decisions of substantial significance for their family lives (Meysen, 2014, p. 550). The most common outcome of early hearings is a referral to counselling centres. The use of joint counselling has become the expected norm. They are available free of charge throughout Germany and can be ordered by the court. Services of the counselling centres are part of the child and youth welfare system, and can also be accessed low-threshold independent of family court proceedings or any administrative decision. In 2014, 151,667 cases of advisory and support by counselling centres were provided due to family conflicts in parental partnerships, after separation and divorce, or disputes about contact and custody (Statistisches Bundesamt, 2016). The concluded family court proceedings concerning contact have plateaued at a level of around 55,000 proceedings since 2010 (Meysen, 2022).

The financial situation and child support is not part of the amicable dispute resolution concept. Child support agencies are separated from services which address post-separation conflicts about contact and custody. Occasional local models of an integrated approach (Mix, 2005) have not been picked up elsewhere. Distinctions between partiality and multi-partiality, adversarial and mediating proceedings, and legal and psycho-social counselling expertise act as stiff formal barriers in family court proceedings as well as counselling practice making holistic family conflict resolutions almost impossible. The indistinct governmental competences do not help either. They are split between the Ministry of Justice being responsible for legal reforms in family law and for family court proceedings and the Ministry for Family Affairs, Senior Citizens, Women and Youth in which resides the governmental competence for policy on single parent families and child support services. As a result the law on child support rarely reflects the requirements and situation of the administrative services but focuses mainly on the wealthier parents who enter the judicial system through lawyers. In the Ministry for Family Affairs, Senior Citizens, Women and Youth one department is responsible for child support (Family Affairs) and another for the administrative child support services as part of the child and youth welfare agencies (Youth). Despite being responsible and financially well-equipped the latter department has not yet initiated a single research or practice development project for the child support services which might be ascribed to a lack of interest because the relevant policy resides elsewhere.

FUTURE CHALLENGES

Single parents and children received constant attention from policy makers. Several departments in the federal government took on the task to improve their situation:

- The Ministry of Family Affairs, Senior Citizens, Women and Youth expanded the provision of advance payments significantly (Family Affairs) and secured access to child day-care from the age of one year on (Youth).
- The Ministry of Labour and Social Affairs refined the basic social benefits and child supplement.
- The Ministry of Justice and Consumer Protection reformed the maintenance law and strengthened the child support requirement as well as alimony for single mothers (or fathers) of young children.
- The Ministry of Finance established a tax relief for single parents.

The variety of measures is not only a strength but also part of the problem. In this fragmented system a coordinated coherent concept is still pending. Several of the necessary changes to enhance the situation of single parents and their children fall through the cracks between the departments' responsibilities within the federal government: child support and advance payments are not passed through but are withheld if single parents receive basic security benefits. Research on the work of the local child support agencies is lacking completely, projects for quality development are not initiated, integrated approaches of post-separation conflict resolution that include child support as well as contact and custody are not yet part of the elaborated German counselling and support services. Single parents with low income still benefit less from specific tax relief than those with higher income. Employment services need to be extended for single parents in the first 3 years after birth; parents as child support debtors need to be prioritised.

Since the diversity of family constellations, in particular concerning shared responsibilities after separation, does not reflect in policy and throughout the legal system, practice manages with work arounds for now. Policy makers should accept the challenge to put the necessary reforms into shape, to address these issues and introduce them to a broad discourse and to adopt the (legislative) resolutions.

Single mothers' economic well-being is suppressed by crisis-driven factors such as the need to provide economies of scale in the household in combination with the full childcare burden. Further, many of them suffer from chronic strain induced by poor qualification and labour market attachment in the pre-separation and pre-birth phase, respectively, both of which are difficult to be solved at short notice. Thus, apart from continuous political need for tailor-made transfers and tax reliefs to ease single mothers' economic situation, poverty prevention deserves more attention in earlier stages of the life-couse: an educational system that leaves no one behind, a policy combatting gender stereotypes in the political, legal, business and societal sphere, and, a continued expansion of institutional childcare and flexible work arrangements lie at the centre of these measures. Hence, there is a lot to be addressed to improve the situation of single parents and their children in Germany.

REFERENCES

Achatz, J., Hirseland, A., Lietzmann, T. and Zabel, C. (2013). Alleinerziehende Mütter im Bereich des SGB II. Eine Synopse empirischer Befunde aus der IAB-Forschung, IAB-Forschungsbericht 8/2013.

Adler, M.A. and Lenz, K. (2016). Conclusion. Comparative father involvement: The dynamics of gender culture, policy and practice. In M.A. Adler and K. Lenz (eds.) *Father involvement in the early years: An international comparison of policy and practice.* Bristol: Policy Press, pp. 231–252.

Anton, J., Hubert, S. and Kuger, S. (2021). Der Betreuungsbedarf bei U3- und U6-Kindern. DJI-Kinderbetreuungsreport 2020. Munich: Deutsches Jugendinstitut e.V. (DJI).

Bastin, S. (2016). Partnerschaftsverläufe alleinerziehender Mütter: Eine quantitative Untersuchung auf Basis des Beziehungs- und Familienpanels. Wiesbaden: Springer VS.

Beinkinstadt, J. (2004). Umgang mit dem Unterhaltsschuldner: Ein Aufruf zur Neuorientierung. Das Jugendamt (JAmt), *77*, pp. 513–519.

Birkeneder, A. and Boll, C. (2021). How causal is separation? Lessons learnt from endogenous switching regression models for single mothers' economic strain in Germany, SOEP Papers on Multidisciplinary Panel Data Research. 1147/2021. Berlin.

Boehm, A.-S., Faetan, N. and Jäger-Maillet, I. (2016). Child maintenance and authentic instruments – A German perspective. In: P. Beaumont, B. Hess, L. Walker and S. Spancken (eds.) *The recovery of maintenance in the EU and worldwide.* Oxford: Hart, pp. 285–310.

Boll, C. (2021). Soziale Disparitäten bei der Nutzung familienbezogener sozialer In-frastruktur. In: Sachverständigenkommission des Neunten Familienberichts (ed.): Eltern sein in Deutschland. Materialien zum Neunten Familienbericht der Bundesregierung. Munich: Deutsches Jugendinstitut. https://doi.org/10.36189/DJI 232021

Boll, C. and Schüller, S. (2021). Shared parenting and parents' income evolution after separation – New explorative insights from Germany, SOEPpapers on Multidisciplinary Panel Data Research, 1131/2021, Berlin.

Bonin, H., Clauss, M., Gerlach, I., Laß, I., Mancini, A.L., Nehrkorn-Ludwig, M.-A., Schnabel, R., Stichnoth, H., Sutter, K. and Wondratschek, V. (2013). Evaluation zentraler ehe- und familienbezogener Leistungen in Deutschland, Endbericht, Gutachten für die Prognos AG. Mannheim.

Böttcher, S. (2020). Kitas und Kindererziehung in Ost und West. Bonn: Bundeszentrale für politische Bildung. www.bpb.de/geschichte/deutsche-einheit/lange-wege-der -deutschen-einheit/47313/kitas-und-kindererziehung (1 Nov. 2021).

Bröckel, M. and Andreß, H.J. (2015). The economic consequences of divorce in Germany: What has changed since the turn of the millennium? *Comparative Population Studies*, 40–3, pp. 277–312.

Bundesagentur für Arbeit (ed.) (2020). Entwicklungen in der Grundsicherung für Arbeitsuchende 2005 bis 2019. Nürnberg. https://statistik.arbeitsagentur.de/ (3 Nov. 2021)

Bundesfinanzministerium (BMF) (2020). Bericht über die Höhe des steuerfrei zu stellenden Existenzminimums von Erwachsenen und Kindern für das Jahr 2022 (13. Existenzminimumbericht). Berlin.

Bundesministerium der Justiz und für Verbraucherschutz (2019). Thesenpapier der Arbeitsgruppe, Sorge- und Umgangsrecht, insbesondere bei gemeinsamer Betreuung nach Trennung und Scheidung. Berlin. www.bmjv.de/SharedDocs/Downloads/DE/ News/Artikel/102919_Thesen_AG_SorgeUndUmgangsrecht.pdf;jsessionid=E2 D34BB3ABF19EC536302E5D087C91B5.2_cid289?__blob=publicationFile&v=2 (31 Oct. 2021).

Bundesministerium für Arbeit und Soziales (BMAS) (Hrsg.) (2017). Lebenslagen in Deutschland. Der Fünfte Armuts- und Reichtumsbericht der Bundesregierung. Bundestagsdrucksache 18/11980 vom 13.4.2017.

Bundesministerium für Familie, Senioren, Frauen und Jugend (BMFSFJ) (2019). Kindertagesbetreuung Kompakt. Ausbaustand und Bedarf 2018. Berlin.

Bundesministerium für Familie, Senioren, Frauen und Jugend (BMFSFJ) (ed.) (2021a). Neunter Familienbericht. Eltern sein in Deutschland – Ansprüche, Anforderungen und Angebote bei wachsender Vielfalt. Stellungnahme der Bundesregierung und Bericht der Sachverständigenkommission. Berlin

Bundesministerium für Familie, Senioren, Frauen und Jugend (BMFSFJ) (ed.) (2021b). Allein oder getrennterziehen – Lebenssituation, Übergänge und Herausforderungen. Monitor Familienforschung, Ausgabe 43 (07/2021).

Dethloff, N. (2015). From separation to stepfamily. A legal perspective. In: U. Zartler, V. Heintz-Martin and O. Arránz Becker (eds.) *Family dynamics after separation*, ZfF Sonderheft 10. Berlin/Toronto, Barbara Budrich, pp. 205–218.

Deutscher Bundestag (2006). Entwurf eines Gesetzes zur Änderung des Unterhaltsrechts. Gesetzentwurf der Bundesregierung. Bundestags-Drucksache 16/1830. Berlin.

Deutscher Bundestag. (2007a). Beschlussempfehlung und Bericht des Rechtsausschusses (6. Ausschuss) zu dem Gesetzentwurf der Bundesregierung – Drucksache 16/1830 –

Entwurf eines Gesetzes zur Änderung des Unterhaltsrechts. Bundestags-Drucksache 16/6980. Berlin.

Deutscher Bundestag. (2007b). Gesetzentwurf der Bundesregierung. Entwurf eines Gesetzes zur Reform des Verfahrens in Familiensachen und in den Angelege-nheiten der freiwilligen Gerichtsbarkeit (FGG-Reformgesetz – FGG-RG). Bundestags-Drucksache 16/6308. Berlin.

Deutscher Bundestag. (2008). Entwurf eines Gesetzes zur Förderung von Kindern unter drei Jahren in Tageseinrichtungen und in der Kindertagespflege (Kinderförderungsgesetz – KiföG). Gesetzentwurf der Fraktionen der CDU/CSU und SPD. Bundestags-Drucksache 16/9299. Berlin.

de Vries, L. (2020). Regenbogenfamilien in Deutschland. Ein Überblick der Lebenssituation von homo- und bisexuellen Eltern und deren Kindern. In: Sachverständigenkommission des Neunten Familienberichts (ed.) *Materialien zum Neunten Familienbericht der Bundesregierung*. München: Deutsches Jugendinstitut. www.dji.de/9_familienbericht (3 Nov. 2021).

Doepke, M. and Zilibotti, F. (2019). *Love, money, and parenting: How economics explains the way we raise our kids*. Princeton: Princeton University Press.

Dorbritz, J. (2005). Kinderlosigkeit in Deutschland und Europa. Daten, Trends und Einstellungen. Zeitschrift für Bevölkerungswissenschaft, (30)4, 359–408.

Eurostat (n.d.). Glossary: Material deprivation. https://ec.europa.eu/eurostat/statistics-explained/index.php?title=Glossary:Material_deprivation (3 Nov. 2021).

forsa. Gesellschaft für Sozialforschung und statistische Analysen mbH (2002). Unterhaltszahlungen für minderjährige Kinder in Deutschland. Berlin.

Geis-Thöne, W. (2019b). Lebenslagen von Müttern an den Übergängen in und aus Alleinerziehung. *IW-Trends, (46)*3, 21–37. https://dx.doi.org/10.2373/1864–810X.19 –03–02 (3 Nov. 2021).

Gerlach, I. (2017). Elternschaft und Elternpflichten im Spannungsfeld zwischen Leitbildern und Alltag. In I. Gerlach (Hrsg.), *Elternschaft. Zwischen Autonomie und Unterstützung* (S. 21–47). Wiesbaden: Springer VS. https://doi.org/10.1007/978–3-658–16032–6_2

Grabka, M.M. and Goebel, J. (2017). Realeinkommen sind von 1991 bis 2014 im Durchschnitt gestiegen – erste Anzeichen für wieder zunehmende Einkommensungleichheit. DIW Wochenbericht, *84–4*, pp. 71–82. http://hdl.handle.net/10419/149855 (3 Nov. 2021)

Hartmann, B. (2014). Unterhaltsansprüche und deren Wirklichkeit. Wie groß ist das Problem nicht gezahlten Kindesunterhalts? SOEPpapers 660/2014. Berlin: DIW. www.diw.de/documents/publikationen/73/diw_01.c.466460.de/diw_sp0660.pdf (31 Oct. 2021).

Heinke, S., Wildvang, W. and Meysen, T. (2021). Kindschaftssachen nach häuslicher Gewalt: Praxishinweise für die Verfahrensführung und Mitwirkung. In: T. Meysen (ed.): *Kindschaftssachen und häusliche Gewalt*. Heidelberg: SOCLES, pp. 96–139.

Hoffmann-Nowotny, H.-J. (1996). Partnerschaft – Ehe – Familie. Ansichten und Einsichten. Zeitschrift für Bevölkerungswissenschaft, 2, S. 111–130.

Hubert, S., Neuberger, F. and Sommer, M. (2020). Alleinerziehend, alleinzahlend? Kindesunterhalt, Unterhaltsvorschuss und Gründe für den Unterhaltsausfall. Zeitschrift für Soziologie der Erziehung und Sozialisation (ZSE), 40–1, pp. 19–38.

Hübgen, S. (2020a). Armutsrisiko alleinerziehend. Die Bedeutung von sozialer Komposition und institutionellem Kontext in Deutschland. Leverkusen: Barbara Budrich.

Hübgen, S. (2020b). Dynamiken des Alleinerziehens – Lebenslagen, Erwerbsverläufe und Transferbezug. Kurzexpertise im Rahmen des Monitors für Familienforschung. Endbericht. Berlin (unveröffentlicht).

Hüsken, K., Lippert, K. and Kuger, S. (2021). Der Betreuungsbedarf bei Grundschulkindern. DJI-Kinderbetreuungsreport 2020. Munich: Deutsches Jugendinstitut e.V.

Institut für Demoskopie Allensbach (IfD) (2020). Lebens- und Einkommenssituation von Alleinerziehenden. Allensbach.

Jähnert, A. and Ziesmann, T. (2021). Bedarfsgerechtes Angebot, In: N. Klinkhammer, B. Kalicki, S. Kuger, C. Meiner-Teubner, B. Riedel, D. Schaft, and T. Rauschenbach, (eds.) *ERiK Forschungsbericht I. Konzeption und Befunde des indikatorengestützten Monitorings zum KiQuTG*. Bielefeld: wbv.

Knappschaft Bahn-See and Minijobzentrale (2021). Mindestlohn steigt zum 1. Juli – Das gilt für Minijobs, Blog, last update 01.07.2021. https://blog.minijob-zentrale.de/mindestlohn-juli-2021/ (3 Nov. 2021).

Knittel, B. (2017). Beurkundungen im Kindschaftsrecht. 8. Ed. Cologne: Reguvis.

Köppen, K., Kreyenfeld, M. and Trappe, H. (2018). Loose ties? Determinants of father–child contact after separation in Germany. *Journal of Marriage and Family, (80)*5, 1163–1175.

Kreyenfeld, M. and Konietzka, D. (2017). Childlessness in East and West Germany: Long-term trends and social disparities. In: M. Kreyenfeld and D. Konietzka (eds.) *Childlessness in Europe: Contexts, causes, and consequences.* Cham: Springer Open, pp. 97–114. https://doi.org/10.1007/978-3-319-44667-7

Leopold, T. and Kalmijn, M. (2016). Is divorce more painful when couples have children? Evidence from long-term panel data on multiple domains of well-being. *Demography, (53)*6, pp. 1717–1742.

Lietzmann, T. (2014). After recent policy reforms in Germany: Probability and determinants of labour market integration of lone mothers and mothers with a partner who receive welfare benefits. *Social Politics: International Studies in Gender, State & Society, (21)*4, pp. 585–616. https://doi.org/10.1093/sp/jxu011

Meysen, T. (2014). § 156 Hinwirken auf Einvernehmen. In: T. Meysen (ed.), *Praxiskommentar Familienverfahrensrecht.* 2nd ed. Köln: Bundesanzeiger, pp. 545–555.

Meysen, T. (2022). Family court proceedings in parent and child matters in Germany: A binding setting for alternative dispute resolution. In: M. Maclean, R. Treloar, B. Dijksterhuis (eds.) *What is a family justice system for?* Cheltenham, UK and Northampton, MA, USA: Edward Elgar Publishing, pp. 235–250.

Meysen, T. and Beckmann, J. (2013). Rechtsanspruch U3: Förderung in Kita und Kindertagespflege. Baden-Baden: Nomos.

Mix, B. (2005). Beistandschaft im Wandel. Ein Beratungskonzept der Stadt Osnabrück, insbesondere im Hinblick auf das Umgangsrecht und dessen Auswirkungen. *Das Jugendamt (JAmt), 78,* 279–283.

Müller, D. and Lien, S.-C. (2017). Arm mit und ohne Arbeit? Lebensalltag von Working-Poor-Familien. Vortrag auf der DJI-Jahrestagung, Konstant im Wandel. Was Familien heute bewegt, Berlin, 21.11.2017. München: Deutsches Jugendinstitut. www.dji.de/fileadmin/user_upload/dasdji/tagungen/2017_Jahrestagung/17_mueller_lien.pdf (3 Nov. 2021).

OECD Social Expenditure Database (n.d.). www.oecd.org/social/expenditure.htm (3 Nov. 2021).

Prognos AG (2014). Gesamtevaluation der ehe- und familienbezogenen Maßnahmen und Leistungen in Deutschland, Endbericht, Studie im Auftrag des BMF und des BMFSFJ, 02.06.2014. Berlin.

Radenacker, A. (2018). Das Scheidungsverhalten in Ost- und Westdeutschland, In: Geisler, E. Köppen, K., Kreyenfeld, M., Trappe, H. and Pollmann-Schult, M. (eds.) Familien nach Trennung und Scheidung in Deutschland. https://doi.org/10.24352/UB-OVGU-2018–096

Saue, J., de Jongh Bekkali, F., Saettem, E. and Rustad, B. (2013). Behördliche Geltendmachung und Vollstreckung von Kindesunterhalt in Norwegen. *Das Jugendamt (JAmt)*, *86*, 368–374.

Schneider, N. (2012). Familie in Deutschland – Stabilität und Wandel. In: Bundeszentrale für politische Bildung (ed.): Dossier, Deutsche Verhältnisse. Eine Sozialkunde. Bonn. www.bpb.de/politik/grundfragen/deutsche-verhaeltnisse-eine-sozialkunde/138019/familie-in-deutschland?p=all (10 Jul. 2021).

Scholz, C. and Wilke, B. (2020). Wahrung des Kindeswohls steht im Zentrum: Bundesjustizministerin Christine Lambrecht zu geplanten Reformen beim Abstammungs- und Sexualstrafrecht. Berlin: BMJV.

Statistisches Bundesamt. (n.d.a). Bevölkerung nach Altersgruppen (ab 2011). www.destatis.de/DE/Themen/Gesellschaft-Umwelt/Bevoelkerung/Bevoelkerungsstand/Tabellen/liste-altersgruppen.html (3 Nov. 2021).

Statistisches Bundesamt. (n.d.b). Startseite/Tabellenaufbau/Eheschließungen je 1000 Einwohner: Deutschland, Jahre. www.genesis.destatis.de/genesis/online?operation=previous&levelindex=1&step=1&titel=Ergebnis&levelid=1625929064974&acceptscookies=false#abreadcrumb (10 Jul. 21).

Statistisches Bundesamt. (2016). Statistiken der Kinder- und Jugendhilfe. Erzieherische Hilfe, Eingliederungshilfe für seelisch behinderte junge Menschen, Hilfe für junge Volljährige. Erziehungsberatung 2014. Wiesbaden: Statistisches Bundesamt.

Statistisches Bundesamt (ed.) (2018) Alleinerziehende in Deutschland 2017. Begleitmaterial zur Pressekonferenz am 2. August 2018, Wiesbaden.

Statistisches Bundesamt. (2019). Statistiken der Kinder- und Jugendhilfe. Pflegschaften, Vormundschaften, Beistandschaften, Pflegeerlaubnis, Sorgerechtsentzug, Sorgeerklärungen. 2018. Wiesbaden. www.destatis.de/DE/Themen/Gesellschaft-Umwelt/Soziales/Adoptionen/Publikationen/Downloads/pflege-vormund-beistandschaft-pflegeerlaubnis-5225202187004.pdf?__blob=publicationFile (31 Oct. 2021).

Statistisches Bundesamt. (2020a). Bevölkerung und Erwerbstätigkeit. Haushalte und Familien. Ergebnisse des Mikrozensus 2019. Fachserie 1 Reihe 3, Tabelle 5.5 Familien (dar. mit Kindern unter 18 Jahren) nach Gebietsstand und Jahren (ab 1996). Wiesbaden.

Statistisches Bundesamt. (2020b). Bevölkerung in Deutschland im Jahr 2019 auf 83,2 Millionen gestiegen. Pressemitteilung Nr. 223 vom 19. Juni 2020. www.destatis.de/DE/Presse/Pressemitteilungen/2020/06/PD20_223_12411.html (31 Oct. 2021).

Statistisches Bundesamt. (2020c). Bevölkerung und Erwerbstätigkeit. Haushalte und Familien Ergebnisse des Mikrozensus 2019. Fachserie 1 Reihe 3.

Statistisches Bundesamt. (2021a). Geburtenziffer 2020 leicht rückläufig. Väter bei Geburt eines Kindes im Schnitt drei Jahre älter als Mütter. Pressemitteilung Nr. 343 vom 16. Juli 2021. www.destatis.de/DE/Presse/Pressemitteilungen/2021/07/PD21_343_12.html (31 Oct. 2021).

Statistisches Bundesamt. (2021b). Verdienste und Verdienstunterschiede. Verdienste 2020. www.destatis.de/DE/Themen/Arbeit/Verdienste/Verdienste-Verdienstunterschiede/verdienste-branchen.html (30 Oct. 2021)

Steinbach, A., Augustijn, L. and Corkadi, G. (2021). Joint physical custody and adolescents' life satisfaction in 37 North American and European countries. *Family Process*, *60*(1), 145–158.

Stichnoth, H. (2020). Verteilungswirkungen ehe- und familienbezogener Leistungen und Maßnahmen. Aktuelle Ergebnisse auf Basis des Sozio-oekonomischen Panels (SOEP) 2017. Expertise für den Neunten Familienbericht der Bundesregierung (unveröffentlichtes Manuskript). Mannheim: ZEW.

Takayesu, M. (2013). Verbesserung der Verpflichtungserfüllung beim Kindesunterhalt durch Erkennen der Bedeutung von Zahlungsbarrieren. *Das Jugendamt (JAmt), 86*, 354–362.

Tamm, M. (2019). Fathers' parental leave-taking, childcare involvement and labor market participation. *Labour Economics, 59*, 184–197.

Walper, S. (2018). Elterliche Sorge und Wohn- bzw. Betreuungsarrangements. In: K. Geisler, K. Köppen, M. Kreyenfeld, H. Trappe, and M. Pollmann-Schult (eds.) *Familien nach Trennung und Scheidung in Deutschland.* Berlin: Hertie School, pp. 16–17.

Walper, S., Entleitner-Phleps, C. and Wendt, E.V. (2016). Brauchen Kinder immer (nur) zwei Eltern? *Recht der Jugend und des Bildungswesens (RdJB), 64*(2), 210–226.

Wegener, S. (2020). § 156 FamFG Hinwirken auf Einvernehmen. In: S. Heilmann (ed.) *Praxiskommentar Kindschaftsrecht.* 2nd ed. Cologne: Reguvis, pp. 1007–1036.

Zoch, G. (2021). Thirty years after the fall of the Berlin wall – Do East and West Germans still differ in their attitudes to female employment and the division of housework? *European Sociological Review, (37)*5, 731–750.

8. Single parent families and the child support system in South Korea

Yiyoon Chung, Yoonkyung Kim, and Eric Lee

INTRODUCTION

The welfare of single-parent families is an important issue in South Korea (Korea, hereafter). In 2020, 4.9 million single-parent families lived with at least one child under age 18 in Korea, which is 7.5 per cent of all families raising minor children (KOSIS, 2021a), and many of these single-parent families in Korea experience economic vulnerability. Since 2016, when the Korean government began to publish statistics on single-parent families with minor children, Korea has ranked as one of the highest OECD countries in poverty for children living in single-parent families (OECD, 2021a). In 2018, the poverty rate for children living in single-parent families was 45.7 per cent, which is more than four times the poverty rate of children living in two-parent families, at 10.7 per cent (OECD, 2021a).[1] There is also evidence that the COVID-19 pandemic hit the welfare of single-parent families even harder than two-parent families (Choi et al., 2020; Son and Moon, 2021).

Several factors account for the relative economic disadvantage of single-parent families in Korea compared to other industrialised countries. First, there are relatively weak welfare provisions available to single-parent families in Korea (Park et al., 2016; Chin et al., 2014). Second, Korea has a larger gender gap in employment and earnings than other OECD countries (OECD, 2022a) including some countries in the Asia-Pacific region (OECD, 2019a).[2] In 2020, the gender wage gap, defined as the difference between median earnings of men and women relative to median earnings of men, was 31.5 for Korea, the largest among the OECD countries (the average of 11.6)

---

[1]   Relative poverty was measured with an equalised post-tax-and-transfer income of less than 50 per cent of the national annual median.

[2]   The analysis by OECD (2019a) compared China, Indonesia, Korea, Japan, Thailand, Singapore, and Vietnam, and Korea showed the highest gender wage gap among the countries examined.

(OECD, 2022a). These large gender disparities affect many single mothers in Korea since most resident single parents in Korea are women (67.4 per cent in 2020), even though the rate of single mothers in Korea is lower than in many other countries (KOSIS, 2021a).

Women in Korea are also less likely to work compared to both men in Korea and women in other industrialised countries, and if they work, they are much more likely to work in unstable, part-time, low-paying jobs (OCED, 2019a). While married women are more likely to stop working (i.e., take a career break) to take care of their children (compared to both men in Korea and women in other industrialised countries), after becoming a single parent, it may be difficult for these mothers to resume work. Relatedly, in 2018, the employment rate for women aged 25–29 and men aged 25–29 was 70.9 per cent and 69.52 per cent, respectively, but the rate dropped to 62.2 per cent for women aged 40–44 while the rate rose to 92.1 per cent for men aged 40–44 (OECD, 2019b). Nevertheless, most single parents are employed. In 2018, 84.2 per cent of single parents were employed (MoGEF, 2018), which is high compared to the 66.6 per cent employment rate for all Koreans aged 15–64, and the 79.0 per cent employment rate for those in their 40s in the same year (MoGEF, 2018).

In Korea, births outside of marriage are relatively uncommon. The proportion of new births to unwed parents in 2019 was only 2.3 per cent (OECD, 2021b), although the rate increased from 1.2 per cent in 2000. This rate is lower than most other industrialised countries; for example, the rate in 2018 was 33.9 per cent in Germany, 39.6 per cent in the United States, and 54.5 per cent in Sweden (OECD, 2021b). In 2019, in Korea, only 0.5 per cent of all parents raising a child under age 18 were unmarried (KOSIS, 2021b). Of this group of single parents, most were divorced or widowed and only 7.2 per cent were never married (KOSIS, 2021b). This low rate of unwed births and unwed single parents in Korea reflects the nation's unique cultural context.

Koreans hold strong cultural beliefs that the traditional two-parent family constitutes a 'normal family' (Chung and Son, 2022; Park et al., 2016). Studies have reported that single parents, especially single mothers in Korea, face significant stigma and discrimination because their families are perceived as 'non-standard' (Park et al., 2016). As a result of the stigma and Korea's strong collectivist and Confucian-influenced patriarchal culture, the societal stigma implicitly and explicitly deters single mothers from revealing their single-parent status in various settings, for example, to friends, extended family, and neighbours, at work, and even in therapy appointments, which may lead to isolation, guilt, and lower levels of civic participation (Chung and Son, 2022). Research has also reported an over-representation of single-parent families among clients in the child protection services system in Korea (Chung et al., 2022), in part because they tend to have fewer financial resources and are challenged with a heavy work schedule.

Despite this gloomy picture, the government has continued to enact stronger policies for single-parent families. A law supporting single parents (single-parent support law, hereafter) was first enacted in 1995, but the benefit was negligible in terms of both eligibility and benefits. The revised law, in 2001, provided cash (initially about $16 per month) to low-income single mothers. Since then, the amount of the benefit has continued to increase from about $50 in 2015 to about $200 for a 'general case' (single parents over age 24) in 2019. This allowance for low-income single-parent families provides a fixed amount of about $200 per month per child for a general case, and $350 for single parents who are younger than 25 years old. Korean single-parent families are currently eligible for the allowance if their family income is under 52 per cent of the designated median income. Interestingly, if the mother is under 25, the eligibility is relaxed to 60 per cent of the designated median income.

The second welfare policy that largely affects single-parent families is the National Basic Living Security System (NBLSS), the nation's representative public assistance program. This policy guarantees a minimum living standard (for all Koreans in principle). Besides in-kind benefits, the guaranteed cash income is 30 per cent of the designated median income and varies by family size. The benefits are calculated as the difference between the guaranteed level and family resources. This program interacts with the child support policy to affect the economic wellbeing of single-parent families. Further description is presented below. A single-parent family cannot receive both the NBLSS benefits and the allowance for a low-income single-parent family. Because NBLSS is generally more generous, only those who do not qualify for the NBLSS apply for the low-income single-parent family allowance. However, starting in 2021, single parents can receive both NBLSS and the allowance for low-income single-parent families, which represents an important policy improvement for single-parent families in Korea. Despite the legal progress, many single mothers are excluded from the public benefit system (Kim et al., 2018; Jun and Chung, 2021), in part because of the strict eligibility requirements for national public assistance programs (Chung and Jun, 2022). Thus, there is considerable room for improvement in public policy for single-parent families.

An additional legal mechanism to support single parents is a revision to the single-parent support law in 2011 that mandates an official survey every three years of a nationally representative sample of single-parent families in Korea. The first survey was in 2012. Since then, three more surveys have been conducted in 2015, 2018, and 2021. The survey is a very comprehensive and unique data source to understand the welfare of single-parent families in Korea including information about childcare, social support, economic wellbeing, and child support.

Single parents, especially single mothers, in Korea have actively led a social movement to empower all single parents and raise public awareness to reduce bias and discrimination against single mothers. They have also participated in decision making on policies that affect their welfare. For example, their political efforts led to a 2018 revision to the single-parent support law. The revised law added statements that single parents and their children should be given the opportunity to participate in decisions about policies designed to support them, and the government should support peer-support groups for single parents. These groups are expected to provide further social support and empower single parents (Son et al., 2019). However, field experts have generally reported that the policies that proactively promote participation in the policy-making process are not well implemented. However, the revised law has symbolic implications for single mothers when making policy demands.

To provide a complete picture of the national context that affects the welfare of single-parent families in Korea and the development of the national child support system from a cross-national comparative perspective, the rest of the chapter includes the following sections: a) Economic and Social Indicators of Korea, b) Cultural Contexts and Family Institutions, c) Legal Changes that Affect the Child Support System, d) Child Support Agency and Performance Measures, e) Child Support Receipt: Incidence and Correlates, and f) The Interaction between the Child Support System and the Welfare System. The chapter concludes with suggestions for future directions for public child support services and income-maintenance policies for single-parent families in Korea.

ECONOMIC AND SOCIAL INDICATORS

Korea is a high-income democracy, and the socioeconomic achievements are well regarded (Yang, 2020). For example, Korea has the 11th largest economy even though it ranks 109th in territorial size and 28th in population size (51.3 million). Korea's life expectancy at birth is 82.7, ranking 9th in the world. However, the fertility rate was 0.92 in 2019, the lowest rate across all OECD countries (OECD, 2022b), which may point to the high cost of raising a child in Korea. To address this problem, Korea recently introduced a child allowance policy that provides $100 per month for a child under age seven, regardless of parents' income levels. As such, there has been a notable increase in public support for families in recent years, but public spending on family benefits is still relatively low in Korea (OECD, 2020). Korea is often categorised as a liberal state in the typology of welfare capitalism (Yang, 2020).

Cultural Contexts and Family Institutions

Korea largely shares a Confucian culture with other East Asian countries
including China, Japan, and Taiwan. Although the influence of Confucianism
has decreased over time, it remains strong in Korea. Thus, this cultural context
shapes gender relations, living arrangements, and social policy differently than
the cultural context of the West (Sung and Pascall, 2014; Skinner et al., 2007).
In Confucianism, 'the family' is based on gender with a generational hierarchy
that subordinates women to their husbands. In addition, the male head of the
household has a disproportionately high level of authority in family matters,
including decisions about children. This model of familial relationships is
quite different from the Western model and strongly affects expectations of
single parenting.

Divorced couples in Confucian cultures tend to have a poorer relationship
than their counterparts in Western cultures, which implies that child support
is more difficult to negotiate and collecting child support is generally lower in
Korea than in Western countries (Chung and Kim, 2019). Confucian culture
stigmatises divorce and reinforces the norm of the traditional two-parent
family, which explains the high proportion of births within marital relationships in Korea. Married couples in Korea also tend to endure a difficult
marriage until the relationship is truly in jeopardy before divorcing because
the social and financial cost of divorce is high. Finally, the traditional divorce
law (i.e., 'fault' divorce) also leads Korean divorced parents to have a poorer
relationship and less contact with their ex-partners after separation or divorce,
compared to single parents in countries that have no-fault divorce policies.
Under traditional family law, couples are more likely to blame each other and
fight fiercely over who is responsible for the dissolution of the relationship to
increase their leverage in determining the division of assets and child custody
arrangements. A poorer relationship and less contact between Korean parents
after divorce can also lead to lower child support for the resident parent.

Legal Changes That Affect the Child Support System

Before the 2000s, if parents were not living together, Korea relegated the issue
of child support primarily to the individual divorcing couple, and did not consider child support a matter of public policy (Chung, 2020; Kim and Chung,
2020). When family law was first written, in 1960, the laws in Korea did not
include any requirement for the child support obligations of non-resident
parents. This omission was partly due to traditional custody practices among
divorced couples. Until 1990, family law in Korea gave the father custody
of the children as the default when couples divorced, and custody was not
negotiated and agreed upon between the couple. In this context, it was deemed

unfair to make non-resident mothers pay for child support because many of the mothers also wanted child custody but did not obtain it due to the legal constraint, and because they tend to be economically disadvantaged (Chung, 2020). The 1990 revision of the family law removed the explicit preference for custody to be given to the father during divorce, and since then, the rate of mother custody has increased. The Supreme Court's 1994 verdict (Supreme Court 1994.5.13. 92S21 Fullbench Ruling Verdict) that awarded resident mothers past support was a transitional verdict in that it dictated that child support liability should be based on the nature of the relationship between the (non-resident) biological parent and the child, regardless of whether and when the biological parent recognised child support liability (Kim and Chung, 2020). However, there was still no law that explicitly dictated or guided specific child support liability.

Partly influenced by the women's movement in the 2000s, policy makers and the public have agreed that there is a strong need for a public response to family issues, in general, and to the persistent economic vulnerability of single-parent families (Chin et al., 2014). To address these issues, in the late 2000s, Korea began to formalise the public child support system. In December 2007, a revision to the family law explicitly made non-resident parents liable for child support (the Civil Law Revision #8720; implemented in June 2008).[3] The revised law stated that couples could no longer obtain an uncontested divorce (which constituted about 90 per cent of divorces in Korea at that time) without reaching an agreement about child custody, access and visitation, and child support. In contested divorces (about 10 per cent of the cases), judges made the decisions about these issues. In 2009, additional legal changes mandated the court to review and confirm all child support agreements made by parents during divorce, which then granted them status as official child support. Before enacting these law changes, child support agreements were not required during the divorce process, which led to few formal child support orders. Kim and Chung (2020) suggested that this law created momentum in Korea's shift from a largely informal, discretionary model to a court-based

---

[3]   The law also required that divorcing couples have a 3-month period of consideration for couples with minor children before completing the divorce procedure. This law might have affected the recent decrease in the proportion of single-parent families among families who raise a child(ren) under age 18. It also led to divorced couples with minor children being a more select group than their counterparts before the law change. As mentioned previously, Korea began to publish the statistics on single parents raising a minor child only from 2016. Previously, it only published statistics for 'single parents' who lived with an unmarried child regardless of the child's age. These earlier statistics included families in which a 70-year-old single mother lived with her divorced son who was 40 years old. Taken together, the exact trend in Korea of the number of single-parent families over a long period is unknown.

scheme in the child support system. The effectiveness of this new system is discussed in detail in the next section.

Further, the revised Family Litigation Act in 2009 enabled family courts to ask non-resident parents to submit information about their assets, provide resident parents with a deposit for child support, garnish a parent's wages (transfer payment directly from the non-resident parent's employer to the resident parent), or apply a penalty such as incarceration (up to 30 days) for nonpayment. Note that unlike automatic income withholding in the United States, the Korean court order for automatic wage withholding applies only to a specific employer (usually after the occurrence of nonpayment); therefore, if a non-resident parent changes the place of employment, the court order becomes unenforceable.

The Korean child support system does not collect or distribute child support. Instead, all transfers are directly from non-resident fathers to resident mothers, unless an income-withholding order by the court directs employers of non-resident fathers to transfer child support amounts directly to the resident mother.

In 2012, family court developed and publicised new guidelines for determining child support amounts and has since updated them three times. However, while families and judges do refer to these guidelines, field experts report that the amount of child support determined by the court depends largely on the discretion of the judge. The guidelines include a recommended range of child support order amounts based on the earnings of both the resident parent and non-resident parent for a standard case. If the child has special needs (for example, medical costs, private education agreed upon by both parents), the guidelines suggest that child support order amounts can be higher than the standard amounts. If more than one child is involved, the child support order amount per child can be lower than the suggested child support amount multiplied by the number of children. Chung (2020) reported that the median range of the recommended child support amount for a child, given the incomes of both parents, is approximately 30 per cent of the non-resident parent's monthly gross income (higher than 30 per cent for low-income non-resident parents and lower than 30 per cent for very rich non-resident parents). For more than one child and special needs children, the order amounts are even higher. Overall, the 'recommended' amounts from the guidelines are unrealistically high for the non-resident parent (Chung, 2020). The guidelines are also not legally binding, so they may not be the standard for actual child support agreements or child support orders. Nevertheless, overall, field experts indicate that the guidelines help increase a resident mother's requested child support, compared to the previous child support order amounts when there were no guidelines (Chung, 2020).

No accurate data is available on shared custody (i.e., the child spends substantial time living with each parent), but this type of arrangement is quite rare in Korea. Thus, there is no explicit documentation of how shared custody is treated in determining child support orders. However, some anecdotal evidence suggests that judges do not consider shared custody in principle as they rarely observe such cases. In contrast, judges sometimes – though rarely – observe split custody (i.e., when one child lives with one parent and the other child(ren) lives with the other parent), and in that case, judges tend to not require child support orders, unless the incomes of the two parents are substantially different, which is reportedly rare in Korea.

The first national survey of single-parent families implemented in 2012 provided empirical evidence that the low rate of child support is a national concern. Partly affected by this, a significant legal change in Korean child support policy occurred in 2014. A new legislation passed in 2014 (Legislation #12532, the Law on Enforcement and Support for Child Support) established the public Child Support Agency (CSA) in March 2015. The goal of this law was to help create a safe environment for children by supporting and enforcing child support; but, notably, the government's cost recovery is not a policy goal. More details on the function of CSA are discussed in the next section. Additional revisions to the Law on Enforcement and Support for Child Support in 2020 and 2021, which became effective in 2021, also strengthened sanctions such as suspension of the noncompliant parent's driver's license, disclosure of the non-resident parent's personal information on a public website, suspension of travelling abroad, or criminal penalties (one year imprisonment or a $9,000 fine) for nonpayors.

Steady demand has also grown for a law on a child support advancement program (or a child support assurance program) in Korea, and several related bills have been proposed to the National Assembly. However, the bills are ambiguous, and the proposed child support advancement program has often been assumed to be a selective program, restricting the services only to those with low income. Thus, these new bills may not be efficient or effective in increasing child support collections and improving the welfare of single-parent families (Chung, 2020). Specifically, it is counterproductive to leave the decision to make child support payments to the discretion of rich and middle-income non-resident parents but then pursue public cost recovery for only low-income non-resident parents (Cancian and Meyer, 2018; Meyer and Cancian, 2012). Thus, a policy priority should be to establish a strong child support enforcement system that applies to all non-resident parents, regardless of their income level.

CHILD SUPPORT AGENCY AND PERFORMANCE MEASURES

Korean CSA mainly provides child support counseling and legal assistance by (1) representing resident parents (for no charge) in court proceedings for child-support disputes, (2) short-term emergency financial assistance to low-income resident parents, which assumes subsequent cost recovery from the non-resident parent, (3) monitoring child support payments for cases for which Korean CSA provide services, (4) establishing an access and visitation program, and (5) researching child support policy issues. The target of the services is divorced or unmarried single parents who are raising a child(ren) age 18 or younger. Notably, parents who are in the process of separation or divorce cannot be served by the Korean CSA because the related law explicitly targets single parents as clients of the agency. Thus there is a demand for the expansion of the agency services to include those who are separating or divorcing. Korean CSA services are always initiated by the resident parent applying for Korean CSA services. The Korean CSA initially provided services to all single parents, regardless of their income levels, but starting in 2021, it restricts services only to those with an income less than 125 per cent of the designated median income.

From 2015 – when the agency was established – to 2021, the Korean Child Support Agency conducted 214,703 online and offline child support consultations and managed 25,791 child support cases (Korean Child Support Agency, 2021). Over the seven years, it has helped collect US $92 million (111,178 million KRW) in child support payments through legal assistance by obtaining and enforcing child support court orders. Child support collection rates improved from 21.2 per cent in 2015 to 38.3 per cent in 2021. However, the statistics shown here are drawn from only the cases that were monitored by the Korean CSA. If mothers had a child support court order but did not use Korean CSA services, the case was not included in these statistics. National statistics drawn from a 2018 single-parent survey are discussed in the next section.

The Korean CSA is not a government agency or an independent public agency, but a part of a public agency named the Korean Institute for Healthy Family. This structure partly reflects the other political influences that go against efforts to make the Korean CSA an independent agency. Compared to child support agencies in other countries with agency-based or court-based child support systems, Korean CSA has a limited ability to identify information about non-resident parents in a timely and efficient manner and impose child support enforcement actions for noncompliant parents. For example, the agency must use an official court process to obtain income and employment information (for noncompliant, non-resident parents) from the administrative records of other governmental departments. This process is complicated, time-consuming, and costly (Chung, 2020).

Although Koreans generally support child support collection, some Koreans have argued that expenditures for Korean CSA are higher than the child support collections that are monitored directly by Korean CSA, suggesting that the agency may be inefficient. However, the statistics are incomplete. Child support collections that single parents receive without using Korean CSA services are not counted as the child support collections that the Korean CSA reports. This argument significantly underestimates the potential social benefits of Korean CSA. Many couples may not directly use Korean CSA services, but they may benefit from the existence of Korean CSA. For example, Korean CSA has increased public awareness about child support, promoted the perception that child support obligations are legitimate, reduced the resident parent's opportunity costs of pursuing child support, and increased non-resident parents' opportunity costs of not paying support. In response to the criticism, Korean CSA funded a cost-effectiveness analysis in 2016 examining the early stage of the child support system. They reported that over the next 10 years, even when taking this approach (ignoring the hidden social benefits of Korean CSA services), the agency will still collect more money than it spends, all of which is transferred to families (Korean Productivity Center, 2016).

Korean CSA has also reported additional achievements of note. The period of short-term emergency financial assistance to low-income resident parents has been extended from 9 to 12 months, and the services for the access and visitation program by the Korean CSA has been expanded. To increase voluntary payments, they have also recently expanded the access and visitation program nationwide in conjunction with local family centers. About 4,900 participants participated in this program from 2017, when the program started, until 2021.

Overall, however, there has been a recent change in the direction of the development of the child support policy from a family supporting approach to a punitive approach. Recent policy efforts in Korea have focused on introducing punitive measures such as revoking the noncompliant parent's driver's license and suspending their ability to travel abroad (in addition to the existing measures for jail sentences). However, punitive measures can be counterproductive (Pate, 2002; Vogel, 2020; Waller and Plotnick, 2001). Meyer, Cancian, and Waring (2020) also reported that suspending licenses is sometimes related to a lower likelihood of beginning to pay. Further, this change has impeded the development of a policy that increases standardised orders and a universal, automatic, efficient collection system.

The Korean CSA scheme has faced both challenges and some success. After it was established, as mentioned previously, Korean CSA services were universally available to all single parents for the first six years, but the services have recently been restricted to relatively low-income parents. In addition, as an organisation, Korean CSA has shrunk in both manpower and budget, although empirical evidence has shown that single mothers using Korean CSA services have higher service satisfaction than single mothers using other legal agencies that are contracted-out and provide single parents legal assistance for child support (KWDI, 2020). Some have still claimed that Korean CSA should focus more on soft programs to enhance family relations while privatising legal services to other legal agencies. Korean CSA's recent emphasis on family relations and voluntary payments may be perceived as relegating the agency to a child support scheme that supports all families, but it may rather be an example that the explicit goals of a policy are not always indicative of the actual function of policy. Korean child support policy continues to develop, and it deserves careful public and scholarly attention and scrutiny.

CHILD SUPPORT RECEIPT: INCIDENCE AND CORRELATES

A national statistic from a survey of representative single parents who resided in Korea in 2018 showed that about 19.6 per cent of all single parents received child support recently, which is a notable increase from 5.6 per cent in 2012. When also considering single parents who did not receive child support recently but had received child support at some point in the past (0.7 per cent in 2012 and 1.6 per cent in 2018) and those who received only a lump-sum payment in the past (6.3 per cent in 2012 and 5.7 per cent in 2018), the rate of any child support receipt by single parents rose to 26.9 per cent in 2018, compared to 12.6 per cent in 2012. These statistics show limited but decent success of the policy efforts. Nevertheless, the rate is still low compared to many other countries with public child support systems, in part because the system has only recently been implemented, and there is still cultural tolerance for nonpayment by non-resident parents. In addition, the quality of parents' relationships after divorce or separation is especially low in Korea (Chung and Kim, 2019). In 2018, only 24.5 per cent of single parents in Korea had a child support order (22.5 per cent with regular orders, 1.9 per cent with lump-sum orders, and 0.1 per cent with both regular and lump-sum orders); for 2012, there is no equivalent data

Korea's cultural context may impact not only the level of child support paid by the non-resident parent, but also the determinants of child support receipt. For example, Chung and Kim (2019) suggested that fathers' discretion, the perceived needs of the children, and fathers' willingness (or unwillingness) to pay support are more important predictors of child support payments in Korea than in the United States.

Kim and Chung (2020) also examined child support receipt among divorced single mothers in Korea and how it changed after the policy reform in 2007 (i.e., mandating that divorcing couples must agree on child support before finalising the divorce), and they found no statistically significant effect. However, the data and methods used in their study were limited. Thus, Kim, Chung, and Vogel (2022) utilised more recent data and a stronger analytic strategy to examine the effects of the recent Korean reform policy package that includes the 2007 legal change as well as the subsequent child support enforcement actions on child support receipt among divorced single mothers. Their results showed a positive effect of national child support enforcement on child support receipt by single mothers.

THE INTERACTION BETWEEN THE CHILD SUPPORT SYSTEM AND THE WELFARE SYSTEM

There is no requirement for welfare recipients to be clients of the child support system. The Korea government does not keep any of the child support received on behalf of single parents to compensate for welfare expenditures. Indeed, it does not have a public system that collects or distributes child support money. However, in Korea, as in the United States, for example, the child support system and the welfare system complements rather than supplements income (Cancian et al., 2008). In determining the eligibility of Korean welfare benefits, all child support received is considered part of the resident parent's income (i.e., Korea has no disregard policy). Further, the representative welfare policy (National Basic Living Security System) guarantees a minimum income, and the benefits are calculated as the difference between the guaranteed level and the family's income, meaning that, for families on welfare, a dollar transferred as child support will take a dollar from welfare support (or possibly negate welfare eligibility).

Additionally, in Korea, there is an allowance for low-income single parent families (a fixed amount of about $200 per month). Like the NBLSA program, the allowance program does not disregard the amount of child support received in determining benefit eligibility (i.e., child support is counted as family income, affecting the eligibility of the benefit), although unlike the NBLSA program, the amount of this allowance benefit is fixed for all families. This welfare system could decrease the incentive for non-resident parents to pay child support because their payments will not benefit their children, as Chung (2016) reported some empirical evidence supportive of this relationship.

CONCLUSION

Significant progress in the child support policy has been made over the past 15 years in Korea as evidenced by the achievements of agencies and the legal system. Changes in family law include legalising child support liability for non-resident parents and strengthening child support enforcement since the late 2000s. These legal changes have somewhat reduced discretion fathers have in making child support payments. However, a child support obligation is still a relatively new concept in Korea. Child support receipt for resident mothers is more likely to be determined at the non-resident fathers' discretion in Korea compared to other countries with stronger child support enforcement (Chung and Kim, 2019).

There is evidence that child support agreements are still infrequent with inconsistent formal child support orders. Qualitative research on the experiences of 17 mothers in Korea who were divorced between 2004 and 2009 and were eligible for child support (Son, 2014) suggests that many of these mothers do not trust the effectiveness of the child support system and believe that non-resident parents will be unable or unwilling to pay despite child support orders. Because many mothers in Korea expect that child support orders will not actually result in payment, they often agree to zero-amount orders to speed up the divorce process (Son, 2014). Results from our recent working papers also show similar stories.

Establishing appropriate child support orders can improve child support compliance (Meyer et al., 2008; Hodges et al., 2020). However, Kim and Chung (2020) suggested that a law mandating that divorcing couples present a child support agreement may not necessarily lead to an increase in child support payments by the non-resident parent if there are no guidelines or enforcement. Family court published child support guidelines, but they are not legally binding. The Law on Enforcement and Support for Child Support legislation passed in 2014 required the Secretary to the Ministry of Gender Equality and Family to establish and release child support guidelines, but this has not happened yet. Thus, the government must develop binding guidelines for child support order amounts that can be effectively used in the field. Implementing measures to enforce and monitor the use of the guidelines is also an important policy task in Korea.

Recent policy efforts in Korea have focused on introducing punitive measures. Although prior literature has reported that punitive measures can be counterproductive (Edin, 1995; Edin and Nelson, 2013; Pate, 2002; Vogel, 2020; Waller and Plotnick, 2001; Meyer et al., 2020), there are no other strong enforcement tools, and cultural acceptance of nonpayment of child support is still relatively strong in Korea. Thus, punitive measures might be less counterproductive. However, it is a concern that this punitive policy may appear to be 'sufficient' in addressing the issue of nonpayment, and thus it could divert the public's focus from the responsibility to enhance child support collection through an effective collection system.

The first priority for the Korean child support policy should be establishing a preventative, simplified, and automated child support system that reduces payor discretion. For example, there could be an automatic income withholding system that would both reduce family conflicts and increase child support collection. Giving Korea CSA more authority to identify non-resident parents' information and process child support cases would also make the agency's efforts more efficient and effective. After establishing an effective national child support collection system, making sure that no non-resident parent with the ability to pay can avoid the payment, the government should consider a universal advancement payment system that targets single parents regardless of their income (Cancian and Meyer, 2018; Chung, 2020). Before introducing a universal child support advancement program, it would help to extend the single-parent support program (not just the emergency support program with cost recovery) by significantly raising (i.e., relaxing) the eligibility requirements (Chung, 2020).

Developing measures to help low-income non-resident parents pay support is also important. There is some evidence that many resident parents are poor, although there are no population-based statistics on the incomes of non-resident parents in Korea. Referring clients to government agencies that offer services designed to improve the employment prospects of low-income fathers could be considered. Although prior research suggests that re-partnering tends to reduce child support payments (Meyer and Cancian, 2012), there is no data on people who are remarried with minor children in Korea. Collecting more accurate data, and evidence-based policy making should be pursued to improve the development of the child support policy and enhance the welfare of single parents and their families.

REFERENCES

Cancian, M., and Meyer, D. R. (2018). Reforming policy for single-parent families to reduce child poverty. *RSF: The Russell Sage Foundation Journal of the Social Sciences, 4*(2), 91–112.

Cancian, M., Meyer, D. R., and Caspar, E. (2008). Welfare and child support: Complements, not substitutes. *Journal of Policy Analysis and Management: The Journal of the Association for Public Policy Analysis and Management, 27*(2), 354–375.

Chin, M., Lee, J., Lee, S., Son, S., and Sung, M. (2014). Family policy in South Korea: Development, implementation, and evaluation. In M. Robila, *Handbook of Family Policies Across the Globe*, 305–318. New York: Springer.

Choi, S., Byoun, S. J., and Kim, E. H. (2020). Unwed single mothers in South Korea: Increased vulnerabilities during the COVID-19 pandemic. *International Social Work, 63*(5), 676–680.

Chung, Y. (2016). Divorced single mothers and their child support receipt in Korea. *Family and Culture*, 28. (Printed in Korean).

Chung, Y. (2020). Child support policy in Korea: History, current policy issues, and future directions, *Modern Society and Public Administration, 30*(3), 219–265. (Printed in Korean).

Chung, Y., Ahn, H., and Lah, T. J. (2022). Child welfare policy and services in Korea. *International Journal of Social Welfare*, *31*(1), 33–44.

Chung, Y., and Jun, M. (2022). A qualitative analysis of the experiences of single parents who received semi-universal benefits during the Covid-19 pandemic: A comparison with experiences receiving public assistance benefits. Working paper. (Printed in Korean).

Chung, Y., and Kim, Y. (2019). How cultural and policy contexts interact with child support policy: A case study of child support receipt in Korea and the United States. *Children and Youth Services Review*, *96*, 237–249.

Chung, Y., and Son, S. (2022). No good choices: Concealing or disclosing single motherhood in Korea. *Social Work Research*.

Edin, K. (1995). Single mothers and child support: The possibilities and limits of child support policy. *Children and Youth Services Review*, *17*(1–2), 203–230.

Edin, K., and Nelson, T. J. (2013). *Doing the best I can: Fatherhood in the inner city.* Oakland, CA: University of California Press.

Hodges, L., Meyer, D. R., and Cancian, M. (2020). What happens when the amount of child support due is a burden? Revisiting the relationship between child support orders and child support payments. *Social Service Review*, *94*(2), 238–284.

Jun, M., and Chung, Y. (2021). The public service users' emotions confronting the state's 'faces.' *Academy of Social Welfare*, *73*(4), 143–171. (Printed in Korean).

Kim, Y., and Chung, Y. (2020). Child support receipt among divorced mothers in Korea: Changes after the 2007 policy reform. *Children and Youth Services Review*, *119*, 105446.

Kim, Y., Chung, Y., and Vogel, L.K. (2022). Effects of the Korean child support reform: Evidence from a recent survey of single parents. Working paper.

Kim, J. E., Lee, J. Y., and Lee, S. H. (2018). Single mothers' experiences with pregnancy and child rearing in Korea: Discrepancy between social services/policies and single mothers' needs. *International Journal of Environmental Research and Public Health*, *15*(5), 955.

Korean Child Support Agency. (2021). Internal statistical data on child support outcomes. (Printed in Korean). Not available online.

Korean Productivity Center. (2016). Economic analysis of Korean Child Support Agency services. (Printed in Korean). Not available online.

Korean Statistical Information Service (KOSIS) (2021a). Single-parent families (unwed, divorced, widows). (Printed in Korean). https://kosis.kr/statHtml/statHtml .do?orgId=101&tblId=DT_1SP1601&conn_path=I2

Korean Statistical Information Service (KOSIS) (2021b). Unwed mothers, unwed fathers by age. (Printed in Korean). http://kosis.kr/statHtml/statHtml.do?orgId=101 &tblId=DT_1SI1601&conn_path=I2

Korean Women's Development Institute or KWDI (2020). An evaluation of the child support system for the past five years and recommendations for future policy development. (printed in Korean).

Meyer, D. R., and Cancian, M. (2012). 'I'm not supporting his kids': Nonresident fathers' contributions given mothers' new fertility. *Journal of Marriage and Family*, *74*(1), 132–151.

Meyer, D. R., Cancian, M., and Waring, M. K. (2020). Use of child support enforcement actions and their relationship to payments. *Children and Youth Services Review*, *108*, 104672.

Meyer, D. R., Ha, Y., and Hu, M. C. (2008). Do high child support orders discourage child support payments? *Social Service Review*, *82*(1), 93–118.

Ministry of Gender Equality and Families (MoGEF) (2018). A study of single-parent families in 2018. (Printed in Korean).

OECD (2019a). LMF1.5 Gender pay gaps for full-time workers, Family Database in the Asia-Pacific Region. http://www.oecdkorea.org/user/nd8662.do?View&boardNo= 00002628

OECD (2019b). LMF1.4 Employment profiles over the life-course, Family Database in the Asia-Pacific Region. http://www.oecdkorea.org/user/nd8662.do?View&boa rdNo=00002628

OECD (2020). Family benefits public spending (indicator). doi: 10.1787/8e8b3273-en

OECD (2021a). CO2.2 Child poverty. OECD Family Database. https://www.oecd.org/ els/family/database.htm

OECD (2021b). Chart SF2.4.A. Share of births outside of marriage. https://www.oecd .org/els/family/database.htm

OECD (2022a). Gender wage gap (indicator). doi: 10.1787/7cee77aa-en

OECD (2022b). Total fertility rate (indicator). https://stats.oecd.org/Index.aspx?Da taSetCode=FAMILY

Park, H., Choi, J., and Jo, H. (2016). Living arrangements of single parents and their children in South Korea. *Marriage & Family Review*, *52*(1–2), 89–105.

Pate, D. J. (2002). W-2 child support demonstration evaluation: Report on nonexperi-mental analyses, volume II: Fathers of children in W-2 families.

Skinner, C., Bradshaw, J., and Davidson, J. (2007). Child support policy: An interna-tional perspective (Research Report No. 405). Department for Work and Pensions.

Son, B., and Moon, H. (2021). Who suffers the most financial hardships due to COVID-19? *Korean Academy of Social Welfare*, *73*(3), 9–31.

Son, S. (2014). Korean divorced mothers' experiences with child support from noncus-todial fathers. *International Journal of Human Ecology*, *15*(1), 38–50.

Son, S., Chung, Y. (Corresponding Author), and Kim, S. (2019). Building social support among single mothers: A case study of a one-to-one peer support program in Korea. *Korean Journal of Family Welfare*, *24*(4), 437–466. (Printed in Korean).

Sung, S., and Pascall, G. (2014). Gender and the welfare states in east Asia. *Gender and Welfare States in East Asia: Confucianism or Gender Equality*, 1–28.

Vogel, L. K. (2020). Help me help you: Identifying and addressing barriers to child support compliance. *Children and Youth Services Review*, *110*, 104763.

Waller, M. R., and Plotnick, R. (2001). Effective child support policy for low-income families: Evidence from street level research. *The Journal of the Association for Public Policy Analysis and Management*, *20*(1), 89–110.

Yang, J. J. (Ed.). (2020). *The small welfare state: Rethinking welfare in the US, Japan, and South Korea*. Cheltenham, UK and Northampton, MA, USA: Edward Elgar Publishing.

9.   The child support system in Malaysia

Zarina Md Nor

INTRODUCTION

This chapter discusses child support issues in Malaysia among previously married couples. There are two separate legal systems governing child support claims: the Shariah court for Muslims and the Civil court for non-Muslims. Mitigating child support matters tend to be difficult among divorced couples. Research shows that, in Malaysia, many divorced mothers do not sufficiently receive child support payments from their former husbands and the effect is more severe for low-income single mother households. This chapter discusses the background of Malaysian society, the roles of culture, religion, dual legal systems, and familial aspects in affecting child support matters.

MALAYSIAN SOCIETY

Malaysia is a multicultural country with a current population estimated at 32.4 million, with an annual growth rate of 1.7 per cent. Malaysia has three main ethnic groups namely the Malay/Bumiputera (68.9 per cent), Chinese (22.4 per cent) and Indians (6.8 per cent). Religious identity remains an important part of Malaysian society. The official religion of Malaysia is Islam and all Malays are born Muslims. Other religions can be freely practised such as Buddhism, Christianity, and Hinduism. In Malaysia, the male population still outnumbers the female population with 17.0 million and 15.5 million respectively, contributing to the sex ratio of 110 males for 100 females (DOSM, 2022a). The gap is narrowing however. In Malaysia, a marriage is only between a man and a woman. Therefore, this ratio indicates that there is a sufficient number of males and females to get married and form a family *ceteris paribus.* Same sex marriage is not allowed, and cohabitation relationship is not legally recognised. Therefore, children are mainly born within a marriage. The concept of a nuclear family in Malaysia refers to a married couple along with their children. If the marriage also involves stepchildren, they will automatically become a part of the family without the need to legally adopt them. An extended family is an important part of the Malaysian family concept, and it includes the maternal and paternal grandparents and their offspring. A married couple and their children will often live with their parents from either side.

The number of marriages decreased from 6.4 per thousand population in 2018 to 5.7 in 2020. The rate of marriage amongst Muslims is higher at 7.3 per thousand compared to 3.1 amongst non-Muslims. Across both groups, the median age for a groom is 28 and a bride is 27 years old. Muslim couples get married earlier, with the median age for a groom at 27 years old, and a bride, 26. A non-Muslim groom is 30, and a non-Muslim bride is 28 years old. The mean age of a mother giving birth to a first child is 27.9 years old. Data on crude birth rates show a decline from 17.2 (2010) to 14.4 (2020) births per thousand population. The fertility of women of childbearing age declined significantly from 4.9 children per woman in 1970 to 1.7 in 2020 (DOSM, 2021). The falling birth rate is more pronounced in urban areas. This may be due to the higher cost of living in urban areas whereby both the husband and the wife in a married couple are working. There is a trade-off between employment and fertility in this situation. The scarcity of childcare and escalating childcare costs do not help either. The higher number of women in the workforce may increase tax collection as long as they are eligible to pay taxes, in the short term. The government has been considering broadening the tax base and implemented the goods and services tax (GST) in 2015, but it was abolished in 2018, reinstating the sales and service tax till now. Malaysia has been running on deficits since 1998 and a declining birth rate may shrink the tax base further in the long run, reducing tax collection which will also be used for welfare purposes such as subsidies, transfers for the poor, and caring for the increasing ageing population. Currently, the Malaysian social support system facilitating for those in need seems to be insufficient as government revenues are lower.

DIVORCE IN MALAYSIA

Divorce rates have risen for Muslims and non-Muslims though the Muslim divorce rate remains at a higher level than that of non-Muslims (Jones, 2021). Earlier research comparing divorces between Muslims and non-Muslims can be found in Kamarudin (1993). In 2020 the median age at divorce for males and females is 37 and 34 years respectively, while most divorces occur between the ages of 30 and 34 years (DOSM, 2021). Table 9.1 shows that Muslims are experiencing disproportionately more divorces per year than their population share. While Muslims comprised 61.3 per cent of the population, they accounted for 83 per cent of divorces in Malaysia in 2020.

Table 9.1   *Number of divorces for Muslim and Non-Muslim population 2000–2020*

	Number of divorces				
Year	Malaysia	Muslim	Percentage	Non-Muslim	Percentage
2000	15,218	13,605	89%	1,613	11%
2006	22,938	17,458	76%	5,480	24%
2010	41,262	32,701	79%	8,561	21%
2016	51,570	40,958	79%	10,612	21%
2019	56,975	45,502	80%	11,473	20%
2020	45,754	37,853	83%	7,901	17%

Note: Lower figures for 2020 are probably due to the movement control order.
Source: Adapted from Jones (2021) and Malaysia Department of Statistics, 2021.

In Malaysia, approximately 0.8 per cent of the population is categorised as divorced or permanently separated. That consists of 1.2 per cent of the female population and 0.5 per cent of the male population. The reasons for such differences cannot be found in the literature but it may be due to the nature and culture of Malaysian society. Firstly, it is easier for a divorced man to look for a new wife compared to a divorced woman. Men might find a potential wife among unmarried women, divorcees, or widows. For a divorced woman, remarriage options can be limited by culture and childcare responsibilities. It is culturally not well accepted for a divorced woman, particularly with children, to get married to a bachelor. The stigma attached to a divorced woman seems to be stronger than that of a divorced man. Stigma is more prevalent among single mothers from lower socioeconomic backgrounds and with dependent children (Rusyda et al., 2011) – ironically, they are the ones who need financial support from a spouse the most. It is common practice in Malaysia to officially or by mutual understanding grant child custody to mothers upon divorce. Oftentimes, they must live with insufficient child support payments or none at all. From a man's perspective, this could become a hindrance as it has higher financial consequences. Secondly, the number of divorces is consistently higher among Muslims. Islam allows polygamous marriage, yet the number of Muslim female divorcees is higher (assumed from the observation). In reality, polygamy is not widely practised among Muslims in Malaysia. The most common polygamous marriage is usually involving only two wives. Hathout (2007) discusses justice and responsibilities in polygamous marriage based on a chapter in the Quran dedicated to women (Surah An-Nisaa). For instance:

> … marry from among women such as are lawful to you – two, or three, or four but if you have reason to fear that you might not be able to treat them with equal fairness,

then [only] one…This will make it more likely that you will not deviate from the right course (An Nisaa 4:3)

In reality, a female divorcee may be open to the idea of being the second wife, but she has to be prepared to face the obstacles that probably come from the first wife, her own family and friends. As a note, there is a stigma related to being the second wife in Malaysian society.

The dissolution of a marriage does not only affect couples but their children as well. Divorces create single parent families, and in particular, single mother households. The number of single mothers and female headed households is increasing in Malaysia. Official data from Malaysia Housing and Population Census in 2010 showed that there was a total of 831,860 women or 2.9 per cent of the population who were either widowed or divorced/permanently separated. A survey called 'Families on the Edge' by United Nations agencies (UNICEF and UNFPA) in December 2020 during the COVID-19 pandemic's conditional movement control order (MCO) found that the income level among female-headed households is 24 per cent lower compared to the end of 2019. Indeed, the pandemic has severe impacts on single mothers raising children on their own (Jusoh and Latada, 2020).

SOCIO-ECONOMIC CLASSIFICATION

Malaysian society is often referred to based on economic status and the government has come up with housing income thresholds dividing the society into the top (T), middle (M) and bottom (B) income categories. Table 9.2 presents the income threshold by household decile group.

Table 9.2   Income classification and threshold, 2019

Classification		Income Range (per month in RM)	Income Range (per month in USD)
T20	T2	> RM15,040	> USD3,581
	T1	RM10,961 – RM15,039	USD2,610 – USD3,581
	M4	RM8,700 – RM10,959	USD2,071 – USD2,609
M40	M3	RM7,110 – RM8,699	USD1,693 – USD2,071
	M2	RM5,880 – RM7,099	USD1,400 – USD1,690
	M1	RM4,850 – RM5,879	USD1,155 – USD1,400
	B4	RM3,970 – RM4,849	USD945 – USD1,155
B40	B3	RM3,170 – RM3,969	USD1,693 – USD2,071

Classification		Income Range (per month in RM)	Income Range (per month in USD)
	B2	RM2,501 – RM3,169	USD 595 – USD 755
	B1	< RM2,500	< USD 595

Note: Exchange rate USD1 = RM4.20 (approximately).
Source: Household Income and Basic Amenities Survey 2019, Department of Statistics Malaysia, 2020.

The B40 households in general are considered poor households. However, the poverty line income for a household is established at RM2,208 (USD526) per month which sits within the lowest decile (The Star, 2020). This poverty line is reasonable given the increasing cost of living in Malaysia. In February 2020, Malaysia has implemented a two-tiered minimum wage of RM1,200 (USD286) and RM1,100 (USD262) based on the place of employment/locality. However, by May 1, 2022, a new minimum wage of RM1500 (USD357) will be implemented (Razak, 2022). Concern remains for those working in informal sectors or self-employed and the possibility of price increases when minimum wage increases, hence escalating the cost of living, and its serious consequences are experienced by people at large (Dass, 2021). Population-wide, more than 50 per cent of households have more than one income earner and in 2020, 45.6 per cent of 7.23 million were outside the labour force due to housework/family responsibilities (DOSM, 2020) which emphasises the need for dual income for a family to survive in current times. For divorced women who do not re-partner, earning capacity is reduced to one earner. In cases where they did not work during the marriage, they may lose their only source of income and are prone to fall into poverty. Finding employment post-divorce is usually harder due to childcare and age factors. This emphasises previous findings on the relationship between single motherhood and poverty in the literature (see: Australia, New Zealand, the UK, Colombia).

Income differences exist among the main ethnic groups in Malaysia. The mean and median income of Chinese households are higher than Malays/Bumiputera and Indians (Table 9.3). The Malays as a group experience lower incomes but higher divorce rates than their non-Bumiputera counterparts. To some extent, this factor could negatively impact their ability to pay child support, particularly among the B40 group.

Table 9.3   *Monthly mean and median income for households by ethnicity*

Ethnicity	Mean		Median	
Malay/Bumiputera	RM7,093	USD1,689	RM5,420	USD1,290
Chinese	RM9,895	USD 2,351	RM7,391	USD1,760
Indian	RM8,216	USD1,956	RM5,981	USD1,424

Source: Household Income and Basic Amenities Survey Report, 2019, Department of Statistics Malaysia, 2020.

The average household size in Malaysia is 3.9 persons. However, single mother households seem to have more children than the national average of two children (Md Nor, 2022). The higher the number of dependent children in a household, the more financial resources are needed for their upbringing. In many cases, single mothers would return to live with their parents post-divorce, particularly among those without proper employment and living in rental properties during the marriage (Md Nor, Mohamad, Vellymalay, Omar and Omar, 2019). This coping strategy may solve their short-term accommodation issue.

It is interesting to note that, according to the 2019 Malaysia Gender Gap Index (MGGI), women have surpassed men in educational attainment, as there is no barrier to education for women in Malaysia. Education is also an enabler for better employment opportunities and women's empowerment. However, the labour force participation rate is rather low for Malaysian women at 51.2 per cent, while for Indonesia it is 53.7 per cent and for Thailand 59.0 per cent, and far below Australia at 61.1 per cent (ILO, 2021). For women's employment, official reports state that housework and family responsibilities are the major reason for those who remain outside the labour force. Recent statistics in 2022 show that 41.7 per cent of those outside the labour force are due to housework/family responsibilities, most probably referring to housewives (DOSM, 2022c). What these statistics reveal is that despite advances in education, social and institutional constraints may pose barriers to women's financial security in the event of a divorce. Many Malaysian women seem to depend on their husbands regarding money matters, which can have significant financial consequences should the marriage end in divorce. The impact of divorce is more severe for women with low educational attainment, minimal job experience and childcare responsibilities. These are the barriers that keep them away from getting good-paying jobs (Md Nor, Abu Hasan, Omar, Vellymalay and Omar, 2018; Mulia, 2017; Lim, Badiozaman and Voon, 2020). Many single mothers choose to be self-employed i.e. working from home, running small businesses or close to home despite the irregular pay and no access to employee benefits due to their parenting responsibilities (Md Nor, 2022; Topimin, Fabeil and Abdullah, 2019). In addition, my observations from extensive fieldwork across Malaysia indicate that single mothers barely have savings for emergencies – they do not even have enough for necessities.

Reflecting on Malaysian households' incomes and costs of living, it becomes apparent that mothers' need for child support and fathers' ability to pay child support may be in direct tension with each other for separated parents in the B40. For higher income groups, parents may have better means of establishing and adhering to child support commitments or orders. Shared custody is yet to be widely practised in Malaysia even though there have been calls to policymakers to delve further into the matter of joint custody (Suzana, Roslina and Najibah, 2017). Currently, the parent without custody will be given visitation rights and access to the children during weekends and school holidays. Before examining these issues in detail, I now turn to describe parents' access to social welfare payments and services that can also help to reduce child poverty through direct and indirect means.

SOCIAL WELFARE

In Malaysia, childcare is mostly the responsibility of the parents. They may opt to provide the childcare themselves or outsource the service to live-in maids, organised childcare centres or informal childcare. Homemaker mothers look after their own children while working mothers may choose formal or informal childcare services. It is common practice in Malaysia to send young children and babies to informal child carers in their own neighbourhood or leave the children under the care of their close female relatives, such as a grandmother or an aunt, or a neighbour who is a homemaker when the parents go to work. There is a cultural belief that children will be better cared for by family or people that they know than within the formal childcare system. Often, familial care or informal care is also cheaper than a formal childcare centre. Government childcare centres are available, but places are very limited given insufficient public investment. When affordable childcare is not available, either through the market or a homemaker relative, mothers often find it more economical to leave their jobs to care for children. It is uncommon for fathers, or a male relative, to take care of the children while the mother goes to work. The responsibility of the wife as the main caregiver remains firm, despite an increasing number of Malaysian women taking up the role as an equal or contributing breadwinner. Given women's main responsibility as caregivers, affordable and accessible childcare is important to enable them to go to work and earn income – and to be able to support themselves in the event of divorce.

Gender Roles, Islam and Divorce

In terms of child support, religion plays an important role as it will determine the jurisdiction that governs the official channel for child support claims. There are two separate legal systems for family courts, namely the Sharia court for

Muslims and the Civil court for non-Muslims. There are 14 States in Malaysia and each State has its own Islamic Law Enactment to regulate Muslims whereas non-Muslims are governed by Federal statutes enacted by the legislature. The divorce process for Muslims and non-Muslims is quite different as Muslim couples have to adhere to Shariah guidelines. A divorce application can be submitted by either a husband or wife to the Religious Department. In Islam, the husband has the right to divorce the wife, however the wife only has the right to apply for a divorce under specific circumstances. The Malaysian Islamic Family Law (Federal Territories) 1984 [Act 303] governs the matters related to the rights of custody and care post-divorce. Caring responsibility for children is stated in Section 81(1), subject to Section 82. Here, a mother is the most entitled of all persons to care for her minor child while the mother is still in marriage and after her marriage is dissolved. However, this does not mean that mothers are always granted caring responsibility. If the court finds that the mother is disqualified to be a custodian, custody will transfer to one of the following in order of priority, namely: maternal grandmother, father, paternal grandmother, older or younger sister from the same parents and others stated in the Act. Section 82 provides that the conditions for becoming the custodian are a Muslim, of sound mind, of an age that qualifies them to give the child the care and affection required, is well behaved in terms of Islamic morals, and living in a place where the child is unlikely to face any adverse moral or physical consequences.

Therefore, mothers are the rightful carers of very young children, but fathers can assume the right to care as children get older – but this does not mean that fathers must take this right up. Once children reach approximately 9 to 11 years old, they are entitled to choose which parent they want to live with. Shared care or moving between residences is not common and decisions about ordinary living arrangements like schooling and social activities are under the mothers' domain. The relationship between the children and the father is usually based on the father's effort and involvement with his children (Turner and Waller, 2017). Oftentimes, the father will get remarried and have other children of his own or have stepchildren that complicate the relationship. Moreover, if a man has more children with his new wife, this may affect the ability and willingness of a father to pay child support to his previous wife.

In Islam, a father is solely obliged to support his children. If the father fails to support his children for whatever reasons, the responsibility moves in the order of the paternal guardians (*wali*). In this case, child maintenance would fall on the paternal grandfather, uncle from the same grandparents, and uncle from the same grandfather. When there are no capable paternal guardians, then the government takes the responsibility to help the family either through a financial institution and property management that administers resources from *zakat* (tithe) which is an obligatory payment made annually on certain kinds of incomes, and *waqf* property which is the property surrendered for public use. Every state has its own *zakat* collection office and those in need, including single mothers, may apply for financial assistance from their respective *zakat* offices.

The amount of child maintenance that must be given by the father to the child depends on the following factors: (a) the income and liabilities of the father; (b) the needs of the children; (c) the age of the children. Child support payments are currently enforced only on the father himself, although Islam has listed that extended family members should be liable for child support payment when the father fails to do so. If it has been a difficult and tedious process claiming child support from the father, such a claim on his extended family members could be much harder. The income and liabilities of the mother are not considered in determining the child support amount from the father because in Islam, a woman should be fully supported by her husband upon marriage. The wife could keep her own money and property and the husband has no right to it as long as she lives. Nowadays, most married couples share their living expenses. Nevertheless, Islam forbids the husband to ask his wife to pay for necessities. It is permissible if it is done at her own free will. Hence there are no instances of child support claims made in Shariah court by a custodian father on his ex-wife. Generally, a child maintenance order is valid until the child is 18 years old, but the father has to take care of his children's expenses for higher education as well. A mediator will be assigned to mediate the negotiation between the divorced couple to agree on the amount of child support and present it to the judge to be sealed as an official maintenance order. The determination of child support amount is subjective; therefore, a proper assessment method is needed (Ahmad et al., 2020). Child support is calculated as debt after a court order. The payment can be made through direct payments or salary deduction/income withholding.

For the non-Muslims in Malaysia, there are two governing laws on family matters: the Law Reform (Marriage & Divorce) Act 1976 (LRA) and the Married Women & Children (Maintenance) Act 1950 (MWCMA). There are two types of divorce: Divorce by Mutual Consent, and Divorce Without Mutual Consent. In the first case, both parties can freely decide on the maintenance of the wife and children, custody and care of the children, and division of matrimonial assets. In the latter case, either party can make an application for maintenance and custody. Where there are two or more children, the court is not bound to place both or all in the custody of the same person but will consider the welfare of each independently (Section 88(4), LRA). The judge may take the advice of a person who is trained in child welfare, interview the child and make a decision accordingly.

A 'child of the marriage' under the LRA includes a child of one party to the marriage accepted as one of the family by the other party and a 'child' in this context includes an illegitimate child of either party to the marriage (s 2, LRA). Section 92 of the LRA provides that except where an agreement or order of court otherwise provides, it shall be the duty of a parent to maintain or contribute to the maintenance of his or her children by providing them with accommodation, clothing, food, and education as may be reasonable having regard to his or her means and station in life. Under Section 3(1) of the MWCMA 1950, the term 'any person' is used. Here, it may seem like a gender-neutral provision that includes a mother and a father. However, this provision is subject to another provision which specifically placed the responsibility to maintain on the father. Support can be found in most cases which established the principle that it is a father's basic responsibility to provide maintenance for his children whether during the marriage or after a divorce between the parents. Previous cases indicate that the mother's duty to maintain is only secondary to that of the father and it may be imposed in special cases (Abdul Hak, Che Soh and Hashim, 2009).

Section 88 (1) provides that a father or a mother may be entrusted with the custody of the child. Only when the parents are determined to be unfit by the court, would a relative of one of the parents be appointed. The relative could be the paternal or maternal grandparent, aunt, uncle or even older siblings. In assessing child maintenance, the court shall have regard to the needs of the child and the means of the parents, taking into account the standard of living the child is accustomed to during the marriage. A father of a divorced couple is now duty-bound to maintain his child not only until the child turns 18, but also until the completion of the child's higher education or training (section 95, LRA).

CHILD SUPPORT IN MALAYSIA IN COMPARISON TO THE INTERNATIONAL CONTEXT

The child support issue in Malaysia focuses mainly on the maintenance of 'child of the marriage', when de facto unions or cohabitant relationships are unacceptable from the religious and cultural perspectives of Malaysian society. Cohabitants have no entitlement to financial claims under civil family law. However, it is wrong to say that there are no children born out of wedlock in Malaysia. The definition of the illegitimate child used by the National Fatwa Council for Muslims includes (1) a child being born out of wedlock, due to adultery or rape, (2) a child born less than six months according to the lunar calendar from the date of intercourse.

As indicated previously, in Islam, paternal lineage is very significant in a child's life as it safeguards the status conferred upon the child through its father within a family. Filiation (*nasab*) under Islamic law generally refers to lineage or descent from a marriage relationship. Nevertheless, a mere maternal lineage without marriage may not confer filiation to a child (Mohd, 2019). It is stated in Islamic rules that the obligation to provide maintenance and subsistence for an illegitimate child from adultery lies with the mother. This is because the filiation of such a child is only with the mother. If the mother is unable to provide maintenance for the child, the obligation passes to the family members of the mother. However, if the child is born as a result of an act of rape, the filiation stays with the father and thus so does the maintenance of the child.

For the non-Muslim, a man could adopt his own illegitimate child born before a registered marriage to the mother who is his current spouse or another woman. Upon marriage, the child will be regarded as a child of the marriage. Therefore, for illegitimate children among non-Muslims, the court may order the father to pay a reasonable monthly allowance (Section 3, LRA). The paternity information for a child born out of wedlock will not be recorded in the birth register, except with a joint application by the mother and the person claiming to be the father of the child and he must sign the birth register together with the child's mother. For Muslims, paternity information for a child born out of wedlock or in a marriage that is less than 6 lunar months is different. Muslims in Malaysia do not follow the convention of paternal surname, they are using their legitimate father's given name instead. For example, the name of a man is Zakaria bin Omar. The man's given name is Zakaria and his father's given name is Omar. Therefore, 'bin' or 'binti' refers to 'the son of' or 'the daughter of' the legitimate father. However, for an illegitimate child, he/she cannot be named as the son or daughter of their biological father. The indication of a child's illegitimacy and the stigma attached to it is a concern amongst the policymakers, religious authority, academia, and society at large. The name and registration issues of illegitimate children have been an ongoing discussion (see Abdul Mutalib and Yahya, 2016).

CHILD SUPPORT POLICY

There is no specific child support policy in Malaysia, but it is governed by the respective provisions in the Family laws for the Muslim and the non-Muslim. In essence, child support in Malaysia focuses on enforcing parental responsibility and improving the wellbeing of the children. Having discussed the laws in the earlier sections, the reality could be quite different. Given social taboos and gender expectations, child support is a delicate and complicated issue. The responsibility to provide care and maintenance always lies with the resident parent irrespective of Shariah or other decrees regarding paternal responsibility for providing resources. In cases where the court makes a ruling on a specific amount to be paid by the father, the amount could be much less than the actual needs of each child. Hence, it remains the mother's responsibility to fill the gap. The role of the extended family is undeniable and is legally enshrined in Shariah law in the case of paternal financial responsibilities and maternal caregiving arrangements when mothers are deemed unsuitable.

Ensuring Financial Support for Children

Another pressing matter is adherence to child maintenance court orders. For Muslims, Family Support Division (FSD) of the Department of Shariah Judiciary Malaysia enforces maintenance orders issued by the Shariah Court. FSD monitors the compliance of maintenance orders by the father post-divorce. For example, when a father refuses to pay the maintenance as per court order, the mother may lodge a complaint with FSD for a follow-up action including hosting a negotiation session involving both parties. If no solution or decision can be made from the session, an enforcement and execution order case will be filed in the Shariah Court. Starting in 2012, FSD has provided the *e-Nafkah* system that serves as a data bank and repository of all maintenance orders issued by the Court. Through the integration of the system, FSD will monitor each case and communicate with the mother of the recipient children, and they will be able to detect the non-compliant and take necessary action. Types of enforcement actions that can be taken by FSD include Judgement Debtor Summons, Judgement Notice, seizure and sale, *Hiwalah* (a contract which causes the transfer of debt from one party to another), and Order of Committal. The issue of 'deadbeat dads' is quite common in Malaysian society. The arrears become a debt and must be paid in full. The mother has the right to file a claim for maintenance arrears through Judgement Debtor Summons and Judgement Notice. If the father fails to pay the arrears, the court could order imprisonment for not more than one month for every month that he fails to pay.

The Federal Constitution has provided that the child maintenance related to Muslims in Malaysia is under the authority of the Shariah court of the respective state. Therefore, the effectiveness of FSD in collecting child support arrears may vary across states. For instance, in 2018 the Shariah court of Penang had collected RM573,297 of child support arrears and most of the cases have been resolved through a judgement notice that comes with imprisonment terms for those who failed to pay and through judgement debtor summons (Ismail and Sulong, 2020). The threat of imprisonment seems to expedite the payment of arrears by the fathers in debt because they are not willing to stay in prison, when they can settle the matter instantaneously or by instalment (Najibah, 2017). Therefore, staffing and resources of FSD need to be strengthened to increase its effectiveness in handling the cases. There are news reports on the consequences of non-compliance to child support orders in the mass media. For instance, there have been cases where some fathers have been imprisoned for not paying child support. While these points provide a message to the public about the responsibilities of fathers and the effectiveness of the court system, they do not provide mothers with additional resources, and instead can cost mothers time and money to pursue justice through the courts. When only the father is willing to cooperate and comply, child support can be settled smoothly with minimal costs.

Over the years, my research has come across many cases of divorced mothers coping with the financial burden of raising their children alone and the consequences of that situation, such as stress and illness (Abd Hamid and Salleh, 2013; Hashim, Azman and Endut, 2015). Many do not claim for child maintenance through courts of law. There are at least three main reasons for such non-action; the fear of losing the children/retribution, the expected complexity and cost of court procedures, and the unaffordability of their former husbands to pay child support. Given the rather conservative society, Malaysian mothers seem to have a strong belief that children should be with them upon divorce. In reference to the first reason, there are many cases whereby the former husband has threatened to take away the children from the mother's care if she formally claims custody and child maintenance. In such cases, the father may agree to pay child support but with no fixed amount or interval, or he may not pay at all. This situation indicates the vulnerability and gendered moral rationality (Duncan and Edwards, 1999) of the mother who prioritises her children's wellbeing over the acquisition of financial resources. As for the father, Malaysian law prioritises their financial autonomy and authority, as has been found in Western contexts (Cook, 2013; Diduck, 1995; Natalier and Hewitt, 2010). Fathers' non-compliance with child maintenance agreements or orders is arrogance at its best, if we may. The second reason refers more to the perceived complexity of court procedures and the potential costs involved. In general, people will avoid going to court particularly for things related to their personal life. Mothers' experiences in dealing with courts in cases of custody and child support describe a lack of information or limited access to information. The interviews done during my field research have revealed the most common comment is that 'the father did not come for the court session'. It is very frustrating to the mothers as going to court may mean that they must leave work, travel quite a distance, and find temporary childcare. This situation emphasises the burdens of claiming child support from the mother's side when facing problematic fathers (Cook, 2021; Natalier and Hewitt, 2010; Turner and Waller, 2017). Herd and Moynihan (2018) have described financial, time and psychological costs as administrative burdens that can prevent people from accessing public systems while Cook (2021) further discusses the onus that separated mothers must bear in navigating administrative requirements of child support payments while separated fathers have it much easier. The third reason may sound so helpless, but the mothers often ask – how could they ask the father for child support when they did not provide for the children even during the marriage? Observation from my fieldwork suggests the causes include unemployment, involvement in substance abuse and imprisonment. This research mirrors the work of Western child support scholars who have also found that women can give up on seeking payments if they know that the father has a limited capacity to earn an income or pay (McKenzie and Cook, 2015). Notably, the mothers' faith and religious beliefs have also helped them in coping with the non-compliance and non-payment of child support as they put it - 'he (the father) will be answerable to God on the day of judgement'.

CONCLUSION

Child support remains a complex, delicate, and marginalised issue in Malaysia. While this edited collection seeks to examine this problem theoretically across countries, in reality, it is the mother who will have to shoulder the financial and caring responsibilities of their children in Malaysia, although both Family Laws in Malaysia require that a father maintains the children. Nevertheless, non-compliance to court orders or non-payment of voluntary maintenance occurs regularly. Real actions in tackling the root cause of child support non-compliance among fathers are lacking. Mothers also need the education to understand and value their rights to acquire child support for their children. This is where the government should play a bigger role. Support is also required to help mothers to turn knowledge about the process into action given that the process involves opportunities for women to be intimidated and oppressed by their former husbands, and women also need financial support to allow them to access judicial processes. Knowledge and financial means are the keys to empowering mothers to fight for their children's rights. However, many women are lacking one or both, especially among the B40. Extended families, particularly women, are also pivotal in helping single mothers get through the hardship of raising their children. At the heart of the issue is the fact that Malaysian society is still very much paternalistic and strongly governed by cultural and religious values.

REFERENCES

Abd Hamid, S.R., and Salleh, S. (2013). Exploring single parenting process in Malaysia: Issues and coping strategies. *Social and Behavioral Sciences, 84,* 1154–1159.

Abdul Hak, N., Che Soh, R., and Hashim, N. (2009). Right of a child to maintenance: Harmonising the laws in Malaysia. http://irep.iium.edu.my/3648/1/9._Article_for _harmonization_-_Right_of_a_Child_to_Maintenance_2009.pdf

Abdul Mutalib, L., and Yahya, A.M. (2016). Isu penasaban anak luar nikah kepada bapa biologi dari sudut pandang siasah syar'iyyah di Malaysia (The issue of the attribution of children out of wedlock to the biological father from the point of view of shariah law in Malaysia). Muzaqarah Fiqh & International Fiqh Conference.

Abdul Talib, M., Abdul Mutalib, N.K., Shahabudin, S.M., and Mahmud, A. (2020). Household income and life satisfaction of single mothers in Malaysia. *International Journal for Studies on Children, Women, Elderly and Disabled, 9*, 75–83.

Ahmad, B., Azahari, R., Ab Rahman, A., and Abdul Wahab, M. (2020). Assessing the rate of child maintenance (financial support) from a Shariah perspective: The case of Malaysia. *Al- Jāmiʻah: Journal of Islamic Studies, 58*(2), 293–322.

Cook, K. (2013). Child support compliance and tax return non-filing: A feminist analysis. *Australian Review of Public Affairs, 11*(2), 43–64.

Cook, K. (2021). Gender, malice, obligation and the state: Separated mothers' experiences of administrative burdens with Australia's child support program. *Australia Journal of Public Admininstration,* 1–21.

Dass, A. (2021). Urgency to Address Rising Cost of Living. https://www.thestar.com .my/business/business-news/2021/10/11/urgency-to-address-rising- cost-of-living

Department of Statistics Malaysia (2020). Household Income and Basic Amenities Survey 2019.

Department of Statistics Malaysia (2021). Labour Force Survey Report 2020. https:// www.dosm.gov.my/v1/index.php?r=column/cthemeByCat&cat=126&bul_id= dTF2dk JpcUFYUWRrczhqUHVpcDRGQT09&menu_id=Tm8zcnRjdVRNWWlp-WjRlbmtlaDk1UT 09

Department of Statistics Malaysia (2022a). Population and Housing Census of Malaysia 2020. https://www.dosm.gov.my/v1/index.php?r=column/cthemeByCat &cat=117&bul_id=akliVWdIa2g3Y2VubTVSMkxmYXp1UT09&menu_id=L0 pheU43NWJwRWVSZklWdzQ4TlhUUT09

Department of Statistics Malaysia (2022b). Marriage and Divorce Statistic 2021. https://www.dosm.gov.my/v1/index.php?r=column/cthemeByCat&cat=453 &bul_id=RWwxcjBJeERmcnNlYnZnYVZYR0VKUT09&menu_id=L0 pheU43NWJwRWVSZklWdzQ4TlhUUT09

Department of Statistics Malaysia (2022c). Labour Force Survey (LFS). https://www .dosm.gov.my/v1/index.php?r=column/cthemeByCat&cat=124&bul_id=bU9ybE FIM2UrUlpxa2g4M1JkOFhTdz09&menu_id=Tm8zcnRjdVRNWWlpWjRlbmt-laDk1UT09

Diduck, A. (1995). The unmodified family: The child support act and the construction of legal subjects. *Journal of Law and Society, 22*(4), 527–548.

Evans, M. (2011). Single mothers in Malaysia: Social protection as an exercise of definition in search of solution. The International Conference: Social Protection for Social Justice, UK. https://www.ids.ac.uk/download.php?file=files/dmfile/Evans 2011Singlemothersandsocialprot ectioninMalaysiaCSPconferencedraft.pdf

Duncan, S., and Edwards, R. (1999). *Lone mothers, paid work and gendered moral rationalities*. London: Macmillan.

Hashim, I.H., Azman, A.A., and Endut, N. (2015). Stress, roles and responsibilities of single mothers in Malaysia. *SHS Web of Conferences, 18*(4). https://www.research gate.net/publication/281736666_Stress_Roles_and_Responsibilities_of_Single _Mothers_in_Malaysia

Hathout, M. (2007). A Quranic Perspective on Polygamy. https://www.islamicity.org/ 3079/a- quranic-perspective-on-polygamy/

Herd, P., and Moynihan, D.P. (2018). *Administrative burdens: Policymaking by other means*. Russell Sage Foundation.

International Labour Organization (2021). Differences Between Male and Female Labour Force Participation Rates. https://www.ilo.org/infostories/en-GB/Stories/ Employment/barriers-women#global-gap/gap-labour-force

Ismail, W.A.F., Baharuddin, A.S., Mutalib, L.A., Mamat, Z., and Shukor, S.A. (2020). A comparative study of the illegitimate child term from Shariah and Malaysia legal perspective. *Humanities & Social Sciences Reviews*, *8*(4), 101–109.

Ismail, M.H., and Sulong, J. (2020). Enforcement child-maintenance payment using judgement debtor summons and judicial notice: A Penang case study. *International Journal of Academic Research in Business and Social Sciences*, *10*(7), 187–200.

Jones, G.W. (2021). Divorce in Malaysia: Historical trends and contemporary issues. *Institutions and Economies*, *13*(4), 35–60.

Jusoh, M.N., and Latada, F. (2020). The challenges faced by single mothers in Malaysia during the Covid-19 pandemic. *Jurnal al-Sirat*, *19*, 80–87.

Kamarudin, Z. (1993). *A comparative study of divorce among Muslims and non-Muslims in Malaysia with special reference to the federal territory of Kuala Lumpur* [Doctoral thesis, University of London]. https://discovery.ucl.ac.uk/id/eprint/13 17888/1/296224.pdf

Lim, W.M., Badiozaman, I.F.A., and Voon, M.L. (2020). Barriers to workforce re-entry among single mothers: Insights from urban areas in Sarawak, Malaysia. *Journal of International Women's Studies*, *21*(6), 427–449.

McKenzie, H., and Cook, K. (2015). 'It should be a big responsibility': Separated low-income mothers' evaluation of child support arrangements and the conduct of fathers. *Australian Journal of Family Law*, *29*, 135–156.

Md Nor, Z. (2022). Precarious employment amongst low income single mothers in Malaysia: The implications on family wellbeing. *E3S Web of Conferences 339, 10th ICMR-2nd INSAEF 2021*. https://www.e3s-conferences.org/articles/e3sconf/pdf/2022/06/e3sconf_10icmr- 2insaef2022_06009.pdf

Md Nor, Z., Abu Hasan, I.S., Omar, B., Vellymalay, S.K.N., and Omar, A. (2018). Financial wellbeing of single mothers in Penang: The sole breadwinner. *Management & Accounting Review Journal*, *17*(1), 35–44.

Md Nor, Z., Mohamad, N.Z., Vellymalay, S.K.N., Omar, A., and Omar, B (2019). When poverty knocks on the door: Sharing the story of low income single mothers in Kelantan. *International Journal of Engineering Sciences*, *12*(2), 50–56.

Mohd, A. (2019). Malaysia. In Yassari N., Möller L.M., and Najm M.C. (Eds.), *Filiation and the protection of parentless children*, 205–229. T.M.C. Asser Press, The Hague. https://link.springer.com/chapter/10.1007/978–94–6265–311–5_8

Mulia, D.S. (2017). Survival strategies of single mothers among Indigenous ethnics in rural areas: Case study in Kota Belud, Sabah. *Jurnal Kinabalu*.

Najibah, S. (2017). Policies and administrative problems related to divorce women regarding to their financial activities. *Journal of Humanities Insights*, *1*(2), 96–103.

Natalier, K., and Hewitt, B. (2010). It's not just about the money: Non-resident fathers' perspectives on paying child support. *Sociology*, *44*(3), 489–505.

Razak, R. (2022). PM Ismail Sabri Announces RM1,500 Minimum Wage to Start May 1. https://www.malaymail.com/news/malaysia/2022/03/19/pm-ismail-sabri-ann ounc es-rm1500- minimum-wage-to-start-may-1/2048317

Rusyda, H.M., Lukman, Z.M., Subhi, N., Chong, S.T., Abdul Latif, A., Hasrul, H., and Wan Amizah, W.M. (2011). Coping with difficulties: Social inequality and stigma-tization on single mothers with low income households. *Pertanika Journal of Social Science and Humanities*, *19*, 157–162.

Subramaniam, M.S. (2019). Custody law and the welfare of child policy in Malaysia. *International Conference on the Best Interest of the Child – Parenting after Divorce*. https://gaikokuho.org/wp-content/uploads/2019/04/EDITED-Custody-Mogana-wo -DOI.pdf

Suzana, A., Roslina, C.S., and Najibah, M.Z. (2017). Application of shared parenting in Malaysia: Appraising the Australian experience. *Pertanika Journal of Social Sciences & Humanities, 25*, 293–300.

The Star (2020). Govt revises poverty line income from RM980 to RM2,208. https://www.thestar.com.my/news/nation/2020/07/10/govt-revises-poverty-line-income-from- rm980-to-rm2208

Topimin, S., Fabeil, N., and Abdullah, A. (2019). Women's business survival: Challenges and strategies for single mother entrepreneurs. *Academic Journal of Business and Social Sciences, 3*, 1–10.

Turner, K.J., and Waller, M.R. (2017). Indebted relationships: Child support arrears and non-resident fathers' involvement with children. *Journal of Marriage and Family, 79*(1), 24–43.

United Nations Children's Fund (2021). Families on the Edge. https://www.unicef.org/malaysia/families-edge

10. The child support system and women's access to child support in Nigeria

Olanike S. Adelakun[1] and Adedayo Adelakun[2]

INTRODUCTION

Child support is a continuous, periodic payment given by a parent, who is usually separated or divorced, or a guardian, for the financial benefit of a child from a marriage or other partnership. Nigeria operates on legal pluralism with statutory law, various customary laws and Islamic law all recognised thereby bringing about complexities in several aspects of personal laws, including child support and maintenance. The complexity of child protection is further manifested in the legislative power division which makes it impossible to have a uniform regulatory regime for child support in Nigeria. This is because there is no uniform federal law on child welfare in Nigeria because child welfare is a matter reserved for the residual list of the Nigerian Constitution, not being a matter listed in the concurrent list. The legislative powers in the Constitution are divided into the exclusive list and the concurrent list with matters not listed in either being the residual list. Matters listed in the exclusive list are legislated upon only by the Federal government and the laws are uniform. Matters listed in the concurrent list are within the legislative powers of the Federal government and the states of the federation. The Federal government enacts laws in this respect for the Federal Capital Territory (FCT) while each state enacts for its respective constituency. This therefore means that each state of the Federation is saddled with the responsibility of enacting appropriate laws for the welfare of the children resident in the state.

This chapter examines child support in Nigeria by providing insight into the determining factors from the plurality of laws. Noting that child support cannot be detached from child custody, the chapter examines the rules governing child

---

[1]   Senior Lecturer, Lead City University, Ibadan, Nigeria
[2]   LL.M Candidate, Lead City University, Ibadan, Nigeria.

custody in Nigeria and consequently how child support plays out according to the rules.

SOCIETAL CONTEXT

Nigeria operates a plural legal system comprising Received English Law (as a result of colonisation), Customary law and Islamic law. These laws operate to reflect indigenous laws and state law. Nigeria, on the Gulf of Guinea, is a big, heavily populated West African country that shares borders with Benin, Niger, Chad, and Cameroon. Standing on a land mass of 924,000 square meters, Nigeria is a 36-state federation with the Federal Capital Territory; the country is a multi-ethnic country with a diverse culture with over 250 ethnic groups and about 521 languages spoken across the country (Mobolaji, et al., 2020). Nigeria is a religiously diverse country, with Islam and Christianity being the two most popular religions. Nigerians are almost evenly split between Muslims and Christians, with a small minority of African traditional religions and other faiths.

Nigeria is one of the countries with the highest fertility rate with a birth rate of 5.32 per woman of reproductive age (O'Neill, 2022). Nigeria has a population of about 206.1 million out of which about 52.4 per cent are children (Commonwealth). It is important to note that this population data is based on projections since the last census conducted in Nigeria in 2006. Nigeria gained independence from the British colony in 1960 and adopted English as its official language. Prior to becoming a stable democracy in 1999, Nigeria went through three years of civil war and various military dictatorships.

While there is evidence of interethnic and inter-religious marriage across Nigeria, the reactions to inter-religious marriages vary across cultures. Among the Fulanis, who are predominantly Muslims, interreligious marriages involving the marriage of a Muslim Fulani woman to a non-Muslim man is prohibited and seen as treason while the marriage of a Muslim man to a non-Muslim woman is encouraged since the woman and her children take after the husband/father's religion (Canada, 2012). However, in the southern parts of Nigeria, religious and ethnic intermarriages are quite common.

Also, internal and international transnational Nigerian families are popular and continue to be on the rise. Approximately one million Nigerians had fled their country to pursue better prospects abroad as of 2010, excluding unauthorised nationals (World Bank, 2011). In addition, many Nigerian children remain behind when their parents travel. Typically, the husband travels outside Nigeria, leaving behind the mother and the children (Caarls and Mazzucato, 2015). Although the exact numbers of children in transnational care are unknown, data show that up to 21 per cent of Nigerian children had at least one biological parent living abroad (NDHS, 2008). The absence of parents has most likely become a regular occurrence in these children's lives. Hacking Immigration Law LLC, an immigration law firm in the United States, reports a high number of Nigerian men filing for divorce shortly after arriving in the United States. This leaves the wife back home with the responsibility of caring for the children of the marriage. It is thus undeniable that children in transnational care are put in a position where the custodial parent or carer has to recover childcare from the parent(s) living apart from the child. This is more essential where the custodial parent is not a working parent.

Importance is placed on the institution of marriage in Nigeria and where a person remains unmarried, such a person stands a chance of being stigmatised. Marriage is tied to creation of family and when an unmarried person gets pregnant, such a person is rejected by family members and the society because pregnancy outside wedlock is perceived as shameful. However, the institution of marriage in Nigeria has experienced fundamental shifts influenced by modernisation and globalisation (Agbontaen-Eghafona, 2021). The Muslim population in the North-east and North-west is significant, and early marriage is common among them with the median marriage age of 16.4 and 15.4 respectively. This means a large percentage of marriage occurs in the teenage years of a girl/woman, thus childbirth starts early in these regions.

While marriage is highly celebrated in Nigeria, in the last couple of decades, the rate of dissolution of marriage and marital separation has taken a spike and it is projected that 32 per cent of marriages will end in dissolution or separation in the first five years while 63 per cent of marriages will come to an end before their 10th year (Olaniyi, 2015). The South and North-east regions had the greatest rates of divorce, while the South-east had the lowest. Previous research reveals that demographic, socioeconomic, and religious factors may be to blame for regional differences (Ntoimo and Akokuwebe, 2010). The high rates of divorce in the Northern regions, notably the North-east, could be attributed to a culture of early marriage, polygamy, ease of divorce among Muslims, and a low rate of education for women and girls (Izugbara and Ezeh, 2010). Approximately one million women between the ages of 20–85 were reported to be either divorced or separated from their husbands in 2014 while about 1.7 million were reported to be widowed (Ovuorie, 2020). As of 2009, over a million women have been reported to be without their husbands in Kano state alone. In 2018, a 14 per cent increase in divorce led to about 3,000 marriage dissolutions recorded in only one judicial district of Lagos State (Economist, 2016) while 4,000 divorce petitions were filed within 2 months in the Federal Capital Territory (FCT) in 2020 (Sunday, 2020). The numbers however reflect only petitions to dissolve statutory law marriage.

Marriage contracts in Nigeria could be by way of statutory law, customary law or Islamic law. Dissolution of customary law marriage or Islamic law marriage could either be orally or initiated at the customary court or Sharia court, respectively. It is therefore impossible to keep track of the statistics of married, divorced, separated or co-habiting persons in Nigeria. For instance, it was reported in Kano that only 32 per cent of marriages survive a period of 3–6 months and many divorced women between the ages of 20–25 have gone through at least three marriages leading to the coining of a term known as 'serially divorced' applied to women below 30 years of age (Yusof and Mashi, 2015).

The rate of remarrying is also unknown. For religious reasons and to prevent promiscuity, it is highly encouraged to remarry in some parts of the North (Solivetti, 1994) to the extent that the government takes up the responsibility of screening suitors and conducting mass marriage for divorced and widowed women (BBC, 2012). The rate of remarriage is often not publicised in other parts of Nigeria. It is therefore safe to say that the true statistics of marriage rate, separation and divorce rate as well as remarriage rate in Nigeria are unknown.

With the prevalence of divorce in Nigeria, there is a corresponding prevalence rate of single parenthood. UNICEF projects the rate of single parenthood in Nigeria to be under 20 per cent (UNICEF, 2013). Similarly, Ntoimo and Odimegwu (2014) project the rate at 16 per cent, while Tribune reports single parenting as 'becoming a norm' (Akintomide, 2017). Also, due to gender roles in Nigerian society, women mostly end up with children as single parents and in most instances, these women are economically disadvantaged with minimal means to care for themselves and their children.

The majority of single mothers have been reported to struggle to provide for their dependents in addition to the social stigma of not living with a man. These factors have been linked to the poor health of children of single mothers due to the inability of the mothers to provide for the nutritional needs of the children compared to children living with both parents (Ntoimo and Odimegwu, 2014). Although there have been interventions aimed at supporting women to attain financial independence, the large population of Nigerian women makes it difficult to reach a larger percentage of the women in need, as a result of which the intervention to support economically disempowered women appears insignificant (Enfield, 2019).

With the unemployment rate steadily increasing from 23.13 per cent in 2018 to 32.5 in 2021 and 33 per cent in 2022 and the poverty line increasing with over 91 million Nigerians living below the line (Ujah and Elebeke, 2022), it is apparent that many Nigerians cannot survive on the minimum monthly wage of N30,000.[3] Even with an average monthly income of N43,200[4] of an

---

[3]   Equivalent of $30 as at October 2023.
[4]   Equivalent of $43.20 as at October 2023.

individual, it is very difficult to survive on this income, especially for a household with dependents. In most Northern households, only the father/husband sustain the family because women are not usually allowed to work, especially in Muslim households, while in most households in the Southern parts both parents mostly contribute to the upkeep of the household. Unfortunately, the threshold of single parenthood falls more on the women in Nigeria and a few per cent of single parents are men, who are likely to be employed or have a steady means of income compared to their female counterpart.

SOCIAL WELFARE CONTEXT

Nigeria, from a legal standpoint, does not have a single legal culture, but rather embraces a variety of legal cultures, which are largely dependent on individual state governments. While common law is prevalent in Nigeria, it is complemented by municipal law, customary law, and Sharia law. This can lead to inconsistencies in the enforcement of some rights, as well as conflicts (Allix, 2021).

However, regulation of statutory marriage and disputes that may arise from such marriage are within the exclusive legislative power of the federal state. Thus the Matrimonial Causes Act (MCA) which regulates statutory marriage and incidental disputes in Nigeria is a federal law which applies uniformly across Nigeria. Thus, the custody and maintenance of children of a statutory marriage are regulated by this law.

Furthermore, Nigeria implemented the earlier ratified UN Convention on the Rights of the Child (CRC) in 2003, in line with the requirement of section 12 of the Constitution, by enacting the Child's Rights Act (CRA). The CRA, being a piece of legislation under the concurrent list, is only applicable in the Federal Capital Territory (Federal capital) and thus has to be explicitly enacted in every state of the federation in order for it to be operational in the states (Adelakun, 2018). As at February 2022, only 28 states out of the 36 states of Nigeria have enacted the CRA with nine northern states outstanding. The basis of discussion in this chapter is therefore focused on the CRA, being the model law for all the states in Nigeria that have adopted the law.

The CRA is the first legislation that provides a rights-based approach to child custody in Nigeria. The CRA established a family court which has jurisdiction in custody placements. The court is empowered to make a custody order including the right of access to a non-custodial parent. The CRA emphasises the best interests of the child to be of paramount consideration in all actions regarding the child.

However, in the event of the dissolution of a customary law marriage of the parents, the children are customarily seen as belonging to the father and thus custody orders favour the fathers (Ntoimo, 2021). The sole custodial right of the father extends to the father's family mainly because Nigeria is largely a patrilineal cultural society. However, a woman may be granted custody of minor children at the time of the divorce, but this is only a temporary arrangement until the child reaches an appropriate age that the father may be able to care for the child (Onokah, 2003). The Supreme court has however ruled that the exclusive custody right of the father over the child of customary law marriage will not be enforced where it is detrimental to the child.[5]

Custody of children of Islamic law marriages, which is predominant in the northern region of Nigeria, is usually granted to the mother in line with Islamic law principles (Adelakun-Odewale, 2014). According to Islamic law, a mother has custody of a male child till age seven, which is presumed to be the age at which the child is capable of taking care of himself and she has the custody of a female child till she reaches the age of puberty (Omar, 2019). The father however has the obligation to support the child fully.

Childcare and maintenance, statutorily, is the primary duty of the parents or guardian of the child. There is minimal childcare support by the state and the support is only limited to children in state care such as orphanages. Also, Nigeria has no social security in the form of unemployment insurance, children's benefits, disability benefits, or food aid. While some ad hoc programs provide assistance, the World Bank reported in 2019 that only 2 per cent of households in Nigeria, and only approximately 4 per cent of the poor, have access to them (Ewang, 2021). With the lack of a more structured method to reach those in need, efforts to scale up cash transfer programs and provide food during the COVID pandemic were severely constrained.

Similarly, there is no requirement for post separation counselling in Nigeria. While there are a few private marriage counsellors in Nigeria, many divorced and separated couples are reluctant to make use of these services due to factors such as lack of finances, stigmatisation, and lack of public support institutions, among others (Bokko, 2014). The downside of this is that several persons may have to go through post-separation depression, including the children, without any form of psychosocial support. This may end up having a long term effect on the resident parent as well as the children.

CHILD SUPPORT

There is no legislation specifically regulating child support in Nigeria but the issue of child support is always linked with the dissolution of marriage or judicial separation as well as child custody, as regulated by the MCA. Hence,

---

[5]   *Febisola Okwueze v Paul Okwueze* (1989) 3 NWLR [pt 109] 321; *Williams v Williams* (1981) 1 QLRN 122.

child support in Nigeria follows the plural laws, depending on the nature of marriage conducted by the parents. In all three forms of marriage in Nigeria, child custody is always a predetermining factor for child support and child custody order is always a consequence of a court order arising from marriage disputes in most cases. However, child custody could be based on mutual agreement of the parents, even in the absence of non-judicial separation (Adelakun-Odewale, 2014).

In determining the joint or sole custody of a child of a statutory marriage, an order of dissolution of the marriage or judicial separation must be sought in a litigious manner in the High Court with the judge having a wide discretion to grant the custody of the child to either the father or mother of the child. Statutory marriage in Nigeria confers equal rights on both spouses in every aspect of the marriage but the court has a responsibility to make a custody order as it deems proper but with regard to the best interests of the child.

Nigerian courts have however been criticised for treating child custody and maintenance issues as 'a matter of right and denial of right almost exclusively for the parties to divorce' (Attah, 2016). This is due to the influence of the patriarchal cultural norms which sees a child as the property of the father on the judicial system. Also, despite acquiring equal rights under statutory marriage, the society places the responsibility of maintaining the wife and children solely on the husband as the head of the household. Courts are therefore cautioned in determining the custody of children solely on the information provided by the parties to divorce or separation proceedings since the relationship between such spouses may have turned sour and custody of the children is often used as a tool of exercising power over each other. It is therefore important for courts to explore the provisions of section 71(2) of the MCA which permits the court to rely on reports made by welfare officers in respect of children to determine the appropriate parent to award custody to. This provision of the law however seems to be under-utilised due to lack of resources and corruption which may make the welfare officer tilt the report towards the party that mobilises him/her.

Establishment of a Child Support Order

A resident parent has a duty to apply for child support along with the child custody application or judicial dissolution of a marriage. However, a judge may, within the wide discretionary powers of the court and without a formal application, make an order as to child support in the best interests of the child. The court also has the discretion to increase the amount of child support from what is claimed by the resident parent where it is in the best interests of the child. However, there is no compulsory duty on the court to make a child support order, especially where the parents have a mutual agreement on the child support arrangement.

Section 14(2) of the CRA recognises child support as a right of the child by providing that 'every child has the right to maintenance by his parents or guardians in accordance with the extent of their means, and the child has the right, in appropriate circumstances, to enforce this right in the Family Court.' The court is empowered to order the non-resident parent to pay a stipulated amount of child support to the resident parent in respect of the child. Unfortunately, the CRA failed to take a stand on the procedure of instituting an action in court by a child to enforce the child's maintenance right. Thus, the requirement of suing through the legal guardian stands.

Statutorily, the court may make a child support order in respect of children of a statutory marriage who are less than 21 years old but where the circumstances justify the court may make such an order in respect of children above 21 years old; for instance, if the child is still in school or has special needs. In this case, the court usually considers the means of the parties, their earning capacity, conduct of the parties and other relevant circumstances (Attah, 2016). Unfortunately, information that assists the court in assessing the circumstances to arrive at a just amount of child support is provided by the parties through their pleadings which may be admitted or denied by the parties and in the absence of sufficient proof, the court is left with no choice but to make an order of child support based on the evidence before it. This is usually more difficult where the paying spouse is self-employed.

Since custody is mostly granted to the father under customary law, the father has no child support claim against the mother, even where the mother is more financially buoyant than the father but where exception is made in granting custody to the mother or where the mother retains custody due to the tender age of the child (for instance before weaning a child), the father is under an obligation to maintain the child. The Nigerian customary rules do not recognise a man's right to claim maintenance from his wife. The divorced wife, on the other hand, has the right to seek support for herself and her children. Similarly under Islamic law, the duty of child support lies with the father until a male child attains puberty and until a female child gets married.

The Federal Ministry of Women Affairs and Child Development (as well as Ministries of the states) have administrative duties to mediate in child support cases by inviting disputing parties and getting the parties to agree on the amount of child support. Where a mother has custody of the child either by court order or private arrangement of the parents themselves, the father is usually made to commit to making a weekly, bi-weekly or monthly payment to a resident mother towards the maintenance of the children. This action is usually initiated by a resident mother by making a complaint against the father at the appropriate department of the state Ministry. Social workers contacted for this chapter revealed that there is no record of a man claiming child support through the Ministry, largely due to the societal perception that the father, as the head of the family, is fully responsible for the maintenance of his children. A father that avoids this responsibility, whether in view of court order or not, is perceived by society as an irresponsible father. The duty of the Ministry is complemented by the National Human Rights Commission of every state as well as several non-governmental organisations and civil societies.

In most cases where a claim for child support must go through litigation, the resident parent bears the cost of litigation. However, where the litigant is entitled to legal aid services, the legal aid is supposed to take up the cost but, in reality, the claimant is still required to pay 'unofficial fees' for filing and logistics. Interviews with single mothers seeking dissolution of their marriages and child support through legal aid in various states revealed that they are required to make payment ranging from N10,000 –N50,000.[6] To many of the interviewees, the reason why they sought legal aid was to save the cost of litigation and several revealed that they will have to forget about the process since they could not afford to make such payment (Adelakun, 2021).

Assessment and Calculation

While the court has wide discretion in making child support orders, there are defined standards for determining the amount to be paid which reflect the means, earning capacity, conduct of the parties and all relevant circumstances. Means of the parties include capital assets and prospective assets as well as pecuniary resources of the parties which may be actual or contingent. Earning capacity of the parties includes the actual and potential earnings of the parties. Furthermore, in calculating child support, on a case-by-case basis, the child's financial needs, income, earning capacity, property, physical or mental disability, and the manner in which the child is being or is projected to be raised must all be taken into account (Adelakun-Odewale, 2014).

In considering the conduct of the parties to determine child support, the misconduct often taken into consideration by Nigerian courts relates to the economic conduct of a party during the period of the marriage or separation. For example, where a father refuses to support the family during the period, the court tends to compensate the resident mother by raising economic fault on the part of the father while the court may order a nominal amount of child support where the father is economically virtuous. While the court may not consider the behavioural misconduct of the parties, the following have been held in

---

[6]   Equivalent of $10-$50 as at October 2023.

Menakaya v Menakaya (1996) to be important in arriving at a just assessment of child support:

(a) The income, earning capacity, property and other financial resources which each of the parties has or is likely to have in the foreseeable future;
(b) The financial needs, obligations, and responsibilities which each of the parties has or is likely to have in the foreseeable future;
(c) The standard of living enjoyed by the family before the breakdown of the marriage;
(d) The age of each party to the marriage and the duration of the marriage;
(e) Any physical or mental disability of either of the parties to the marriage;
(f) The contributions made by each of the parties to the welfare of the family including any contribution made by looking after the house and caring for the family; and
(g) In the case of proceedings for divorce or nullity of marriage, the value of either party to any benefit like a pension, which by reason of the dissolution or annulment of the marriage that party will lose the chance of acquiring.

Although the means and income of the parties must be taken into consideration in determining child support, parties have a duty to make this information available and, where this is not done, the resident parent may apply to the court to get a certificate of means of the other parent which is done by assessing the capacity of the parties to earn as well as the resources of the parties. The court may also take evidence on oath from the parents and failure to disclose may lead to prosecution for perjury but this appears to be ineffective because parties still lie under oath and many get away with it without being prosecuted (Adelakun-Odewale, 2014).

While there is no minimum or maximum bar to the amount of child support order that the court or administrative body may make, the child support may be an order for a lump sum or a weekly, monthly, yearly or other periodic amount as may be determined. Also, the order may be to secure the lump sum or periodic amount. The order may also relate to executing a deed or release of title document or to appoint or remove a trustee. The child support order may be paid directly to the resident parent or to the trustee or appointee of the court or any other authority as the court may deem fit.

The approach to calculating child support under customary law is fairly similar to the provision in the MCA. The amount that the father had agreed to before the divorce or separation would serve as a starting point for determining the amount of maintenance to be paid. The court dismissed a father's claim for child support from the estranged wife but rather made an order of child support against him in *Ejimbe v Ejimbe* (1989). Under the principles of Islamic law, which is prevalent in northern Nigeria, parents are at liberty to agree on the amount of child support but where the parents cannot reach an agreement, the *Kadi* (Sharia court judge) or the *Sheik* that solemnised the marriage, after evaluating the father's means, must decide on the sum for child support. The father's status and the child's previous standard of living would be taken into account when calculating child support based on this approach (Adelakun-Odewale, 2014).

Collection

Evidence abounds that parties that are responsible for payment of child support in Nigeria (often the fathers) mostly default on such payments and the resident parents (mostly the mothers), rather than go to court to enforce payments, often struggle to raise their children on whatever income that they are able to make in addition to family support (Uzodike, 1990). This further highlights the gap in the lack of specific law to recover child support. Nigeria ratified the CRC as well as the African Charter on the Rights and Welfare of the Child (ACRWC) and gave domestic effect to these instruments in 2003 by enacting the CRA. However, Nigeria is not a party to child support specific international instruments such as the Hague Convention on the International Recovery of Child Support and Other Forms of Family Maintenance and Hague Convention on the Civil Aspects of International Child Abduction.

Thus, the basic laws that regulate child support in Nigeria are the MCA, MCR, CRA, Child Rights Laws of various states, customary law and Islamic law. Hence, the lack of uniformity in child support laws and process is a major hindrance to effective child support determination and recovery in Nigeria.

When a party fails to pay child support as directed by the court, the resident parent may make an *ex parte* application to the High Court for an attachment of earnings order. Such *ex parte* application will be supported by an affidavit stating the details of the child support order, the outstanding amount, details of actions taken by the applicant to recover the outstanding amount, as well as details of the employer of the defaulting parent and the place of work. The court will thereafter evaluate the application and supporting affidavit and where satisfied, make an attachment of earnings order. Where this order is made, the applicant must file a copy of the order with the court's Registrar, who will ensure that a sealed copy of the order is served on everyone who is obliged by law to receive a sealed copy.

Where it can be established that a person has defaulted in four weekly instalments or two instalments in other periodic payments or where it is clear that the defaulter has wilfully and persistently refused to pay child support, the court may order the defaulter's employer to deduct the child support directly from the defaulting parent's earnings. The order to the employer shall indicate the amount and the court's officer to whom payment shall be made. Where an employer fails to comply with the earnings attachment order, such employer shall be prosecuted and if convicted, be liable to pay a fine not exceeding N200 and the employer may raise a defence of taking reasonable steps to comply with the order. In reality, these provisions of the law are not usually invoked to compel a defaulting parent to pay child support. While there is a gap in the literature as to the factors responsible for this, it appears that the stigmatisation associated with single motherhood, cost of court processes and the delay in court matters, which may drag on for years, may be attributed to the failure of parties to take advantage of the law. Again, the fine for defaulting (maximum of $0.48 without option of imprisonment) is so insignificant that it is not worth exploring legal options to get a defaulting parent to pay. Since the law is ineffective, it is not surprising that many defaulters will flaunt the law just to 'punish' the resident parent. In most cases, where the court denies a father of custody and awards a child support order against the father, the father 'deals' with the mother by refusing to comply with the child support order, especially where the mother is economically incompetent. This is a strategy used to compel the mother to take the children back to their father so that the children will not suffer hardships.

Possibly, the attitude of defaulters would differ if the punishment is stringent such as imprisonment and publishing the names of defaulters in a child support defaulter database. Unfortunately, the lack of specific legislation and effective recovery mechanisms on child support have rendered this aspect of child protection unrealistic in Nigeria. Furthermore, a defaulter is permitted to raise a defence of 'reasonable steps to comply with the order' but the MCA fails to explain the steps that will be deemed reasonable in this context. It is also disheartening that despite the embrace of technology in every sphere of life in Nigeria, there have been no steps taken technologically to keep records of child support orders and to facilitate hitch-free payments. Currently, all Nigerians are required to have a National Identification Number (NIN) which is linked to every government database and every registered sim card as well as banking details of every Nigerian who operates a bank account in Nigeria. Also, the requirement of a Bank Verification Number (BVN) which creates a banking database of all bank users is an essential database to ensure that no individual operates bank accounts under different names. If the political will is present to effectively protect the best interests of the child in respect of child support, efforts should be made to sensitise the public on the importance of payment of child support as well as the need to report defaulters. Where this is done, child support orders can be linked directly to the bank of the defaulting party.

Where a child support order is made by a foreign court, the order may be registered in a High Court in Nigeria if the foreign court is in a country that has a bilateral agreement with Nigeria. Where the order is registered in a High

Court in Nigeria, the order will have the same effect as if it was made by a Nigerian court and the amount due may be recovered as a judgement debt. Thus, the procedure for recovery of judgement debt could be by attachment of earnings, garnishee order or by any means approved by the court.

Where a child support order is made by customary court, the order is usually to make the payment to the court from where the resident parent makes collection. Where a party defaults, the customary court tries to mediate and appeal to the father to make payment but where he continues to comply, he may be remanded for a few days to ensure that he pays. Where this approach fails, the mother may continue to appeal to the father's relatives or resort to public shaming. Where all approaches fail, the mother is left to care for her children by whatever means she can and the state is not of much help in this aspect. A similar approach applies in the northern region where parties in question are subject to Islamic law.

In recent times, there have been several interventions by the government, international organisations as well as NGOs by way of livelihood projects targeted at improving the economic abilities of women in Nigeria. With the reality that single parenthood is rapidly on the increase with a majority being single mothers without means of livelihood, the need for entrepreneurship empowerment, rather than dependence on a recalcitrant ex-husband/partner, is gradually gaining ground (Kayode, 2018).

STICKING POINTS AND FUTURE CHALLENGES

Having established that the diversity and multi-ethnic nature of Nigeria contributes to the law and welfare of the child, the approach to child welfare differs in Nigeria. Also, factors such as teenage pregnancy, divorce, separation, transnational families, widowhood and more recently, choice has contributed to an increase in the rate of single parenthood in Nigeria. Unlike in the 1980s and 1990s where grandparents stepped in to care for children, the economic situation of Nigeria makes it quite difficult for extended family relatives to continue the trend of care like it used to be. The unemployment rate has also contributed to the inability and refusal of non-resident parents to support their children and the institutional framework for recovery appears to be very weak, thereby leaving many children with only one parental support or to cater for themselves. The lack of a social security system in Nigeria also affects the ability to have a structured child support system in place.

It is therefore pertinent to take legislative steps to move child welfare to the exclusive list of the Constitution such that the Federal Government will be able to make uniform child protection laws that recognise the diversity of the Nigerian population. There is also a need to establish a structured institutional framework that will make use of technology to track child support orders and to make recovery easy. Finally, there is a need to move away from the approach of child welfare from 'ownership' approach to a 'rights' approach in order to safeguard the growth and development of every child in Nigeria.

REFERENCES

Adelakun, O. S. (2021). The influence of community leaders on the Criminal Justice System of gender-based violence in West Africa: A case study of Nigeria and Ghana. *Organization, 4*.

Adelakun, O. S. (2018). Application of the subsidiarity principle in intercountry adoption in Nigeria: Lessons from South Africa. *Journal of Comparative Law in Africa, 5*(2), 22–44.

Adelakun-Odewale, O. (2014). 'Recovery of child support in Nigeria' in *The recovery of maintenance in the EU and worldwide*. Oxford: Hart Publishing.

Agbontaen-Eghafona, K. (2021). The changing phases of African marriage and family: Perspectives on Nigeria in the African context http://www.pass.va/content/scienzesociali/en/events/2019–23/family_ecology/agbontaen-eghafona.html. Accessed 12 January, 2022.

Akintomide, B. (2017). Perils of single parenting. *Tribune* https://tribuneonlineng.com/perils-single-parenting/. Accessed 12 January, 2022.

Allix, L. (2021). Children of Nigeria: Realizing children's rights in Nigeria. *Humanium* https://www.humanium.org/en/nigeria/ Accessed 17 September, 2021.

Attah, M. (2016). *Family Welfare Law in Nigeria.* Benin: Ambik Press.

BBC. (2012). 'Nigerian Kano divorcees marry in mass ceremony' *BBC* https://www.bbc.com/news/world-africa-18072118. Accessed 12 January, 2022.

Bokko, I. T. (2014). Marriage and divorce counselling strategies in Borno State, Nigeria. *Sokoto Educational Review, 15*(2), 63–68.

Caarls, K., and Mazzucato, V. (2015). Does international migration lead to divorce? Ghanaian couples in Ghana and abroad. *Population, 70*(1), 127–151.

Canada: Immigration and Refugee Board of Canada. (2012). 'Nigeria: social attitudes toward religious intermarriage; treatment of intermarried couples and their children by society and the authorities; protection and services available to intermarried couples' https://www.refworld.org/docid/50c8482d2.html. Accessed 8 February, 2022.

Constitution of the Federal Republic of Nigeria, 1999.

Enfield, S. (2019). Gender roles and inequalities in the Nigerian labour market. K4D Helpdesk Report. Brighton, UK: Institute of Development Studies. https://assets.publishing.service.gov.uk/media/5d9b5c88e5274a5a148b40e5/597_Gender_Roles_in_Nigerian_Labour_Market.pdf. Accessed 12 March, 2022.

Ewang, A. (2021). 'Hunger during the pandemic shows Nigeria's social security gaps' *Human Rights Watch,* https://www.hrw.org/news/2021/08/19/hunger-during-pandemic-shows-nigerias-social-security-gaps#:~:text=Nigeria%20has%20no%20social%20security,Nigeria%20had%20access%20to%20them. Accessed 19 December, 2021.

Izugbara, C. O., and Ezeh, A. C. (2010). Women and high fertility in Islamic northern Nigeria. *Studies in Family Planning, 41*(3), 193–204.

Kayode, G. M. (2018). Entrepreneurial empowerment of single mothers in Ekiti State, Nigeria. *IOSR Journal of Research & Method in Education, 4*.

Matrimonial Causes Act 1977.

Matrimonial Causes Rules 1977.

Mobolaji, J. W., Fatusi, A. O., and Adedini, S. A. (2020). Ethnicity, religious affiliation and girl-child marriage: A cross-sectional study of nationally representative sample of female adolescents in Nigeria. *BMC Public Health, 20*(1), 1–10.

NDHS. (2008). 'Nigeria demographic and health survey 2008' http://www.dhsprogram .com/. Accessed 21 January, 2022.

Ntoimo, L. F. C. (2021). 'Customary law in Nigeria favours men over children in custody cases' *The Conversation* https://theconversation.com/customary-law-in -nigeria-favours-men-over-children-in-custody-cases-154420. Accessed 16 September, 2021.

Ntoimo, L. F. C., and Akokuwebe, M.E. (2010). Prevalence and patterns of marital dissolution in Nigeria. *Nigerian Journal of Sociology and Anthropology, 12*(2).

Ntoimo, L. F., and Odimegwu, C. O. (2014). Health effects of single motherhood on children in sub-Saharan Africa: A cross-sectional study. *BMC Public Health, 14*(1), 1–13.

O'Neill, A. (2022). 'Fertility rate in Nigeria 2009–2019' https://www.statista.com/ statistics/382212/fertility-rate-in-nigeria/. Accessed 3 February, 2022.

Olaniyi, A. A. (2015). Analytical study of the causal factors of divorce in African homes. *Research on Humanities and Social Sciences, 5*(14), *18.*

Omar, M. L. (2019). 'Custody and guardianship of children: Shari'a perspective' (Paper presented at the Refresher Course for Judges and Kadis at the Nigerian Judicial Institute, Abuja, 11–15 March, 2019) https://nji.gov.ng/wp-content/uploads/ 2019/03/CUSTODY-GUARDIANSHIP-FINAL.pdf. Accessed 23 October, 2021.

Onokah, M. C. (2003). *Family law.* Ibadan: Spectrum Books.

Ovuorie, T. (2020). The challenge of single mothers in Nigeria (Part 2) *HumAngle* https://humangle.org/the-challenge-of-single-mothers-in-nigeria-part-2/. Accessed 12 January, 2022.

Sasu, D. D. (2022). Forecast unemployment rate in Nigeria 2021–2022 *Statista* https://www.statista.com/statistics/1119227/forecast-unemployment-rate-in-nigeria/ . Accessed 13 February, 2022.

Solivetti, L. M. (1994). Family, marriage and divorce in Hausa community: A sociological model. *Africa, 64*(2), 252.

Sunday, T. (2020). 4,000 divorce cases in 2 months: Which way family values? *Blueprint* https://www.blueprint.ng/4000-divorce-cases-in-2-months-which-way-fa mily-values/. Accessed 12 January, 2022.

The Commonwealth, 'Nigeria,' https://thecommonwealth.org/our-member-countries/ nigeria. Accessed 17 September, 2021.

The Economist (2016). 'Divorce in Nigeria: Rings fall apart – official statistics vastly understate Nigeria's divorce rate.' 7 July, 2016. https://www.economist.com/middle -east-and-africa/2016/07/07/rings-fall-apart. Accessed 12 January, 2022.

Ujah, E., and Elebeke, E. (2022). '91m Nigerians fall below poverty line – NESG' *Vanguard* https://www.vanguardngr.com/2022/01/91m-nigerians-fall-below-poverty-li ne-nesg/. Accessed 13 February, 2022.

UNICEF. (2013). *Improving child nutrition: The achievable imperative for global progress.* New York: United Nations Children's Fund.

Uzodike, E. N. (1990). Custody of children in Nigeria: Statutory, judicial and customary aspects. *The International and Comparative Law Quarterly, 39*(2), 419.

World Bank. (2011). *Migration and remittances factbook 2011.* Washington, DC: World Bank.

World Bank. (2021). 'The World Bank in Nigeria' https://www.worldbank.org/en/country/nigeria/overview#1. Accessed 18 January, 2022.

Yusof, R., and Mashi, A. L. (2015). An assessment of 'Zawarawa' mass marriage programme, in Kano State, Nigeria. *International Journal of Social Science and Humanity*, 5(10), 849.

11. United Kingdom and the child support system

Christine Skinner

INTRODUCTION

This chapter provides information on the socio-economic circumstances of single parents in the UK and the operation of the child support system, which is called the Child Maintenance Service. It begins by setting the societal population context before discussing the key future challenges faced in the UK regarding child maintenance (child support) policy.

SOCIETAL CONTEXT

Population Size

The UK population has been steadily increasing despite the total fertility rate remaining consistently low. The population size was 66.4m people in 2018, projected to rise to 69.4m in 2028. Of the four countries that make up the UK, England's population is the largest at 56m people, followed by Scotland at 5.4m, Wales 3.1m and Northern Ireland 1.9m (ONS, 2019). This latest data was published in October 2019, prior to the COVID-19 pandemic and before Brexit, which means that future projections on death rates and migration flows will be substantially different. Note that statistical data on England and Wales are often combined and unless otherwise stated, this chapter will focus on England and Wales not least because they share the same legal and child maintenance systems (Scotland and NI schemes differ slightly) (ONS, 2019).

The total fertility rate in England and Wales has remained below replacement level since 1973. Currently it stands at 1.65 children per woman and continues to fall (ONS, 2020a). In the late 1990s however, political concerns arose about a sub-section of the single parent population, teenage single parent families. Their overall numbers were increasing and the UK had the highest teenage pregnancy rates in Europe. This alarmed politicians who were concerned about the sexual behaviour of teenagers and their assumed ignorance re contraception, their morality and the impact on their life chances of becoming a teenage parent. A Teenage Pregnancy Strategy was set up in 1999 to reduce the rates and by 2018 they had fallen in England and Wales by 62.7 per cent (ONS, 2020b). This was considered a great policy success and there has been less interest in teenage pregnancy rates since. Whilst recognising teenage parents may face different challenges compared to others (education for example), they are included under the overarching term single parent for the rest of this chapter.

Families

There were 19.4 million families in the UK in 2020, up by 7.4 per cent from 2010 (ONS, 2021). The majority of families with dependent children are couple families, with 1–2 children being the most common family size. According to Dromey, Dewar and Finnegan (2020), there were 1.8m single parent families in 2019 in the UK, equivalent to 22 per cent of all families with children. Most (54 per cent) had one child and by far the majority (86 per cent) were headed by women. Importantly, single parent families may also form part of a separated family unit, but not all separated families consist of single parents. It is therefore difficult to measure the size of the separated family population, partly because there is no legal requirement to report separation. The UK therefore relies on estimates using the Family Resources Survey for Great Britain (which excludes Northern Ireland). In 2020, 2.4m separated families with 3.6m children were estimated to live in Great Britain (DWP, 2021a) – a substantial population. Most official data divides families into single parents and couples; 'separated families' are not delineated. Whilst many separated families contain single parents, it is single parent families that are at greater risk of poverty compared to couples even though their employment rates are similar.

Parental Employment

The majority of single parent families are in employment (around 68 per cent), as are mothers in couples (around 78 per cent) (Dromey, Dewar and Finnegan, 2020). Yet, whilst the employment gap between them has narrowed over time, single mothers earned just about half as much as mothers in couple families as they are overrepresented in part-time employment. This is partly because the difference in hourly rates of median pay between full and part-time workers is high and stood at 49 per cent in 2019 (£9.94 for part-time workers and £14.82 for full-time workers). Single parents are also more likely to stay stuck in low pay employment; 33 per cent earn below the 'voluntary living wage' (see definition below) (Dromey, Dewar and Finnegan, 2020, p.8). The pandemic also had a bigger impact on single parents compared to others. Between February and June 2020 single parents' working hours reduced by an average of 26 per cent compared to 21 per cent for couples. Their employment rate and weekly pay was also more severely affected (Dromey, Dewar and Finnegan, 2020, p.11), increasing their risk of poverty to which we now turn.

Poverty

Before considering poverty rates for single parent families, it is important to clarify the measures and the terminology used to protect people's earnings as these can be confusing. For example, the 'voluntary living wage' (sometimes called the 'real living wage') was introduced by the Living Wage Foundation to encourage employers to pay wages based on real living costs (£9.50/hour in 2020). It differs from both the National Minimum Wage (introduced in 1999) and the National Living Wage (introduced in 2016) which are both legally binding. Since April 2020, eligibility for the National Living Wage is for employees aged over 23 years: paid at £8.91/hour. The National Minimum Wage is for employees under 23 years of age and is banded by age group (£8.36 for 21 or 22 year olds: £6.56 for 18 to 20 year olds and £4.62 for those younger than 18 years or apprentices). The Joseph Rowntree Foundation's (JRF) analysis of poverty in the UK in 2020–21, demonstrated that pre-pandemic both the national minimum wage and national living wage had been effective in reducing the rates of hourly low pay since 2014, but had a more modest impact on increasing weekly incomes as low paid employees worked fewer hours (JRF, 2021, p.15). Even so, JRF argue that poverty rates had not changed much over the last 15 years once housing costs are taken into account (based on a relative poverty measure of having less than 60 per cent of the median income 'after housing costs' (JRF, 2021, p.15). Most poverty analysis uses an after housing costs measure, whereas the UK government tends to use before housing costs measures which under-represent poverty rates (Kenway, 2021).

JRF's analysis states that, pre-pandemic, more than one in five people lived in poverty and that both child poverty and in-work poverty were rising. Whilst overall rates of in-work poverty stood at 13 per cent in 2018–19, single parent families suffered the highest rates, with between 25 and 35 per cent experiencing in-work poverty depending on their employment sector. This is partly due to their underemployment and the barriers they face regarding transport and childcare issues (JRF, 2021, pp.24–28). More specifically, the Child Poverty Action Group estimates the child poverty rate, which stood at 49 per cent for all children in single parent families in 2019–20. Overall, there were some 4.3 million children in the UK living in poverty (31 per cent of the child population using a before housing cost measure). Therefore, paid work is not sufficient protection from poverty, with 75 per cent of all children in poverty living in

a household with at least one earner. The rise of in-work poverty is a result
of deterioration in terms of employment, greater employment insecurity,
stagnation in wages, high housing and childcare costs as well as insufficient
social security benefits to supplement low wages (CPAG, 2021). Despite the
majority of single parent families being employed, they work part-time, are
stuck in the low pay sector and around a third experience in-work poverty. This
highlights the difficulties in combining working and caring as single parents.
They have a greater reliance on formal childcare services and social security
benefits than might be the case for couple sole earner families, because one
parent can provide childcare while the other parent works. It is important
therefore to consider the welfare context affecting single parents' employment
opportunities: specifically childcare provision and social security benefits that
provide subsidies to cover some childcare expenses.

SOCIAL WELFARE CONTEXT

Childcare Provision

In the UK, childcare services are run on a mixed economy basis with the
private, voluntary (not for profit) and state sectors running alongside one
another. There is a universal free early-education entitlement of 15 hours
per week for all 3 and 4 year olds, and if their parents are working, there is
an extended 15 hours entitlement per week in England, giving potentially 30
weekly hours of free childcare for working parents during term time (38 weeks
per year). Some children aged two years in low-income families are also entitled to 15 hours of free childcare, but only where their parents are receiving
means-tested social security benefits. There is also a subsidy for eligible childcare costs for all working families in receipt of benefits; up to 85 per cent of
costs are covered up to a pre-set maximum limit (£175 per week for one child
and £300 per week for two or more children).

   Most families, therefore, can receive some help with childcare for children
under school age. However, families with children under 2 years of age are
particularly badly hit because there is no free entitlement available to them,
although if they receive benefits they can still access the childcare subsidy.
However, the subsidy has not kept pace with actual childcare costs which have
risen above inflation. In 2020 a part-time nursery place for a child under two
years of age was 5 per cent higher than the previous year with parents paying
an average of £6,800/annum (Coleman et al., 2020). For single parent families
working full-time with a child under 2 years of age, they could pay as much
as £100 per week to top up the childcare subsidy (Davis et al., 2021, p.11).
Typically, the UK has the highest childcare costs in the OECD, even after
accounting for benefit transfers and free provisions (OECD, 2020). Provision

is also patchy: just over half of local authorities in England (56 per cent) reported they had enough childcare to meet the needs of full-time working parents. Even fewer local authorities in England had sufficient after school provision for children aged 5 to 14 years in all areas (ranging from between 14 per cent to 32 per cent) (Coleman et al., 2020). A lack of affordable childcare is still a significant obstacle to overcome for single parent families trying to combine working and caring, especially when their children are very young. Therefore, many still have to rely on social security benefits if unemployed or to supplement their earnings.

Social Security Benefits

Most recently, the social security benefit system has undergone a radical transformation as it was believed the system had become too complex and expensive to administer. Six highly specific in-work and out-of-work means-tested benefits were combined into a single Universal Credit. Both employed people on low incomes and the unemployed are eligible for Universal Credit. It provides a safety net minimum income and a top-up for low wages. The roll out of Universal Credit has taken a long time; it began in 2013 and is not expected to be completed until 2024, when all legacy benefits will be migrated over (Mackley, 2021). It is a completely online system by default and is paid monthly in arrears (rather than weekly or fortnightly as before under many legacy benefits) and advocacy groups believe it causes budgeting problems for claimants. In February 2021, over 5 million households were claiming Universal Credit and 3.2 million were claiming legacy benefits (Hobson, 2021). This however represents a massive surge of over 3 million claimants as a result of the pandemic starting in March 2020 (Mackley, 2021).

A primary aim of Universal Credit is to ensure people are better off in paid work than on benefits. To make work pay, claimants can work any amount of hours at the same time as receiving Universal Credit with it tapering off as earnings rise. For single parent families, Universal Credit payments alongside the childcare subsidy were intended to facilitate their entry to employment. However, a conditionality framework also underpins eligibility for Universal Credit. The framework sets out claimants' work-search requirements or requirements to increase earned incomes to a set threshold. The unemployed are expected to make work search activities 'a full-time focus'. Failure to meet these requirements results in benefit sanctions. Under Universal Credit these welfare-to-work conditions were extended and intensified and are intended to be punitive and stigmatising. Single parent families are now subject to more stringent and harsher penalties than was the case under the previous benefit system (Andersen, 2020). Even though single parents are treated almost equally to other types of claimants regarding work expectations, they are supposed to be treated more flexibly. For example, childcare constraints that hinder their employment or stop them from meeting the earnings thresholds should be recognised at the discretion of 'work coaches' in Jobcentres and sanctions should not be applied. These measures were intended to recognise the particular challenges facing single parents to simultaneously be the main breadwinner and main carer. However, longitudinal and cross-sectional studies have shown that the work coaches do not understand the flexibility rules well enough resulting in the sanctions regime being unfairly applied to single parents. Moreover, Universal Credit does not achieve its aim of supporting single parents into work and causes undue distress and creates short- and long-term financial hardship (Johnsen and Blenkinsopp, 2018; Rabindrakumar and Dewar, 2018). According to JRF (2021), four in five people living in single parent families are in receipt of income-related benefits and these benefits have been ineffective in preventing families falling into poverty. This is despite the supportive effects of a high percentage of childcare costs covered under the Universal Childcare subsidy. There is also another way in which UK policy has attempted to boost the incomes of single parent families: through the child maintenance system. Child maintenance policy aims to enforce the private financial responsibilities of separated parents to pay maintenance for their children. This policy has however had a chequered history with different aims and outcomes regarding the reduction of poverty.

UK CHILD MAINTENANCE SERVICE IN THE INTERNATIONAL CONTEXT

Overview and Policy Aims

The UK child support system has been mired in controversy ever since the creation of a dedicated agency to assess and enforce child maintenance obligations in 1993 – The Child Support Agency. Introduced under a Conservative government, the original policy main aims were to increase the amounts of child maintenance paid by separated parents (mainly fathers) whilst simultaneously reducing the fiscal costs of paying social security benefits to single parents (mainly mothers). Part of the rationale for the agency was to ensure parents met their private responsibilities. At the time, the first national survey of single parent families showed that only one third received any maintenance and mostly via agreements ordered by the courts or made voluntarily (Loft, 2021). Child poverty reduction was however an assumed policy aim, because the agency was designed to increase payments, especially for single parent families dependent on social security benefits (who were forced to comply with the agency). However, reducing fiscal costs became paramount and this was achieved in multiple ways: by increasing the numbers of single parents on benefits applying to the agency (due to it becoming compulsory), by increasing the average amounts to be paid by fathers and most importantly by retaining all the maintenance payments where the receiving parents were on benefits. Therefore, children in the poorest families (single mothers on benefits) actually received none of the maintenance that was paid and separated fathers were effectively reimbursing the state. Consequently, incentives to comply with the agency were minimal and arguably this was a major factor in the policy losing its legitimacy in the eyes of the public. Many protest groups of angry fathers emerged objecting to paying maintenance that did not benefit their children.

Given the controversy generated by the policy, the Child Support Agency was subject to near constant policy and regulatory reform. However, this exacerbated the problems, not least because by 2003, two separate policies with different operational procedures were being run concurrently (Loft, 2021). Errors were amplified leading to maladministration, the backlog of uncompleted cases increased and a mountain of unrecoverable maintenance debt grew into billions of pounds (HOC, 2022). A major independent review was conducted in 2006 resulting in the Henshaw report (see Loft, 2021). Finally following the Henshaw report the lack of incentives to comply was given some recognition. In part this was due to the fact that the reduction of child poverty had become an explicit policy goal under a Labour government. Correspondingly, two important changes were introduced in 2008: the withdrawal of the compulsion for single parents on benefits to apply to the agency and the full pass through of maintenance payments to receiving parents. This helped reduce some poverty because parents could now keep all the maintenance paid without it reducing their benefits, but this worked only if maintenance was actually paid. Nearly two thirds of parents using the agency did not receive any child maintenance, about the same proportion as in 1993 when the agency first started operations. Clearly non-compliance had become an intransigent problem and correspondingly it became more costly for the state to pursue payments. By 2010, the incoming Conservative-led coalition government considered the Child Support Agency to be a toxic brand directly contributing to the problem of non-compliance and also to increasing parental conflict. In 2012 it was radically overhauled, this time into an entirely new rebranded scheme – The Child Maintenance Service.

The 2012 Child Maintenance Service effectively turned policy round full circle as responsibility for making child maintenance agreements was handed back to parents. All separated parents, including those claiming social security benefits, were incentivised to collaborate to make private agreements completely outside the statutory service (DWP, 2021c: para 22). Compliance was thought to be better under private agreements and it was assumed most parents could reach agreements outside the system. There was no mediation built-in to help parents make agreements (although parents could be signposted to other specialist services). The service was intended to be a back-up, available only when parents needed it (for example if non-compliance with private agreements occurred). The intention was to focus resources on the 'harder' cases needing 'Collect and Pay' services. Ten years on, in 2022, the Department for Work and Pensions responsible for the Child Maintenance Service explained to the National Audit Office that the overall objective of the 2012 reforms were to:

• increase numbers of effective maintenance arrangements for children
• increase the numbers of 'voluntary' (i.e., private) arrangements
• 'reduce dependency on the state through a smaller, more efficient' service (NAO, 2022, p.6).

Notably, reducing the costs to the state is still an expressed objective. Arguably, this fiscal objective sits in contention with getting effective maintenance for children; one may not be achievable without damaging the other.

The importance of protecting the state is woven through operational procedures. For example, operationally, the move towards private agreements was achieved via a new gatekeeping structure, the Child Maintenance Options service, sitting alongside a new system of charges and fees. The options service controlled entry to the statutory Child Maintenance Service by encouraging parents to seek private agreements outside the scheme in the first instance and to make 'Direct Pay' arrangements themselves to transfer maintenance. Otherwise, if parents wanted to use the Child Maintenance Service's 'Collect and Pay' scheme, they would face a system of fees and charges (DWP, 2021a). The service went wholly online in August 2019, and it still applies a simple percentage-based formula to the paying parent's income only. To keep the calculation straightforward, the receiving parent's household income is disregarded, and the calculation is based on the payers' earnings data held by His Majesty's Revenue and Customs. Parents can use the Child Maintenance Options calculated amount as a guide, or they can agree their own amount. All previous Child Support Agency cases were migrated through this gatekeeping structure (completed in 2018) with only those parents who had a proven history of domestic abuse being allowed direct entry to the new statutory service free of charge. In these operational ways the service was streamlined and the caseload substantially reduced. The National Audit Office latest report (March 2022) shows that savings of 40 per cent in real terms was achieved in 2021 compared to the administrative costs of running the previous scheme in 2010–11 (NAO, 2022). Clearly, the state's interests have been protected, although the administrative costs are still rising, up from 35 pence for each £1 of maintenance recovered to 36 pence per £1.

Overall, it is hard to see how this 'light touch' 2012 scheme could fulfil its stated aim: 'to maximise the number of effective child maintenance arrangements' (HOC, 2022, p.3). Indeed, 10 years on, although more streamlined, this more residual back-up system is not working. Only 38 per cent of parents have a private agreement and 44 per cent have none. Furthermore, the remaining 18 per cent with a statutory agreement is much less than the 33 per cent predicted to need the service. This equates to around half of separated families with no maintenance agreement for some 1.8 million children (HOC, 2022). Debts in unpaid maintenance under the new scheme's 'Collect and Pay' service are soaring again, running at over £1million pounds per week in October 2021 (HOC, 2022, pp.4–5). Moreover, assessments showing recovery of £972.7 million of maintenance in 2020/21 is arguably grossly overinflated (DWP, 2021d). For example it is assumed that maintenance paid via 'Direct Pay' is satisfactory and fully compliant, even if parents agree to pay nothing. This assumption is based on the rationale that if parents were dissatisfied they would apply for the statutory service to use 'Collect and Pay' (DWP, 2021a). Consequently, there is no administrative monitoring of what is actually paid and received under 'Direct Pay'; nonetheless, it is still counted in the total figures:

- £783.6m from Direct Pay
- £189.1m from Collect and Pay (DWP, 2021d).

Thus, 80 per cent of the total recovered maintenance amount of £972.7 million is based mainly on assumptions and not on administrative data. Even so, there are some beneficial aspects of the UK child maintenance service compared to other countries, especially in relation to poverty reduction potential.

Compared internationally, the 2012 scheme is distinct because receipt of child maintenance payments is not included in calculating social security benefit entitlements, in effect decoupling child maintenance from the benefit system, at least for receiving parents. Thus, single parents on benefits will gain extra income above their benefit entitlements which has been shown to help lift many out of poverty, but only if maintenance is actually paid. In some other countries, the interaction between child support and benefit systems results in parents gaining no extra income from child maintenance payments (see Hakovirta et al., 2020). Comparatively therefore the UK scheme offers some poverty reduction potential, even if that is not currently a policy aim. However to maximise this potential, non-compliance has to be tackled. More controversially perhaps, it is one of only a few countries where the receiving parents' income is completely disregarded when calculating child support amounts (Denmark and Iceland also do this). Countries more commonly apply an 'incomes share model' that assesses both parents' incomes (Hakovirta and

Skinner, 2021). Though not without its problems, the income shares model is considered by some as 'fairer' because it takes into account the resources of both parents to provide (Cook and Skinner, 2021). Rather than assessing both parents' incomes which would introduce greater complexity, the UK service is focused more on streamlining and simplification to keep running costs low.

In sum, many of the major challenges that existed originally in the UK child maintenance schemes endure. Now however, parents are left to make their own private agreements, or have to pay fees to seek statutory help. Two of the most tricky and tenacious problems are non-compliance and poverty. Whilst single parent poverty is an ongoing problem as noted above, there is no explicit aim to reduce it within the 2012 child maintenance policy. Yet, poverty and non-compliance are closely entwined (especially if the impact of paying on paying parents is also considered) and these are likely to be major future challenges. In addition, a new separate policy on domestic abuse presents challenges ahead as it has important implications for the Child Maintenance Service. Each issue is now discussed in turn.

FUTURE CHALLENGES

Non-compliance and Arrears

A perennial problem for the UK's child maintenance systems is non-compliance and the build-up of arrears. As discussed above, the debts from unpaid maintenance are still rising alarmingly under the 2012 scheme. This is despite streamlining of services which were designed to dedicate more resources to focus on harder cases and enforcement. As noted, the rates of compliance are only accurately known for the minority of cases on the 'Collect and Pay service' (34 per cent) (DWP, 2021b). Of the 156,600 paying parents on Collect and Pay in the quarter ending September 2021, only about half (49 per cent) paid 'in full' (defined as paying 90 per cent or above) whilst 28 per cent paid nothing and 23 per cent paid something (Foley and Foster, 2021). Compliance rates look even worse however, if one considers that paying 'in full' is set at 90 per cent and also that rates are inflated by the percentage of paying parents in the service facing direct deductions to their social security benefits. These parents are automatically compliant as maintenance is removed at source, min-imising the workload on the service to track them down. Usually they represent between 21–24 per cent of paying parents, but under the pandemic this rose sharply to 40 per cent by September 2020 (Foley and Foster, 2021). The rise in non-compliance and arrears has led many to criticise the service and call for yet further radical reform to involve the state more in private agreements to help tackle single parent poverty (See Hansard debates 21st Jan. 2021 and 24th

June, 2021). Concerns have also been raised about the impact of the service on paying parents' poverty.

Poverty

Child maintenance policymakers in the UK have dallied with the poverty question for a long time as no explicit poverty reduction goal was set consistently. Contrastingly, reduction of fiscal costs has been an enduring policy theme. Even so, the question of poverty cannot be avoided when enforcing private obligations in separated families as to do so raises moral, ethical, legal and political dilemmas. The dilemmas arise from the interconnectedness of four key and often competing financial interests at play in child maintenance: those of the paying parent (in the UK mostly fathers), the receiving parent (mostly mothers), the state and the eligible child. The conundrum is how to balance the needs of separated parents, the child and the state whilst simultaneously alleviating poverty, or at least avoiding making it worse. In order to consider the full effects on poverty however, it is necessary to not only look at single parent families but also to include an examination of the impact on payers. Otherwise, the service may simply reshuffle poverty across separated families' households. There is however limited research on the effects of payments on paying parents.

A comparative analysis of paying fathers in the US, UK and Finland did show poverty rates were increased for payers across all three countries. Although, fewer fathers were pushed into poverty by making payments than single mothers were lifted out of poverty from receiving payments. Specifically for the UK, poverty rates increased among all paying fathers by 1.9 percentage points (a 30.6 per cent increase) (Hakovirta, Meyer, and Skinner, 2019). UK policymakers have hitherto shown little interest in the poverty effects among payers and currently rely on outdated income thresholds (not changed since 1998) to assess affordability to pay. Low income parents now pay more than was originally planned when the thresholds were set up because the lower income thresholds have remained static (SSAC, 2019). Also, benefit recipient paying parents have the minimum amount of £7 per week child maintenance deducted at source from their benefits (and a further 20 per cent collection fee of £1.40/week if they have arrears) (Foley and Foster, 2021). Thus, incomes of benefit recipient payers fall below the minimum benefit safety net. This not only raises the question of affordability for low income payers, but also about fairness among the paying population as a whole – that is if higher income earners are also advantaged because the upper thresholds remain low relative to average incomes. The threshold problem prompted a consultation in 2021 to explore more accurate ways to match incomes to assessments. Consideration was given on how to include 'unearned income' into the calculation, which is more susceptible to fraud as parents seek to reduce their liabilities by not reporting it. In this regard, some £10.9 million of fraud was found in around 1,400 cases in 2020–21 (NAO, 2022, p.11). At the lower income level, the consultation also wanted to respond more speedily to drops in income of the self-employed (NAO, 2022). There was however no mention of defining a poverty minimum for payers; yet 44 per cent of payers in the Collect and Pay service were in receipt of benefits (NAO, 2022, p.13).

Certainly, the Social Security Advisory Committee (an independent statutory body) were concerned enough about the poverty of paying parents that they tried to investigate how both the social security and child maintenance systems treated paying parents and the impact this might have on their poverty (and also on their ability to share care) (SSAC, 2019). However, they were unable to make any recommendations regarding benefit rules because they discovered there was no overarching strategy for separated parents within the social security system and no 'clear articulation of the Westminster government's objectives' either (SSAC, 2019, p.9). They also discovered that a poverty threshold for payers is undefined within the Child Maintenance Service. The SSAC recommended that a cross-departmental strategy be set up for separated families that should focus on the welfare of both separated parents and their children as a whole. In response, the Department for Work and Pensions (responsible for the Child Maintenance Service) pointed out that a cross-departmental group for coordinating programmes aimed at reducing parental conflict already existed, but they agreed to discuss this recommendation further with SSAC (DWP, letter from Minister May 2020). As yet no holistic policy aimed at improving the well-being of separated families has emerged. This is perhaps unsurprising given that the original policy aim in 1993 was to make errant fathers pay maintenance primarily to help reduce fiscal costs of providing benefits to single parents. Thereby, the interests of separated parents (mothers and fathers) were dichotomised in divisive ways from the very beginning. Arguably this has haunted policy developments ever since. This has important ramifications for how the Child Maintenance Service will deal with domestic abuse, to which we now turn.

Domestic Abuse

In 2019 a new Domestic Abuse Act was passed. Among other things, it provided clear definitions of abuse and considered the support offered by government agencies to survivors and victims of abuse. The Child Maintenance Service has come under scrutiny in this regard, not least because a recent survey by 'Gingerbread' and 'Mumsnet' found that 86 per cent of single parents say the service has allowed their ex-partner to financially control or abuse them post-separation (Gingerbread, 2020). Financial abuse is explicitly defined under the Act and the deliberate withholding of child maintenance payments is regarded by many as an example (Rabindrakumar, 2019, p.4). Whilst victims of abuse are fast tracked through to the Child Maintenance Service, the service will apply 'Direct Pay' approaches in the first instance (for example, by setting up direct debits from the paying parent's bank account). It will not move to 'Collect and Pay' until there is actual default on 'Direct Pay' and this action can take months (NAO, 2022). This minimalist approach coupled with ineffective enforcement action has led to severe criticism that the service allows abusive partners to use the scheme as 'a weapon' and thereby it assists ongoing abuse (Hansard, 21 Jan. 2021: Col 1211). Consequently, the Department for Work and Pensions are initiating an independent review exploring how the Child Maintenance Service supports survivors and victims of domestic abuse (Hansard, 24 June, 2021: Col 172GC).

It is a moot point to note that domestic abuse is a long standing problem for the UK child maintenance schemes. Currently, in 2020–2021, between 58 per cent and 60 per cent of the caseload involved domestic abuse cases having risen steadily from 28 per cent in March 2015 (DWP, 2021b). Now that financial abuse is defined explicitly under the 2019 Act it is likely that managing it will become a major challenge for the Child Maintenance Service. It may well force reconsideration of having a standalone administrative agency focused solely on child maintenance, because not only does the current scheme seemingly fail to adequately safeguard victims of abuse seeking maintenance, it offers little direct holistic services to help separated parents reduce conflict or reach agreements. Many parents are choosing not to use the service and any imbalance in power that allows one parent to dictate child support terms on the other is left unchecked if the receiving parent does not apply to the statutory service. Even if they do apply, the new lighter touch approach makes it relatively easy to default on payments; a fear expressed by single parent advocacy groups like Gingerbread. Certainly, survey evidence demonstrated that only 58 per cent of parents were still on Direct Pay after 13 months, and of those 36 per cent either received lower amounts or it was paid late (NAO, 2022, p.12). The Child Maintenance Service does not understand why fewer than expected numbers use the service and consequently the National Audit Office has recommended more research to investigate barriers to take-up (NAO, 2022). Ironically, a new service that was designed specifically to reduce its caseload is now concerned that not enough of the parents who should receive maintenance are using the service. The dilemma of balancing the competing interests of the state and separated parents has not been solved. Most recently however, the Department for Work and Pensions put out a call for evidence on child poverty and the Child Maintenance Service (May-July 2022). The call is wide ranging and among other things will explore the poverty of separated families (includes both parents), effectiveness of the Direct Pay and Collect Pay services and the role the service plays in 'dispute resolution' for separated families.

CONCLUDING DISCUSSION

The UK Child Maintenance Service is on the cusp of yet another round of potentially radical reform. Pressure for policy change is rising due to the failure of the 2012 scheme to halt the build-up of arrears and reduce non-compliance, but also because the new Domestic Abuse Act has necessitated an independent review exploring how effective the Child Maintenance Service is at protecting victims. Notwithstanding potential changes to the formula or regulations to reduce non-compliance and fraud, perhaps one of the biggest future challenges for child maintenance and single parent families is how well does the 2012 scheme fit with societal norms regarding the gendered division of labour in families?

Currently, the 2012 scheme operates a breadwinner model of family life with only the paying parents' (mainly fathers') incomes being assessed. Whilst administratively more straightforward and supposedly more efficient than adopting an incomes shares approach that assesses both parents' incomes, this simpler assessment protocol has still not improved compliance rates. At the same time, the service is not completely out of step with UK norms, because parents in intact families do adopt a gendered division of labour in the form of a one and a half earner model. Arguably, whilst this may work when two parents in intact families can share earnings and caring responsibilities without the need for large amounts of formal childcare, this has more negative consequences on separation. Because as we have seen, single parent families rely mostly on part-time employment which cannot lift them out of poverty and formal childcare services are inadequate and costly making full-time employment more difficult, especially when children are very young, under two years of age. Additionally, if the limited evidence provided by Gingerbread (2020) on the extent of financial abuse regarding child maintenance holds true, the economic disadvantage already experienced by women in single parent families creates and/or facilitates a power imbalance between parents on separation. This imbalance is potentially exacerbated and sustained by the Child Maintenance Service, albeit inadvertently. Simultaneously, poorer paying parents seem insufficiently protected from falling into poverty.

In the future, a completely fresh approach to supporting separated families might improve the well-being of separated parents and their children; one that not only provides more holistic targeted services but is also disentangled from the fiscal cost reduction goals attached to the efficient management of social security institutions. The narrowly confined role for the UK state in transferring maintenance money from one separated parent to the other has not worked effectively hitherto. Various child support schemes, all embedded within social security institutions, have failed to produce the desired results. This is despite the implementation of numerous policy adaptations created under different political ideologies. However, developing a more holistic policy for separated parents would suggest an expanded role for the state. Not only might this involve development of more services but given the gendered power and income imbalances between separated parents, one that more closely engages with risks around domestic abuse. This extension of the state into the lives of separated families may be unpalatable on political and fiscal grounds. However, it is probably inevitable given the potential for the Domestic Abuse Act to expose the true extent of abusive behaviours (particularly financial abuse) and the fact that the Child Maintenance Service is embroiled in these relationships in any case.

REFERENCES

Andersen, K. (2020) Universal Credit, gender and unpaid care childcare: Mothers accounts of the new welfare conditionality regime. *Critical Social Policy*, *40*(3), 430–449.

Coleman, L., Dali-Chaouch, M. and Harding, C. (2020) Childcare Survey 2020, London: Coram Family and Childcare Trust. Accessed 15.7.21. https://www.fam ilyandchildcaretrust.org/childcare-costs-surge-over-double-rate-inflation

Cook, K. and Skinner, C. (2021) Technical fixes as challenges to state legitimacy: Australian separated fathers' suggestions for child support policy reform. *Social Politics: International Studies in Gender, State and Society*, *28*(2), 501–520.

CPAG (2021) Poverty facts and figures. Accessed 15.7.21 https://cpag.org.uk/child -poverty/child-poverty-facts-and-figures.

Davis, A., Hirsch, D., Padley, M. and Shepherd, C. (2021) A minimum income standard for the United Kingdom in 2021, York: JRF.

Dromey, J., Dewar, L. and Finnegan, J. (2020) Tackling single parent poverty after coronavirus, Leicester: Learning and Work Institute, Gingerbread, and Joseph Rowntree Foundation.

DWP (2021a) 'Separated Families Statistics: April 2014-March 2020'. Accessed 22. 12.21, https://www.gov.uk/government/statistics/separated-families-statistics-april -2014-to-march-2020/separated-families-statistics-april-2014-to-march-2020

DWP (2021b) 'Child Maintenance Service statistics: data to September 2021 (experimental)' Accessed 22.12.21, https://www.gov.uk/government/statistics/child -maintenance-service-statistics-data-to-september-2021-experimental/child- maintenance-service-statistics-data-to-september-2021-experimental

DWP (2021c) 'Open consultation child maintenance: modernising and improving our service' para 22 (no page) Accessed 21.12.21, https://www.gov.uk/government/ consultations/child-maintenance-modernising-and-improving-our-service/child -maintenance-modernising-and-improving-our-service#executive-summary

DWP (2021d) 'Client Fund Accounts'. London: DWP.

Foley, N. and Foster, D. (2021) Child maintenance: Fees, enforcement and arrears, London: House of Commons Library Briefing Paper.

Gingerbread (2020) Data released today from Mumsnet and Gingerbread show stark findings on CMS. Accessed 22.12.21, https://www.gingerbread.org.uk/what-we-do/news/mumsnet-gingerbread-survey-findings-released/

Hakovirta, M. and Skinner, C. (2021) Shared physical custody and child maintenance arrangements: A comparative analysis of 13 countries using a model family approach. In L. Bernardi and D. Mortelmans (Eds.) *Shared physical custody: Interdisciplinary insights in child custody arrangements*. Cham, Switzerland: Springer.

Hakovirta, M., Meyer, D. and Skinner, C. (2019) Does paying child support impoverish fathers in the United States, Finland and the United Kingdom? *Children and Youth Services Review, 106*, 10448.

Hakovirta, M., Skinner, C., Hiilamo, H. and Jokela, M. (2020) Child poverty, child maintenance and interactions with social assistance benefits among lone parent families: A comparative analysis. *Journal of Social Policy, 49*(1), 19–39.

Hansard, House of Commons (Debate 21 Jan. 2021, Volume 687) Covid-19: Child Maintenance Service. Accessed 15.7.21, https://hansard.parliament.uk/Commons/2021–01–21/debates/0E3957B0-D917–4B4B-9D08–0C7F6486B4AB/Covid-19ChildMaintenanceService

Hansard, House of Lords (Debate, 24 June, 2021, Volume 813) Child Maintenance Service. Accessed 15.7.21, https://hansard.parliament.uk/Commons/2021–01–21/debates/0E3957B0-D917–4B4B-9D08–0C7F6486B4AB/Covid-19ChildMaintenanceService

Hobson, F. (2021) Universal Credit: Ten years of changes to benefit claims and payments. London: House of Commons Library.

House of Commons (HOC) (2022) Committee of Public Accounts: Child Maintenance, Ninth Report of Session 2022–23. Accessed 29.6.22. https://committees.parliament.uk/publications/22699/documents/166898/default/

Johnsen, S. and Blenkinsopp, J. (2018) Welfare Conditionality: final findings lone parents, York: ESRC. Accessed 15.7.21. www.welfareconditionality.ac.uk

JRF (2021) UK poverty 2020/21. Accessed 15.7.21. https://www.jrf.org.uk/report/uk-poverty-2020–21

Kenway, P. (2021) Back to the 20th Century: Our Child Poverty Disaster, Blog for CPAG. Accessed 19.7.21. https://cpag.org.uk/news-blogs/news-listings/back-20th-century-our-child-poverty-disaster

Loft, P. (2021) Insight: 30 years of the Child Support Act, London: House of Commons Library. Accessed 29.6.2022. https://commonslibrary.parliament.uk/30-years-of-the-child-support-act/

Mackley, A. (2021) Coronavirus: Universal Credit during the crisis, London: House of Commons Library.

NAO (2022) Child Maintenance: Report by the Comptroller and Auditor General, London: National Audit Office. Accessed 30.6.2022. https://www.nao.org.uk/wp-content/uploads/2022/03/Child-Maintenance-Summary.pdf

OECD (2020) Is Childcare Affordable? Policy Brief on Employment, Labour and Social Affairs. OECD: Paris.

ONS (2019) National population projections: 2018 based. Accessed 19.7.21. https://www.ons.gov.uk/peoplepopulationandcommunity/populationandmigration/populationprojections/bulletins/nationalpopulationprojections/2018based

ONS (2020a) Births in England and Wales 2019. Accessed 19.7.21. https://www.ons.gov.uk/peoplepopulationandcommunity/birthsdeathsandmarriages/livebirths/bulletins/birthsummarytablesenglandandwales/2019

ONS (2020b) Conceptions in England and Wales: 2018. Accessed 19.7.21. https://www
.ons.gov.uk/peoplepopulationandcommunity/birthsdeathsandmarriages/concepti
onandfertilityrates/bulletins/conceptionstatistics/2018

ONS (2021) Families and Households in the UK: 2020. Accessed 19.7.21. https://www
.ons.gov.uk/peoplepopulationandcommunity/birthsdeathsandmarriages/families/
bulletins/familiesandhouseholds/2020

Rabindrakumar, S. and Dewar, L (2018) Unhelpful and unfair? The impact of single
parent sanctions. London: Gingerbread.

Rabindrakumar, S. (2019) Direct pay: Innovation or failure? London: Gingerbread

SSAC (2019) 'Separated parents and the social security system: Occasional Paper No.
22'. London: SSAC.

12. The child support system in the United States of America

Alisha Griffin

INTRODUCTION

In this chapter, child support policy in the United States of America (U.S. hereafter) is explored across historical, social, and familial domains. There are many influences and events pushing and changing the world we live and work in. To explore those influences and the potential and trending concerns and changes to the U.S. Child Support and social welfare programs, it is important to understand the context, history and journey that has locked them together and brought the programs to 2022.

FAMILIES IN THE U.S.: THE SOCIAL AND ECONOMIC CONTEXT

Family Composition

The family structure in the United States continues to undergo great change. The U.S. Census has conducted, for the past 60 years, the Annual Social and Economic Supplement (ASCS). Its reports show that in 1968, 85 per cent of all children under the age of 18 lived with two parents and by 2000 it was less than 70 per cent (United States Census Bureau, 2021). Today, although the most common living arrangement for children is still with two parents, it has decreased by 15 per cent. Children living with a mother only has more than doubled and the number of children living with a father only has more than quadrupled to 21 per cent and 4.5 per cent respectively. The report also shows that the ages of the children play a role in those differences. Children aged 0–5 are most often (50 per cent) living with two parents. For children aged 12–17, it is more likely that they live in a one parent household or are living with no parent. Although the two-parent living arrangement is still the most common overall, there are variations by race and origin. Asian children show the greatest likelihood to live with married parents, Hispanic children were the most likely to live with unmarried parents. Children who live with the mother only are represented as follows: 25 per cent black, 13 per cent white and non-Hispanic and 21 per cent Asian. Average household size has declined from 3.6 in 1940 to 2.5 in 2020, and there has been an even greater shift to living more independently or with non-family members.

Child Birth Rate

Prior to 2020, the average birth rate in the United States had been declining steadily since its peak in the 19th century. By 2020 it had dropped to 1.64, the lowest rate ever recorded (Osterman et al., 2022). There has been a brief spike associated with the 2008 recession. Factors like increases in delayed marriage, economic instability, and expanded contraceptive access and use have created a continual decline. Birth rates have now been dropping regularly for the past 13 years at an average of 2 per cent per year (CDC, 2022). In 2019, the overall birth rate decline was 4 per cent, the largest in five decades and across all races. In 2020, the total number of births for all races declined again to 3.6 million with 1.8 million being white, 528,000 black, 26,000 Native Americans, 218,000 Asian and 863,000 Hispanic (CDC, 2022).

While it is evident that the birth rate will continue to decline, this has not appeared to be attributable to any one demographic, economic, or policy change. An exception to this may be seen in the future due to the recent U.S. Supreme Court's overturning of Roe vs Wade. The largest decrease in birth rate overall is to women under 30 (Population Reference Bureau, 2021). In light of these decreases in marriage, birth rates, and fewer intact two-parent households, it is pertinent to interrogate the economic wellbeing and rates of poverty among these families.

Work and Income

Before the advent of the COVID-19 pandemic the nature of work in the U.S. was changing, as more people took up 'gig work' or independent contracting. The Bureau of Labor Statistics (BLS), (U.S Bureau of Labor Statistics, 2022) highlighted the rise in self-employment and demographic shifts, which were ultimately made easier by the advances of technology. In recent decades, women's education and earnings have grown in relation to that of men. As more women are completing advanced educational degrees and building earnings capacity, the statistics reflect the impact of these advances on women's choices of when and whether to begin a family.

Poverty and Economics

In 2015 U.S. Congress directed the National Academies of Science, Engineering and Medicine to conduct a comprehensive study of child poverty and the cost to the nation for not addressing child poverty effectively. The U.S. Census (2020) estimated that in 2015 over 20 per cent of the nation's children were poor. In 2021, the average poverty rate for all families across the nation was 15.7 per cent and for children it was 37.9 per cent (U.S. Census Bureau, 2022). Recent reports support this finding, showing that children remain the poorest age group in the U.S. (Children's Defense Fund, 2021). American families are considered to be living in poverty if they have an annual income below the Federal Poverty Line of $25,701 for a family of four, which amounts to less than $2,142 a month, $494 a week, or $70 a day. One in six American children (approximately 11.9 million) live in poverty. Black children (30.1 per cent), American Indian/Alaska Native children (29.1 per cent), and Hispanic children (23.7 per cent) experience disproportionately higher rates of poverty compared to white children (8.9 per cent).

The ongoing impacts of childhood poverty can be experienced through diminished academic performance, and subsequently, difficulty finishing high school, gaining employment, economic hardship, and interactions with the criminal justice system (CDF, 2021). Despite decreases in family size, birth rates and improved economics, poverty has not decreased. Amid current economic challenges, families are struggling with sharp increases in the prices of gas, food, household goods, and transportation. While these changes are being felt across all income levels, those at the mid and lower income levels are the most seriously impacted.

THE U.S. CHILD SUPPORT PROGRAM STRUCTURE

The U.S. Child Support program is made up of 50 States, 4 Territories, 60+ Native American recognised tribal agencies (State) and a federal Office of Child Support Enforcement (OCSE) (Office of Child Support Enforcement, n.d.). Given the structure of each state's program and the political influences in that state, the makeup and sharing of duties vary widely. For example, the designation of that single lead agency in each state varies; the majority fall under the umbrella of Health and/or Human Services, but others are based in judicial domains (Attorney General or Justice) and some fall under revenue / tax-based authorities. The next demarcation point comes from the choices the State has made as to the balance of administrative and judicial control over the program. Another split will depend on whether the state is heavily county-based, thus considered to be state-directed but county or locally administered. Others may have regional setups or maintain a fully centralised state-operated program.

The program structure will also influence the way practice and policy are implemented; thus, states generally refer to themselves operationally as either judicial, administrative, or quasi-judicial and even then, within each of those demarcations, each has slightly different structures. While child support programs must comply with federal law, regulation, and performance, how they are enacted is State, Territorial, or Tribal specific (Office of Child Support Enforcement).

Historical Development of U.S. Child Support Policy

Historically, child support policy stemmed from traditional beliefs established by settlers and the founding fathers that if a 'family', primarily a mother and her children, had lost the financial support of the breadwinner due to death or injury then charitable services were provided by the community, to whatever extent available. However, if the father, or even in rare cases the mother, were to leave or fail to support, the treatment was more prosecutorial, and actions were taken involving measures like forced work, stocks, and debtors' prison to enforce the need to support (CDF, 2021). Subsequently, the responsibility for finding and enforcing a parent's failure to provide child support was the responsibility of local law enforcement and courts. The emphasis on criminal enforcement is seen in the first model child support act that the Commissioners on Uniform State Laws developed in 1910, such as the Uniform Desertion and Non-Support Act. This act made it a criminal offense to fail to support or to desert a wife and children (Office of Child Support Enforcement, 2021).

Post-World War I, with the growth of disabled returning soldiers and families left without support, the philosophy and belief structure that criminalised failure to support and familial desertion were codified in federal law and policy by The Social Security Act in 1930. The Act created the national program known as Aid to Families with Dependent Children (AFDC) with the purpose of helping separated mothers stay at home with their children. The authority to address or prosecute for non-support by parents remained with the courts (The Social Security Act, 1935). Subsequently, the first federal laws establishing a child support program came with the amendments to the Social Security Act (SSA) in 1950 requiring the State welfare agency to have a separate responsible unit responsible for notifying appropriate law enforcement officials and for requesting the courts to act. Also, in 1950, the Uniform Reciprocal Enforcement of Support Act (URESA) was approved. URESA superseded the Uniform Desertion and Non-Support Act. URESA established a uniform process for a custodial parent to apply to the courts of another state to establish or enforce a support order without traveling to that state. It also protected the applicant from becoming subject to the jurisdiction of that other state's courts for any purpose other than the support proceeding. All states and US territories were required to and did enact some form of URESA or similar legislation. Since the states were not obliged to enact URESA exactly as written and approved, the Uniform Act was therefore never truly uniform (Office of Child Support Enforcement, 2021).

In 1975, Public Law 93–647 amended the Social Security Act to formally create a separate Title to the Social Security Act, Title IV-D for Child Support Enforcement, and a new Federal Office of Child Support Enforcement (OCSE). All States were required to have the single organisational lead agency as specified in CFR 302.10: 'To establish and collect child support, accessing employment information and utilising a variety of enforcement tools to secure support orders.' The 1975 legislation also formalised and expanded both federal and state roles with respect to child support responsibilities and expectations. It also established a requirement for performance, annual reporting, and an incentive system directly tied to improved performance. Critical to this new framework was a public policy requirement that any family, as a condition of receiving AFDC or 'welfare' benefits, must cooperate with information to identify and locate the absent parent(s) and to enable the collection of child support. Any child support collected was to be paid to the State as an offset for the benefits given.

The caseload for AFDC was 3.4 million cases on behalf of 8 million children (Office of Family Assistance, 2004). Eighty-three per cent of all cases were due to an absent parent but only about 21.9 per cent had a child support order (IRS, 2018). Throughout the 1970s and 1980s, again numerous new requirements and tools were added to enhance and enable the Child Support program to locate parents and establish and enforce child support. States were now also required to enforce medical support and spousal support where it was tied to a child support order. Enforcement was enhanced through garnishment and the attachment of wages, and the ability to intercept tax returns at both State and Federal level.

Prior to 1988 both child support orders and the amounts were still the sole jurisdiction of the Courts in most states and were based on or dependent on the facts or information available and presented to the court. The Child Support Amendments of 1984 required all states and territories, 'as a condition of receiving federal funds, to develop mathematical calculations to determine appropriate child support awards.' Again, these numerical formulas were only advisory, so they varied by jurisdiction. To remedy this situation the Family Support Act of 1988 was passed (FSA, 1988). It 'required that the guideline calculation create a rebuttable presumption that it is the appropriate amount of support.' The guideline formulas were, at minimum, required to take into consideration incomes of both parents, costs of raising children, and the costs of living.

Today, U.S. states use three basic guideline models: the Melson formula, the Income Shares formula, and the Percentage of Income formula. The Income Shares model is used most widely as the current model in 42 States, Guam, and the U.S. Virgin Islands. The Percentage of Income model has two variations and is used in 6 States. The Melson model is used by 2 States and by the District of Columbia. In the Income Shares model, the income of both parents is considered and is based on the perspective that the child(ren) should receive the same proportional level of support from the parent's income as if the parents had not separated. Shared parenting time and custody are taken into consideration. The percentage of income is based solely on the paying parent's income and applies a percent factor to that income for the support. The recipient parent's income is not considered. The Melson formula was a predecessor of the Income Shares Model and is considered a more complex version of the Income Shares Model. It includes additional considerations like the self-support needs of each parent and standards of living of both parents and the children. Most guidelines application includes some level of consideration or adjustment for shared custody or shared parenting.

FSA 1988 also required that, in any case where paternity was contested, states had to require all parties to take a genetic test at the request of any party. It set a new standard for performance for paternity establishment, requiring that States had to have a paternity establishment percentage of 50 in the first year after FSA'88 was enacted, increase by 3 percentage points from FY1988 to FY1991, and improve every year thereafter by at least 3 per cent or face a program penalty. The law also established the first 'pass through' to families on AFDC. When a collection was made on an AFDC case, the first $50 dollars was payable to the family and would not minimise any of the social welfare benefits received by the family.

In response to concerns among congress and key administrators, on how to stem the growth and address the continued rise of poverty and welfare cases, the Personal Responsibility and Work Opportunity Reconciliation Act (PRWORA) was drafted in 1996 to address this nationwide 'welfare crisis' (PRWORA, Public Law 104–193, 1996). This federal act is generally considered to be the most sweeping social welfare landmark legislation in the United States. The purpose of the legislation was to:

1. provide assistance to families,
2. end dependency on government by promoting work and marriage,
3. prevent and reduce the incidence of out of wedlock births, and
4. promote two parent families and ultimately reduce reliance on social welfare and poverty (PRWORA 1996).

Best known as 'the Welfare to Work' law, this legislation had a major impact on all programs in the Health and Human Services domain. It also brought many other systems and programs to the table to work with child support, particularly around the areas of parentage and enforcement. PRWORA, along with the Uniform Interstate Family Support Act (UIFSA), is one of the uniform acts drafted by the National Conference of Commissioners of Uniform Law (NCCUSL), known today as the Uniform Law Commission (ULC). UIFSA continues to ensure that orders can be properly established and modified and enforced on cases within the U.S. States and Territories. When more than one state is involved in the establishing, enforcing, or modifying a child or spousal support order, only the law of that state can be 'applied to requests to modify the order of child support, unless the courts of that state no longer have original tribunal jurisdiction (CEJ) under the Act.' UIFSA also allows for the establishment of direct income withholding which is known as an interstate enforcement mechanism. Direct income withholding provides a caretaker parent or child support program to send an income withholding order 'to the employer of the obligated/payor parent, that requires that employer to withhold pay for the benefit of the child(ren) and send it directly to the parent or State requesting it.'

Key to the implementation of the 1996 legislation is that it required States to have procedures and enact State and any local regulations required for implementation, including for UIFSA, by March 31, 1998, or face loss of federal funding for both child support enforcement and social welfare programs. Interestingly, the 1997 Annual Report to Congress, prior to the required dates for full implementation of PRWORA, reported that the child support caseload had already been reduced to 19 million cases, 1 per cent lower than 1996 and 11 per cent lower than 1993. It also noted that there had already been some progress based on earlier improvements, as more than 1.2 million children had paternity established and collections had increased by $4.2 million. But clearly it was not sufficient, and the past need and concerns continued to be of major focus and a top priority for the nation.

Highlighted below are some of the key provisions of the 1996 PRWORA legislation that are important as we talk about the future. But as indicated previously, sources such as the Code of Federal Regulations, or the websites of both programs provide extensive detail on the legislative history.

- Aid For Dependent Children became the Temporary Assistance for Needy Families (TANF) program. It required families receiving assistance to comply with child support, and to go to work or school (work requirements) in order to receive benefits and established time limits by which a family or individual must be independent, or benefits were reduced or eliminated. Penalties were also to be assessed on the recipient. The concept was that families should only need temporary welfare benefits if they went to work.

- Programs under Title IVE (child welfare/ foster care) and Title XIX (Medicaid) were now required to cooperate by automatically referring their cases to child support for establishment and collection against the benefit received or the cost for care of the child.
- Increased noticing, confidentiality provisions, publications of services, standardising forms, and other similar aspects aimed at standardising operations were to be developed and utilised.
- Families who did not receive services through any of the programs that required referral but needed child support established or enforced were now able to apply directly to child support and receive services.
- All collection and disbursement of support were centralised.
- Employers are required to identify employees for location and report new hires to child support and provide health care for children subject to the child support order whenever healthcare was available for the employee.
- It required the social security number for all individuals be added to all professional, drivers and occupational licenses, registrations, death certificates, and many other documents which allowed for improved location and enforcement.
- Required data matching and intercepting of funds for collections with banks, stocks, bankruptcies, insurance settlements, and many other sources for payments and leverage over delinquent payors.
- Established a mechanism with the Department of State to deny, restrict, or seize passports.
- Upgraded and enhanced computerised systems to meet all these requirements and track the case management, payments, and disbursements.
- Created the authority for establishing and recognising Tribal Child Support programs.

A companion bill passed two years later, the Child Support Performance and Incentive Act of 1998 (CSPIA) is particularly significant to the framework and operation of today's State, Territorial, and Tribal child support programs. The new performance categories of CSPIA were paternity establishment, order establishment, collection on orders, collection on debt owed (arrears) and cost effectiveness. Each performance measure was defined in the law for the purposes of equity of measurement and the required reporting period was the federal fiscal year (Office of Child Support Enforcement, 2020). All programs needed to meet these new expectations by the deadline date in 1998, or risk substantial penalties. All these new tools and requirements certainly had a significant effect on both child support and the social benefit/welfare programs. The effect was felt at both the State and local levels as well as in the public and private arenas as all these external sources came into compliance with the new laws.

The combined legislative framework stemmed from a long history of social concerns and State innovative practices. Today, there is much debate as to the effectiveness of the legislation and strong, but varied, interest in revisiting its foundations and its orientation to family and family policy for the future.

By 2000, just two years after the compliance date, the number of families on TANF had been reduced from the 4.7 million in 1995 to 3.5 million and the families seeking service continued to decline and by 2014 it was 1.9 million. The caseload in 2000 for Child Support shows similar drops but also a significant change in whom the program was serving and to whom collections were being distributed. By 2000, the overall caseload of child support had dropped to 17.4 million with 3.3 million currently receiving TANF or other social welfare benefits, 7.9 million were former recipients of assistance (6 per cent growth), and 6.2 million had never received assistance (2 per cent). Collections were \$19 billion with 51 per cent going to never assisted families, 42 per cent to formerly assisted families and 7 per cent to currently assisted families.

Caseloads have continued to steadily decline at the National and State level so that, 20 years later, in 2020, TANF caseloads are 885,000 for 1.5 million children and child support caseloads are at 13.2 million. This is a 12 per cent decline over all categories in the program. Each State's caseload decline over the 20 years has been different ranging from 0.5 per cent to more than a 27 per cent decrease. Collections made and distributed are \$31.4 billion. The performance also has shown a marked change; 87 per cent of all cases have an order and over 79 per cent of cases receive a collection (Office of Child Support Enforcement, 2020b; TANF, 2020). In the review of the data, there were two trends: first, more families had left welfare/TANF or did not seek the services offered by the program; and second, the child support programs had become more effective in establishing paternities and orders and collecting on those orders than they were in 1975 or in 1996. The child support caseload distribution showed that more collections were going to families who had left welfare and to families who never had been on assistance. The latter was particularly true in states that had enacted laws where all divorce and custody orders were automatically referred to the Title IV-D child support program. As the caseloads declined and changed, there were issues and concerns being raised from both the involved programs but also from researchers and advocates regarding several aspects of the child support and the benefits programs and how to position, adapt and/or restructure them for the future.

With the child and family poverty rates continuing to grow, and other indicators of child and family health showing deterioration, many practitioners, advocates and legislators began to examine the current structure asking key questions like were the services not needed, why were they not being utilised, were these the right services, and what changes should be made? There are many other factors of both an economic and social nature affecting the state of today's family. To what extent are those trends influencing today's programs and the future of social service and child support programs, and what changes if any should we be considering as we move forward?

Most experts point to the key contributing factors for the decline in applications or participation on welfare to the time limits placed on families receiving benefits, the poor quality of work available, the restrictions on education or training counting toward participation and/or not actually leading to job acquisition or income, and the required cooperation with child support. Additionally, the national restrictions on legally present immigrant families that exclude them from receiving TANF, Medicaid, or Food Stamps (SNAP) increase the poverty. Some States have reduced services due to funding or to changes in State level policies which have further limited access to benefits and have further impacted the poor in those States. The TANF program today serves less than one of five poor children, and the families who do receive services today are truly considered deeply poor. Besides TANF and other benefit programs being reduced in the number of families who qualify and receive services, participation rates have also shrunk as families do not see the benefits as helpful or providing the needed level of assistance. What impact does this have on families and the child support programs and what changes will be needed?

CONSIDERATIONS AND CHALLENGES

Children and families today are very much in need of services and economic support. The economy, generational differences, COVID-19, and many other factors are influencing the delivery expectations for services. What is needed to address the changed and changing needs of families and children? Many professionals throughout the human services, social services, and child support communities have begun to both assess and address the need to change. There is significant focus and energy in trying to craft new policies and practices that look at and are responsive to a 'whole family' framework; a comprehensive system that aligns systems and services together to meet the needs of all family members rather than pitting services and members against each other (Dutta-Gupta, 2019; Urban Institute, 2022).

For many years now, experts across many disciplines including State and Federal administrations have pointed to the need to revisit the TANF program. For starters it has been flat-funded since the original 1996 legislation requiring States to add funds to keep the program available at any level and many States have had to reduce the already limited services. Advocates and practitioners point to many elements that require rethinking, new policy, and new practices as well providing additional supportive services in areas of work, housing and education, to name a few (APHSA, 2020; Green, 2021).

Childcare and child tax credits need to be comprehensively funded; currently the United States comes in at the bottom of all developed countries in spending on children. Additionally, the existing policies of mandated referrals to child support and the structure of that mandate should also be reconsidered. Given the complexity of the changes needed as well as the other issues currently facing the country, including the significant changes to the economy and the fears around recession, climate change, and the general politically turbulent climate, there have been no full bills developed as yet.

CHILD SUPPORT MOVING FORWARD

As discussed with the review of the history of the development of the program, the child support program became an essential core program for ensuring parents supported their children through utilisation of a multitude of enforcement techniques. This focus was in keeping with the preference of the country on reducing welfare dependency and federal and state budgets but not necessarily with addressing the underlying issues. Some of those original concerns around poverty and welfare are still dominant concerns today, not only for child support programs but also for other professionals and family advocates throughout the U.S. All the impacts that families are dealing with in regard to the changes to family structure, economy, and logistics, the child support program and many other programs like TANF, social service, health and welfare programs are also experiencing. However, there are many emerging additional concerns for all, like race, diversity and equity, engagement, service tailoring, technology and systems and maintaining performance and funding that are dominating the discussions within the child support community. It will require time and deliberation to advance a new structure for any or all these programs.

A stated goal of child support programs throughout the country has been to have both parents support their children. That goal has not changed, but the path to achieving it will require change. Given all these changes to family, work and expectations discussed so far, the future program will require striking balances and utilising new techniques in engaging parents, enforcement practices and how program conformity can be maintained for equity but allow State and local variations.

NEW PRACTICES FOR THE FUTURE

Engaging Both Parents

One of the early hallmarks, but also a point of concern and criticism, regarding the child support program's performance, was the effectiveness of the combined process between TANF and the other mandated referring agencies which brought families directly into the CSE program (Gerrish, 2017). It was seen also as a process that drove families apart. There was no allowance made for unmarried parents to have orders that supported the family living together, providing support through other means like food, household goods, or services like day care and still allow the receipt of benefits. The lack of cooperation resulted in reduced incomes or benefits for the parent needing support, the parent providing support, and the government. A multitude of programs on the federal, state and county level have begun the engagement of both parents early and often throughout the life of the case. Engaging the parents in all aspects is beneficial for families. It provides for equity, clarity, and fairness. This engagement is evidencing itself in the areas of communication, order establishment, guideline revisions and enforcement. This change is also improving and broadening the methods used for communication through more enhanced account and case service options and websites.

Order Establishment

Recently many programs have begun to redevelop their communication and program structure, while also rethought the order establishment process to do more negotiated or consent order processing. In this process both parties are included, brought together where possible, and provided the opportunity to try to come to an agreement on an order. The role of the child support program is becoming more one of a facilitator rather than an adversary. If agreement is accomplished, then the child support agency can execute the order administratively with court approval. If agreement is not reached, then the regular process of going to court can proceed. This process works in the modification process as well reducing administrative process but most importantly it reduces major negative impact to either parent.

While guidelines are required to be updated every 4 years, most quadrennial reviews have looked primarily at inflation, updating job information, and consumer price indexing to make sure that the formulas keep step with the economy and cost of raising a family.

Recently the National Parents Organization (NPO) issued a report that catalogued and ranked the shared parenting models of all States guidelines. This is a good example of how much more vocal parents and other organisations become in having a voice in and working with agencies on how child support operates in the future. Efforts are needed to determine the methodologies required to ensure that they are operationally appropriate for today's needs and can be adapted as required in the future.

Work

As programs have begun to look at methods to improve their work with families, they have identified community resources and services that would be beneficial in improving and supporting families as well as the programs' performance by providing access to work and training programs. Currently states cannot use federal Title IV-D funds to pay for work opportunity/training programs unless they receive a waiver. As a result, such programs are funded through other avenues and most child support customers have had limitations with accessing them. Recently the National Council of Child Support Directors (NCCSD) issued a report that shows how twenty-two states have begun or established programs that assist the paying parent in gaining or improving their employment and therefore their ability to pay. Ultimately this effort can provide benefit to both families.

Tailoring Enforcement

There are numerous tools for enforcement that the program has been given over the course of the years. While some are limited by time or other involved jurisdictions, like annual tax intercepts at the federal and state levels or others are dependent on certification by courts or other agencies, the larger majority have often been applied broadly at a point set by the State for successive non-payment, often two missed payments. Many programs are now questioning that thinking and have started to develop broader guidance and utilise new tools toward a more tailored approach to enforcement. In other words, they are trying to apply the right enforcement technique to the right person at the right time. A good example of this is the historic use of automatically suspending a person's driver's license. This certainly may get the person's attention, but it is often compounded by the fees and other actions that the licensing authority may take and may hamper the ability of the parent to work and ultimately to pay support. Applying enforcements in a more tailored way can also work more effectively in the efforts to engage the parent and ensure more consistent support.

Some of these new methods and practices are within the State's authority to manage and adjust its program if it continues to meet all applicable federal and state law and regulations. While there has been broader recognition at the State level as to the benefits of this change, there is now recognition and acknowledgment and support emerging at the federal level to examine these more closely to see how or if adjustments need to be made in existing policy, rules and regulations. The federal government and other organisations have been supporting innovation where possible by giving grants and waivers to States to enable them to make changes and document the need for legislative and funding changes in the future.

Equity and Fairness

Overarching through all these areas of improvement are the concern and focus on equity and fairness in how the program operates and treats individuals. Overwhelmingly most of the families who have been involved in the program have been low-income families. It is important to listen to parents who have been involved in the child support program and hear from them. The importance of listening to their lived experiences and circumstances helps craft the right response to obtaining the goal of the parent's support. Much of the way the program was built created an environment that did not talk to parents nor understand what kind of impression the program was conveying from beginning to end. This need for heightened awareness and a review of policy and practice is not unique to child support but is being raised at almost every level of service provision throughout the United States.

Performance Program and Practice

As stated earlier but simplified here, State performance is judged on five key factors: (1) Of children born to unmarried parents, how effective are they in getting the parentage of those children established? (2) Of the cases that come to them, how many do they get orders established on? (3) Of the cases having an order and needing a collection, how effective is the program at getting that collection? (4) Of the debt owed on all cases, how effective are they at getting that debt collected? And lastly (5) how efficient and effective are they at operating the program? Most of these performance measures are tied to the federal fiscal year (October 1 – September 30th) for counting purposes and then States are audited on the information they provide. Once the audits are completed then the State is eligible for a share on an incentive payment based on those five factors.

There is some consensus that the first four standards are very good indicators that can produce solid benefits for families. For example, children who have parentage established can benefit greatly by being able to maintain connectedness to family members, eligibility for other programs/services, like veterans benefits or access to genetics and other beneficial health information.

Orders established generally yield income for the family. Certainly, the more a family can receive the income due from a support collection on an order the more they may be able to meet the family's needs, to rise out of poverty and maintain a positive environment for the children. The concerns with all these standards is equity, fairness and in particular how orders are set, and enforced.

There is, of course, strong discussion as to whether these are the right measures, if there should be others added or different ones developed altogether. Some believe that the measures themselves may not be the problem but how they have been implemented and that they create negative pressure points. In particular the two collection measures are often criticised because the collection for a family receiving benefits is most often returned to the state and federal government to offset the benefits given currently or in the past. Today, several programs working together are trying out a process that allows for these collections to be returned to the family in an effort to improve family economics and participation. Clearly by the goals and standards set by the 1996–1998 legislation, the program has been highly effective and these performance standards have quantified it. But 25 years later, it may require a different lens and goal adjustment.

The political and social culture of a nation is most often determined by which assumptions or concepts dominate the social policy at that particular time in history. The United States has always valued individualism and freedom along with the values of fairness, equality, self-determination. Different times will change the emphasis and which dominate. It would appear that the emphasis that dominated the late 1990s and early 2000s is not the same emphasis that is driving the country today. How that shift affects our service delivery and what changes need to be made is a process that has begun. It needs to involve families, practitioners from child support and other programs, researchers, advocates and politicians. Child support practitioners and leaders would seem to be taking measurable and well-founded efforts to explore what parents and families want, have opened a dialog with parents and many others both within and outside of the program and they have begun to explore and test new methodologies and practices.

Ultimately any change will require larger and more substantive research and discussion with a broad spectrum of individuals and programs to ensure that any changes made are solidly aligned to the goals of improving services and supporting families to meet today's and the future needs of families but also are well-structured in laws and regulations that support and enhance the practice.

REFERENCES

APHSA (2020). Laying the Tracks for an Equitable Recovery and Long Term Repair. Brookings Institute. https://files.constantcontact.com/391325ca001/301df042–8d7e -4a16–8db5–1103a8f4824b.pdf

Centers for Disease Control and Prevention (2022). *Quarterly Provisional Estimates for Selected Birth Indicators, 2020-Quarter 1, 2022.* https://www.cdc.gov/nchs/nv ss/vsrr/natality.htm (Accessed 18 August 2022).

Children's Defense Fund (2021). The State of America's Children 2021. https:// www.childrensdefense.org/wp-content/uploads/2021/04/The-State-of-Americas -Children-2021.pdf (Accessed 28 September 2022).

Dutta-Gupta, I. (2019). Improving TANF's countercyclicality through increased basic assistance and subsidized jobs. https://www.brookings.edu/research/improving -tanfs-countercyclicality-through-increased-basic-assistance-and-subsidized-jobs/

Gerrish, E. (2017). The effect of the Child Support Performance and Incentive Act of 1998 on rewarded and unrewarded performance goals. *Journal of Policy Analysis and Management*, 36: 65–96. https://doi.org/10.1002/pam.21957

Green, C. (2021). Reimagining SNAP Administration through a Human-Centered Lens. APHSA. https://aphsa.org/APHSABlog/mhhspp/reimagining-snap-administration-t hrough-human-centered-lens.aspx

IRS (2018). IRS Disclosure Policy Guidance: Use of Federal Tax Information (FTI) for Child Support Enforcement Purposes. https://www.irs.gov/pub/irs-utl/using-federal -tax-info-for-child-support-enforcement.pdf (Accessed 28 September 2022).

Office of Child Support Enforcement (n.d.). https://ocsp.acf.hhs.gov/irg/welcome.html (Accessed 28 September 2022).

Office of Child Support Enforcement (2020a). Child Support Performance and Incen- tive Act of 1998. https://www.acf.hhs.gov/css/policy-guidance/child-support-perf ormance-and-incentive-act-1998 (Accessed 28 September 2022).

Office of Child Support Enforcement (2020b). Office of Child Support Enforcement Preliminary Report 2020. https://www.acf.hhs.gov/sites/default/files/documents/oc se/fy_2020_preliminary_data_report.pdf1998 (Accessed 28 September 2022).

Office of Child Support Enforcement (2021). Essentials for Attorneys in Child Support Enforcement. 4th ed. www.acf.hhs.gov/css/training-technical-assistance/essentials -attorneys-child-support-enforcement (Accessed 28 September 2022).

Office of Family Assistance (2004). Caseload Data 1975 (AFDC Total). https://www .acf.hhs.gov/ofa/data/caseload-data-1975-afdc-total (Accessed 28 September 2022).

Osterman, M., Hamilton, B., Martin, J., Driscoll, A. and Valenzuela, C. (2022). Births: Final Data for 2020. *National Vital Statistics Reports*, *70*(17). https://stacks.cdc.gov/ view/cdc/112078

Parkinson, C. (2020). COVID-19, educational attainment, and the impact on American workers. *U.S Bureau of Labor Statistics.* https://www.bls.gov/opub/mlr/2020/ beyond-bls/covid-19-educational-attainment-and-the-impact-on-american-workers .htm (Accessed 18 August 2022).

Personal Responsibility and Work Opportunity Reconciliation Act, (1996). PUBLIC LAW 104–193—AUG. 22, 1996 110 STAT. 2105 https://www.congress.gov/104/ plaws/publ193/PLAW-104publ193.pdf (Accessed 18 August 2022).

Population Reference Bureau (2021). Why is the US Birth Rate Declining? www.prb .org/resources/why-is-the-u-s-birth-rate-declining

Temporary Assistance for Needy Families (TANF) (2020). https://www.acf.hhs.gov/sites/default/files/documents/ofa/fy2020_tanf_cascload_children_0.pdf (Accessed 18 August 2022).

The Social Security Act of 1935 (1935). https://www.ssa.gov/history/35act.html (Accessed 18 August 2022).

United States Census Bureau (2021). *Annual Social and Economic Supplement (ASEC) of the Current Population Survey (CPS)* https://www.census.gov/programs-surveys/saipe/guidance/model-input-data/cpsasec.html (Accessed 18 August 2022).

United States Census Bureau (2022). 2020 Census Results. https://www.census.gov/programs-surveys/decennial-census/decade/2020/2020-census-results.html

Urban Institute (2022). TANF Isn't Improving Participants' Employment Outcomes. Could Sectoral Work Programs Be the Answer? https://www.urban.org/urban-wire/tanf-isnt-improving-participants-employment-outcomes-could-sectoral-work-programs-be (Accessed 27 January 2023).

U.S Bureau of Labor Statistics (2022). *Labor Force Statistics from the Current Population Survey.* https://www.bls.gov/cps/demographics.htm (Accessed 18 August 2022).

13. Sticking points, blind spots and ways forward

Kay Cook, Adrienne Byrt, and Thomas Meysen

INTRODUCTION

This collection has advanced comparative research on child support policy by locating ten individual child support systems within wider socio-political contexts. Our approach has enabled comparisons across systems that interrogate child support alongside a suite of other social policies. These frameworks situate children's and single parents' economic welfare within the context of state, market and family sources of expected support, including the culturally-specific gender and family logics that underpin them. Taking this approach, each chapter illustrated how the country's suite of relevant welfare and family policies shape the possibilities or limits of post-separation child support policy. Together, the collection identifies key sticking points and blind spots within policies across all countries, while also bringing to light the predominance of gendered single parenthood. Policies are often failing to even acknowledge or address the inequity of gendered caring burdens. No state examined here has managed to level them out.

Across all countries, the child support system is falling short of meeting the needs of single parents, predominantly mothers. The chapters expose failing, inadequate, or incohesive child support systems. For example, Australia has an incapable, Canada an outdated, and Germany a fragmented system with a need for cohesive policy (Table 13.1). In the UK the child support system seems to be detached from the reality of the lives of single parents resulting in a lack of access to adequate care and benefits. In the US a reliable infrastructure of all things falls short of the families who need support most. Colombia is in need of reform given socioeconomic disadvantage and intricacies of the system. Nigeria is in need of a consistent approach, lacking uniformity across payment calculations. Malaysia has issues with the societal approval of extramarital motherhood, with non-compliance and enforcement. South Korea has an advancing system with still infrequent payments and support. Only Finland

Table 13.1   *State of child support systems and policies to address the gendered burdens of single parenthood*

Developing system	Established system with shortcomings	Elaborated system
Colombia, Malaysia, Nigeria, South Korea	Australia, Canada, Germany, UK, US	Finland

takes most of the burden off single mothers with the state giving child support guarantee, but non-compliance remains a core issue.

As set out in Chapter Two, irrespective of empirical context, it is overwhelmingly mothers who are positioned as responsible for children's welfare. When parents separate, and the traditional gendered division of labour persists across contexts, mothers must find new ways to resource this caring work. However, while simultaneously being positioned as carers, single mothers also face income insecurity and a lack of supportive policies. While child support is viewed as a means of bridging the shortfalls that exist between mothers' available time, income generating capacity and parental responsibilities, it too falls short of being able to remedy the unwinnable triple bind that sole mothers experience, as it relocates responsibility for securing child support with already time and resource poor women.

TRIPLE BIND OF SINGLE MOTHERS

The triple bind of securing caring resources, achieving financial resources through employment, and the burdens of activating the system (Nieuwenhuis and Maldonado, 2018) highlights the tension between private and state responsibility for children of separated parents. States' desire for expenditure reduction collides with the need to alleviate poverty for single mothers and their children. As explored in Chapter 2, applying a gender lens to the triple bind brings to light the disproportionate burden endured by mothers post-separation. Across the countries included in this collection, the tensions between caregiving, adequate employment, and pursuing child support payments or social benefits create ongoing administrative burdens for single mothers. Single mothers must navigate one bind at the expense of another. Women contend with caring crises as they reduce work hours to meet their caregiving demands, all while being made responsible by the state to pursue child support payments from non-compliant payers. Low wages and earning capacity, expensive or inaccessible childcare, and tenacious and stigmatising gendered expectations shape the contexts within which single mothers are expected to raise, and provide for, their children post-separation. Against this backdrop, incohesive child support policies continue to responsibilise women as they navigate systems that do not centre their – or their children's – basic needs.

Securing Caring Resources

As evidenced in this collection, accessible and affordable childcare remains out of reach for single mothers in most countries included. The exorbitant cost of childcare in Australia and the UK can prove prohibitive, and the financial consequences might be experienced by mothers through reduced work hours. In Canada, affordability and a lack of consistency in service delivery compounds the difficulties parents face accessing childcare. Here, the COVID pandemic brought to light the caregiving burden endured by mothers, in particular, and highlighted the need to reform the system. Finland stands to host the most accessible childcare scheme, as low-income families are given access to free early childhood education and care. German mothers still take on the majority of childcare, and lower use of formal childcare before the age of 3 for children exacerbates lower rates of employment among single parents in the early years of their children's life. In both Malaysia and Nigeria, the state assumes no responsibility for providing support to families to access childcare.

Table 13.2   Availability of affordable publicly funded childcare for children of single mothers/parents

None	Limited availability	Availability free of cost
Malaysia, Nigeria	Australia, Canada, Colombia, Germany, South Korea, UK, US	Finland

As Table 13.2 illustrates, only Finland provides a low-cost way for single mothers to manage the gendered demands and limitations on their working life. Only Finland provides widely available free childcare. While Korea also offers universal, public childcare, 90 per cent of centres are privately operated (Lee, 2022) and families overwhelmingly choose to take up childcare places in private centres due to quality concerns. As such, while free of cost childcare is available, in practice, policy limitations and implementation failures have meant that such places are not socially acceptable. In all other countries, low-cost childcare was either severely limited, unavailable, or only regionally provided for.

Reflecting on the low value and unreliability of child support payments in light of inaccessible or expensive childcare highlights the importance of the welfare state in resourcing women's caring work. However, as we now turn to explore, the welfare state was also often unsupportive, leaving women to enter a gendered and often discriminatory labour market in order to secure sufficient resources to support their unpaid caring work.

State and Market Forms of Financial Support

Single mothers face considerable limitations on their earning capacity as a result of career interruptions, the need to fit employment around their children's schooling and health care needs (Nieuwenhuis and Maldonado, 2018), and as a result of systemic biases that manifest in such forms as the gender wage gap (OECD, 2022). The chapters in this collection illustrate women's marginal position when it comes to securing resources to support their caring work. For single mothers, inadequate employment opportunities and the persistence of the gender pay gap shape women's earning capacity in all countries included in this collection.

As outlined in Table 13.3, the Malaysian and Nigerian states provide very few payments to support single mothers' caring work. Rather, single mothers are rendered responsible for securing their income through the labour market. There, however, women face considerable barriers, which lowers their income security and makes combining their caring and employment responsibilities extremely challenging. Malaysian, Nigerian, and partly South Korean women endure social stigma if they do become single mothers, with benefit systems failing to provide women with financial security given this marginalised social status. Traditional gender roles shape women's departure from employment when they become parents in Korea, and in turn, they may struggle to find adequate employment once they are single. Furthermore, building on the previous section, a lack of accessible childcare hinders single mothers' employment opportunities in all nations.

While Finland, Germany and South Korea provide payments to support single mothers' caring activities, these payments are not sufficient to alleviate financial stress even in circumstances where single mothers are employed. In Finland, for example, high levels of poverty persist among single mothers despite high levels of employment. Payments position women as carers first and would-be employees second. The gender wage gap reinforces this notion. In complete contrast, it seems, is Australia. Here, the benefit system seeks to move single mothers into employment as a priority, as work tests apply to those with school-aged children. Caring work is not sufficient to warrant state support. Women who do move into employment face a lower gender wage gap than the OECD average, but high childcare costs, child support obligations that reduce as women's income increases, and inadequate state support make this triple bind a challenge.

Canadian single mothers have high labour-force participation rates, yet they too must endure an entrenched gender pay gap – one higher than the OECD

Table 13.3   Context of income opportunities available to single mothers

	Limited benefits provided to support single mothers	Benefit system supports single mothers as carers	Benefit system supports single mothers as would-be workers
Comparatively low gender wage gap		Colombia	Australia
Comparatively high gender wage gap	Malaysia, Nigeria	Finland, Germany, South Korea	Canada, UK, US

Note: Where available, OECD (2022) gender wage gap figures were used to categorise countries as higher or lower than the 2021 OECD average wage gap of 11.9 per cent.

average – in addition to the expectation that single mothers on welfare must participate in work-seeking or education in order to justify welfare receipt. How these mothers contend with the demands of finding adequate childcare to meet such expectations remains problematic. While Canada, the UK and the US position single parents as would-be workers within their benefit systems, regarding payments as contingent on previous or prospective employment activity, these countries each report higher gender wage gaps than the OECD average. Each of these countries also provides only limited public childcare, meaning that working mothers must use their limited incomes on childcare costs, diminishing the resources available to support their household. Colombia provides payments to single parents to support their caring work. Seemingly, in direct contrast to Canada, the UK and the US, Colombia is reported as having a comparatively low gender wage gap of 3.2 per cent (OECD, 2022). However, this figure excludes the highly informal workforce described in Chapter 5. While Colombian women are more educated than men, they too endure a persistent gender pay gap in a highly informal workforce. In this context, child support schemes are based on parental income, yet the informal and inadequate employment opportunities put effective provision of child support on shaky ground.

Single mothers residing in the countries examined here thus find themselves in a largely unwinnable bind: to seek employment to cover the shortfall in state or familial support, only to find that employment also fails to adequately acknowledge or resource women's unpaid caring responsibilities. The systemic issues shaping single mothers' access to adequate employment are, evidently, ubiquitous across familial, religious, and neoliberal states. The gender pay gap, traditional gender roles, and inadequate, informal work leave single mothers with little capacity to adequately provide for their families without government or child support. Single mothers are in turn bound to accessing adequate childcare to meet their families' needs in cases where non-resident parents fail to comply with child support payments and where governments provide little to no financial support. The tensions entrenched in the gendered triple bind maintain a stronghold over the financial safety and well-being of single mothers and their children.

Navigating the Child Support System

Policies often do not take into account what it takes for single mothers to provide the financial resources for her household and the child. Fathers as (primary) breadwinners are the patriarchal norm in most countries of this collection which keeps many single mothers dependent on men's financial authority and manifests gender roles (Australia, Canada, Colombia, Korea, Malaysia, the UK, the US). Sometimes employment services are for fathers not (so much) single mothers (US). The focus lies on fairness for paying fathers while actively excluding mothers' experiences and burdens (Australia).

Child support as part of the financial basis for single parent households relies on compliance with agreements or orders. To reach them, most states included in this collection support single parents with administrative or court services. While in Colombia several agencies administer to single parents' needs, services are not accessible for or eligible to all single parents in Korea and the UK. In Canada, services are restricted to enforcement in case of non-compliance. Single mothers bear the full burden and costs of court proceedings in Malaysia and enforcement services are only provided if an order is issued. The Nigerian Federal Ministry acts as mediator in case of non-payment, a theoretical option for most mothers.

Many states privatise the economic well-being of single parents. The primary goal of policy is the reduction of state's expenditures (the UK), the private financial responsibility (the US and to a lesser extent Canada) or an increase in the paying fathers' liability (Australia). In Nigeria, the state stays completely out and, as in Colombia and Malaysia, counts on extended families as sources. However, in Korea compliance is the state responsibility, in Finland and Germany the state compensates for or supplements unpaid child support. As Skinner highlighted in her chapter, the expectation that separated parents can reach agreements privately is overshadowed by the entanglement of non-compliance and poverty – not only – in the UK. For these single mothers, pursuing child support payments again intensifies the tension endured between their need for employment, accessible and affordable childcare, and policies that centre their and their children's needs.

Broadly, inadequate policies shape non-compliance and exacerbate the impacts of the gendered triple bind for single parents, respectively burdening predominantly single mothers. Child support payment compliance and enforcement in case of non-compliance are contentious across most countries of this collection. The administrative burdens associated with pursuing child

Table 13.4   *Matrix of level of privatisation of financial well-being of single parent households and state support*

	Active privatisation/ low state responsibility	Implicit privatisation/ limited state responsibility	No privatisation/ full state responsibility
No support	Nigeria		
Limited support	Malaysia	Canada, Korea, UK	Germany
Proactive support	Australia, US	Colombia	Finland

support payments cost single mothers time and diminish their capacity to seek or carry out paid work. In states with child support agencies or services within a court-based system (all but Nigeria), the relief of the claiming burden often is hidden behind technical solutions, and single parents' needs are captured by the system. Canadian and US single parents can pursue enforcement of child support payments, but the breadth of administrative work to mobilise the process of claiming and adjustment remains individualised and burdensome. Non-conformity with the paternalistic rules and procedures can lead to an exclusion from the system. Expectations for accuracy and transparency cannot be met, and parents face a risk of having to repay social security payments (Australia). The costs of court proceedings or the risk of bearing the costs stay with single parents (Colombia, Germany, Malaysia, Nigeria). Seeking assistance may incur transportation costs, a loss of time off and an onus on gathering proof of the case (Colombia).

Single mothers, and to a far lesser extent single fathers, are the group most hit by or at risk of poverty in all the countries of this collection. Social benefits play an important role to address the hardships single mothers and their children face. Nevertheless, several states do not provide for any specific benefits for this circumstance (Australia, Canada, the UK, the US). Poor families often fall through the cracks in the US. In Colombia, targeted or specific additional programs for single mothers are limited, furthermore, child welfare and child support are even disconnected. Malaysia and Nigeria do not provide for (reliable) benefits at all. In Korea, short term emergency financial assistance is restricted to single parents with low income. Germany prioritises and privileges single parents in several aspects of the social security net and pays so called advance payments in case of non-compliance regardless of the individual financial situation. Finland is the only country to provide a child support guarantee in line with the intention to provide for all children. Child support payments do not lead single mothers and their children out of poverty due to claw back by the state if social benefits are paid or there is a full reduction of state benefits (Australia, Canada (most provinces), Finland, Germany, the US) with direct effects on failing to reduce poverty (Hakovirta et al., 2020).

As the preceding section has revealed, there are many alignments, misalignments, overlaps and tensions between countries identified as liberal, conservative, Nordic, and religious policy regimes. These comparisons advance the conceptual possibilities for future comparative post-separation family policy research and practice and broaden the scope of family and welfare policies to be included therein. In the final sections of this collection, we now turn to identify possible directions for such future work.

MOVING CHILD SUPPORT FORWARD

Chapters 3–12, as well as the synthesising outlined above, identify avenues to advance child support and related policies in ways that better meet the needs of children living in separated parent households. These proposals range from wholesale structural reforms through to technical, or administrative changes to program settings and criteria, through to education programs and calls for more research. Running through all of these proposals, however, is a thread of discontent with the current situation that sees children living in single parent families disproportionately likely to live in poverty and their mothers disproportionately responsible for their predicament.

The Australian, Canadian, German, Nigerian and UK chapters each call for sweeping reforms that reframe how children are regarded in policy frameworks, be they calls for a child rights' approach or for gender equity. Each set of recommendations acknowledges the need to rethink how children living apart from their previous breadwinner are financially supported – and how their previous caregiver may be better supported to take on these dual roles. As has been central to several chapters, these issues cannot be solved within the child support system alone. Rather, as Canada, Finland, Germany, and the UK chapters explore, fundamental changes are required to childcare, workplace and social security systems to support both parents to work and care, both prior to and following separation. These proposals may include universal childcare, guaranteed incomes, and workplace flexibility that recognise all workers' dual responsibility to care.

Other countries, such as Colombia, South Korea, Malaysia and the US, foregrounded administrative or educative solutions to the problems currently experienced within the child support scheme, with the US calling for more research to understand the pain points and failures of complex systems. While these solutions speak to a different scale of the problem – namely how to ensure women take up the rights afforded to them within the system – they invariably point to the same issues outlined by the triple bind, namely the complexity and bureaucracy of systems, women's lack of resources, and their caring responsibilities. Proposals to provide education (Chapter 9), outreach services (Chapter 5) or simpler systems (Chapter 8) to connect women with child support agencies, all speak to the competing demands of limited time and resources with which women must attend to their myriad responsibilities. Making systems easier to access, however, will lessen only one of the triple binds that single mothers experience; namely the persistent demand to navigate complex systems in order to secure sufficient resources.

CONCLUDING REMARKS

This collection sought to move beyond an examination of child support as a solitary policy, and rather, view it as one component within the system of support available to children in separated families. Single parents – most typically mothers – seeking to resource their children's care must not only navigate child support in order to obtain funds directly from their ex-partner, but they must also navigate state support in the form of subsidised childcare, income support or other payments and subsidies, as well as private resources in the form of care providers, employers and often legal systems. These vast fields of administrative work require time, knowledge and energy which deplete the available resources mothers have available for their children. Where the child support system fits into this complex web is what each individual chapter, and the consolidatory chapters sought to explore.

Child support can play a significant role in reducing child poverty (Hakovirta et al., 2020; Hakovirta and Skinner, 2021; Skinner, Cook and Sinclair, 2017; Skinner et al., 2017), but these effects are more muted when systems are difficult to access, fail to ensure compliance, do not guarantee child support income, or can be used to manipulate women's income or access to other payments. These administrative burdens can diminish the role that child support could play, as women turn away from state systems, as has been found in a range of Liberal states with complex administrative systems (Cook, 2022; Edin, 1995; Harris, 2015; Meyer et al., 2015; McKenzie and Cook, 2015). When women do not access child support systems, these payments have no poverty reduction effects.

What the chapters in this collection reveal is a need to return to the fundamental purpose of child support and re-evaluate whether the system as a whole, or the current settings within, are meeting this objective. Are complex program rules, costly and time-consuming paternity, legal or administrative procedures, or inconsistencies with gender norms working against the assumed function of the scheme? Following Carol Bacchi's (1999; 2009) approach to discerning the precise nature of policy problems from their solutions: what is the problem that child support seeks to remedy? The inconsistent and contradictory settings found across contexts make this question difficult to answer. Working the other way, if the program seeks to reduce child poverty – as many such schemes originally, or currently, purport – then this complex array of requirements that often cut across or compete with other policy objectives may be muddying the waters. As this collection has shown, there are fundamental interplays between the array of policies that shape women's capacity to earn and care, and as such, an ecological approach to mothers' resourcing is required.

REFERENCES

Bacchi, C. L. (1999). *Women, policy and politics: The construction of policy problems.* Sage.

Bacchi, C. (2009). *Analysing policy: What's the problem represented to be?* Frenchs Forest: Pearson Education.

Cook, K. (2022). *The failure of child support: Gendered systems of inaccessibility, inaction and irresponsibility.* Bristol: Policy Press.

Edin, K. (1995). Single mothers and child support: The possibilities and limits of child support policy, *Children and Youth Services Review, 17*(1), 203–30.

Hakovirta, M., Skinner, C., Hiilamo, H. and Jokela, M. (2020). Child poverty, child maintenance and interactions with social assistance benefits among lone parent families: A comparative analysis. *Journal of Social Policy, 49*(1), 19–39.

Hakovirta, M. and Skinner, C. (2021). Shared physical custody and child maintenance arrangements: A comparative analysis of 13 countries using a model family approach. In L. Bernardi and D. Mortelmans (Eds.) *Shared physical custody: Interdisciplinary insights in child custody arrangements.* Cham Switzerland: Springer.

Harris, D. A. (2015). 'You just have to look at it as a gift': Low-income single mothers' experiences of the child support system. *Journal of Poverty, 19*(1), 88–108.

Lee, S. H. (2022). Why the initiative of free childcare failed to be an effective policy implementation of universal childcare in South Korea. *Journal of Asian Public Policy, 15*(3), 558–574.

Meyer, D., Cancian, M. and Chen,Y. (2015). Why are child support orders becoming less likely after divorce? *Social Service Review, 89*, pp. 301–34.

McKenzie, H. and Cook, K. (2015). 'It should be a big responsibility': Low income payee mothers' evaluations of their child support arrangements. *Australian Journal of Family Law, 29*, 135–65.

Nieuwenhuis, R. and Maldonado, L. (2018). The *triple bind of single-parent families: Resources, employment and policies to improve well-being.* Bristol: Policy Press.

OECD (2022). *Gender wage gap.* OECD better policies for better lives: Gender equality. https://www.oecd.org/gender/data/gender-wage-gap.htm

Skinner, C., Cook, K. and Sinclair, S. (2017). The potential of child support to reduce lone mother poverty: Comparing population survey data in Australia and the UK. *Journal of Poverty and Social Justice, 25*(1), 79–94.

Skinner, C., Meyer, D., Cook, K. and Fletcher, M. (2017). Child maintenance and social security interactions: the poverty reduction effects in model lone parent families across four countries. *Journal of Social Policy, 46*(3), 495–516.

Index